God
Outwitted
THE STORIES
OF MY LIFE
Me

God
Outwitted
THE STORIES OF MY LIFE
Me

MAXIE D. DUNNAM

Seedbed

All Scripture quotations, unless otherwise indicated, are taken from the Holy Bible, New International Version®, NIV®. Copyright © 1973, 1978, 1984, 2011 by Biblica, Inc.™ Used by permission of Zondervan. All rights reserved worldwide. www.zondervan.com The "NIV" and "New International Version" are trademarks registered in the United States Patent and Trademark Office by Biblica, Inc.™

Scripture quotations marked ESV are taken from The Holy Bible, English Standard Version. ESV® Permanent Text Edition® (2016). Copyright © 2001 by Crossway Bibles, a publishing ministry of Good News Publishers.

Scripture quotations marked (Mof) are from the James Moffatt, *A New Translation of the Bible, Containing the Old and New Testaments*. New York: Doran, 1926. Revised edition, New York and London: Harper and Brothers, 1935. Reprinted, Grand Rapids: Kregel, 1995.

Scripture quotations marked "Phillips" are taken from The New Testament in Modern English, copyright 1958, 1959, 1960 J.B. Phillips and 1947, 1952, 1955, 1957 The Macmillian Company, New York. Used by permission. All rights reserved.

Scripture quotations marked NRSV are taken from the New Revised Standard Version Bible, copyright © 1989 National Council of the Churches of Christ in the United States of America. Used by permission. All rights reserved.

Scripture quotations marked KJV are taken from the Holy Bible, King James Version, Cambridge, 1796.

Scripture quotations marked The Message are taken from THE MESSAGE. Copyright © by Eugene H. Peterson 1993, 1994, 1995, 1996, 2000, 2001, 2002. Used by permission of NavPress. All rights reserved. Represented by Tyndale House Publishers, Inc.

Printed in the United States of America

Front cover portrait of Maxie Dunnam by Anthony Thaxton
Cover design by Strange Last Name
Page design and layout by PerfecType

Dunnam, Maxie D.
  God outwitted me : the stories of my life / Maxie Dunnam. – Frankin, Tennessee : Seedbed Publishing, ©2018.

  pages : illustrations, portraits ; cm.

  Includes bibliographical references.
  ISBN 9781628244281 (paperback)
  ISBN 9781628244298 (mobipocket ebk.)
  ISBN 9781628244304 (epub ebk.)
  ISBN 9781628244311 (updf ebk.)

  1. Dunnam, Maxie D. 2. United Methodist Church (U.S.)--Clergy--Biography. 3. Asbury Theological Seminary--Presidents--Biography.   I. Title.

BX8495.D86 A3 2017   287/.6/092   2017961085

SEEDBED PUBLISHING
Franklin, Tennessee
seedbed.com

To my wife, Jerry, and my children, Kim, Kerry, and Kevin—
everyday witnesses to God's grace outwitting me

CONTENTS

FOREWORD

Years ago I had the unenviable task of introducing Maxie Dunnam to a large group of people gathered for a weekend of preaching and teaching. I stood before the group and asked, "How does one introduce their hero?" After that I broke down and began to cry. Unable to speak, I motioned for Maxie to take the stage and sat down.

It's precisely how I feel again all these years later as I am charged to write an opening word to his stirring autobiography, *God Outwitted Me: The Stories of My Life*. The great Danish theologian Søren Kierkegaard once said something to the effect that life must be lived forward but could only be understood backward. It's an apt agenda for a memoir. As Maxie has surveyed the circuitous and unpredictable journey of his life, a singular theme threads the whole story: "God outwitted me!" It is indeed a summative phrase for the stories of his life. Back to my quandary: How does one introduce their hero?

We could recount what he called his "barefoot days of the soul" as a child in Perry County, Mississippi. We might sit on the banks of that cold creek of his baptism or wander up to the clearing on the hillside where his beloved parents are buried. We could tell the stories of the hidden place where he suffered the scourge of poverty, which became the wounds of deep inferiority, which today he bears as the redeemed scars of glory and the source of his greatest riches.

We would need to tell the story of his courageous stand against racial discrimination and injustice in the early days of the civil rights movement that earned him his exile from the state of his birth to the far western boundary of the country. It brings to mind the words of the Mexican proverb, "They tried to bury us. They didn't know we were seeds." Indeed, this journey westward would become the story of multiple church plants and the depths of soul only suffering can bring.

This introduction must take us back to the heartland of this nation to Nashville, Tennessee, where he served a distinguished tour of duty as world editor of the *Upper Room*. Here he penned what would become, by most standards, his magnum opus. *The Workbook of Living Prayer*, what many thousands would come to know as their awakening to prayer, ultimately became an international best seller, reaching well more than a million souls. In many ways his profound journey became the answer to his ponderous question, "What if there are some things God either will not or cannot do until and unless his people pray?"

It was during those *Upper Room* years that he and a few friends founded the Walk to Emmaus, a spiritual renewal movement that hundreds of thousands now count as the decisive turning point in their life and faith. Because Maxie knew the rising tide of faith would depend on the deepening currents of orthodoxy, he gave himself to the arduous work reclaiming the "faith once handed down to the saints." Again, he and a band of brothers and sisters followed the Spirit into the waters of theological pluralism and denominational chaos and founded the Confessing Movement, contending for the ancient creeds, the authority of Scripture, and the uniqueness of Jesus Christ.

This journey would take him all the way to the obscure town of Wilmore, Kentucky, to serve as the fifth president of Asbury Theological Seminary, a bastion of evangelical faith forged in the fire of the Holy Spirit. He led the seminary to unprecedented expansion, planting a campus in Orlando, Florida, and launching one of the first and finest online learning platforms in theological education.

While Maxie would count his decade at the helm of Asbury Seminary as his greatest contribution to the church, if we want to understand his greatest passion we need to go to Memphis, Tennessee. Maxie has given the better part of three decades of his life to building up the body of Christ in what may be regarded as one of America's most troubled cities. Through his dozen years as the senior minister of Christ United Methodist Church, he led God's people to work together in ways that fostered a demonstration plot for God's kingdom. And immediately upon finishing his tenure at the seminary he made a beeline back there to serve the church and the city he loves so much.

Maxie has loved Jesus and he has loved the church in ways we can only describe as extraordinary. Yet in all of this, through seasons of both heartbreak and happiness, Maxie has most deeply loved the little community of faith that was his first and will be his last—his family. His bride of more than sixty years, Jerry, a celebrated artist, has literally and figuratively provided all the color to their shared calling. Then there's Kim, Kerry, and Kevin, about whom there are enough family stories alone to warrant another book.

In his short and magical biography on St. Francis of Assisi, G. K. Chesterton offered this captivating logic:

> If St. Francis was like Christ, to that extent Christ was like St. Francis . . . Now in truth while it has always seemed natural to explain St. Francis in the light of Christ, it has not occurred to many people to explain Christ in the light of St. Francis . . . St. Francis is the mirror of Christ rather as the moon is the mirror of the Sun. The moon is much smaller than the Sun but it is much nearer to us; and being less vivid it is more visible. Exactly in the same sense St. Francis is nearer to us, and being a mere man like ourselves is in that sense more imaginable.[1]

The last half of the twentieth century reeked of counterfeit Christian leaders. Christian celebrities and capitalists, pragmatic CEOs, and throngs of company pastors littered the landscape of the church. The quest for crowds far exceeded the love of people. The closer one came the more disillusion magnified. Where were the kingdom heroes? In a sea of slickly imaged Christian leaders, Maxie and Jerry Dunnam have provided a mirror of Christ. In becoming so vulnerably near and authentically real they have shown us who Christ could become in our lives.

Maxie was not a man for the people as much as he was a man for the person. Chesterton noted of St. Francis:

> What gave him his extraordinary personal power was this; that from the Pope to the beggar, from the Sultan of Syria in his pavilion to the ragged robbers crawling out of the wood, there was never a man who looked into those brown burning eyes without being certain that Francis Bernardone was really interested in him; in his own inner individual life from the cradle to the grave; that he himself was being valued and taken seriously . . .[2]

I once heard Maxie introduced in this fashion, "In life you meet two kinds of people. You encounter many persons and walk away saying, 'What a great person that is.' You encounter a select few from whom you walk away saying, 'What a great person I am.' Maxie Dunnam is clearly in the latter category of people."

It's no secret that Maxie Dunnam had a love affair with Charles Schultz's famed comic strip *Peanuts*. One of Maxie's favorite entries opens with Snoopy pondering a deep question: "Why were some created humans and others created dogs?" The next frame repeats the question as Snoopy's consternation grows. "Why were some of us created dogs and others humans?" The final frame closes with Snoopy joyfully dancing to these words, "Why should I have been the lucky one!?" It's a question Maxie has asked himself on many occasions and in many places.

My first encounter with Maxie Dunnam happened when I was a student at Asbury Seminary serving as his yard man. Today I am his publisher. It's an understatement to say that God has outwitted me! "Why should I have been the lucky one?" I think that's how I'd like to introduce my hero.

As we explore the well-lived life of this giant in ordinary, may we find ourselves outwitted by this outwitting God. And may the ponderous question of that joyful beagle be ours: Why should we have been the lucky ones!?

John David "J. D." Walt Jr.

Pentecost 2017

Introduction

Many know the name Brother Lawrence. If you have not read his book *The Practice of the Presence of God*, you have probably heard a preacher or teacher speak of him. He served in the kitchen of his monastery and said he experienced the presence of God as clearly when he was washing pots and pans as he did in the Blessed Sacrament of Holy Communion. What an inspiring story!

But it is another claim and story of Brother Lawrence that has gotten my attention. Like many others, he entered a monastic order believing that he was giving up this world's happiness to become a monk. But there he discovered a much deeper happiness than he had ever imagined. One day when he was praying and reflecting on the dramatic turn of events in his life, he shouted out, "God, You have outwitted me!"

Isn't that a delightful phrase? What a testimony to the providence of God, the working of God's grace in our lives. It's my testimony; God has outwitted me over and over again. I think of those times as a kind of parenthesis in my ongoing life. When you are reading and a parenthesis is inserted into an otherwise understandable and grammatically complete sentence, pay attention; the author wants you to understand what is being said. Parentheses often occur in our life stories. We are headed in a particular direction, and something is interjected that sends us in another direction we had not even considered. What has gone on before and what goes on after is understood only if we pay attention to, and grasp the meaning of, the parenthesis.

I believe God puts parentheses in our lives to give us the opportunity to grow, change directions, clarify vision and mission, and fulfill the plan he has for us. All the parentheses in my life are required to tell the story.

For at least twenty years now, many (including publishers and my family) have asked, "When are you going to write an autobiography? When are you going to tell your story in a book?" I have resisted that because I have written a lot and have shared in a personal and confessional way. My story has been told in my writing as I have lived it. Also, I feel presumptuous to think that a book recording the narrative of my life (where I was born, and to whom; where I was educated; where I have lived and the jobs I have had; who I know and who has known me; a catalogue of dates and places) would be read. But more, I've doubted it being worth reading. More presumptuous would be writing a book about my accomplishments. Those who really matter know whatever accomplishments I have had.

My wife, who is the major contributor to this enterprise, tipped the scales. She is a storyteller, a far better one than I, and she loves a good story, especially if it sparkles with humor. She has no patience with people who toot their own horn. But she knew the stories, the parentheses, the times when God outwitted us and made our lives what they are. "You must share our journey, but please, make it *the rest of the story,* not the too typical, where I have been and what I have done." Then came the final straw that pushed me over the edge. "If for no other reason," Jerry added, "for our children and grandchildren."

After a lot of resistance, I'm still reticent, though as I have gotten into it my excitement has grown. Maybe it is still a crumb of resistance left over that makes me insistent on calling it a *memoir,* not an *autobiography.* The difference in the definitions of the words are so slight, you may think I'm being hypersensitive. An autobiography is a more or less detailed account of the events and circumstances of a person's life. Though *memoir* is a synonym for biography, words like *memory, remembrance,* and *reminiscence* are in the definition. I'm doing more than giving an account of events and circumstances; I'm reminiscing and reflecting. Some may even say I'm "preaching and teaching" about my experiences.

Many times when I go someplace to preach or teach, some person will greet me with a word like this, "I know you, I read your book," and they will name the book. I take that as a great affirmation. I want people who read the books I have written, and hear me when I teach and preach, as well as in personal conversation, to have at least a sense of who I am. I tell stories and share experiences, believing that they add flesh to the bones of my efforts at communication. I want people to understand and our stories are often the key to their getting the message.

So, some of you will find a story or an experience you have heard me share, or you may have read it in a book I've written. But pay attention, it may be a *parenthesis* to give meaning to something altogether different than before, or provide the meaning that was never there.

As I have reflected and written, I have begun to think that I have lived a kind of *hinting life.* I mean that my life is a "hint" of what it could have meant, what it might have been, and what the Lord calls us all to. The best definition of *hint* is "a slight indication." Synonyms for it are *inkling, intimation, cue,* and *clue.* So my life has been an inkling, an intimation, a cue. . . . Do you get it? . . . A hint, sometimes weak and only a slight hint; sometimes strong and a bold hint; but always flowing out of my commitment to live in Christ.

CHAPTER ONE

The Great Depression

The Great Depression was still the defining dynamic of the nation when I was born in Demer, Mississippi, on August 12, 1934. The Depression was caused by the stock market crash of October 29, 1929 (known as Black Tuesday). It was the worst depression of the twentieth century, affecting people worldwide. Unemployment in the United States rose to 25 percent.[1]

The Depression made worse the poverty that would have defined my family's life even without it. I doubt if we would have had electricity in our house before I was nine years old or indoor plumbing before I was eleven, even if the Depression had not come.

President Franklin D. Roosevelt, seeking to deal with the crippling amount of unemployment and poverty, established the Rural Electrification Act of 1936. The program resulting from this act gave federal loans to states to provide electrical distribution systems to rural areas. Always on the short end of the stick, it didn't get to some of us in Perry County, Mississippi, until the early forties.

We had moved from Demer, in Neshoba County, Mississippi, when I was two. I was too young to know what was going on, but I was told we moved at least three times before we settled in our own house on Camp Eight Road in Perry County six years later. I don't know how he did it, but somehow my father purchased twenty acres of land and built the first house we ever owned. It was eight miles from Richton, the largest town in Perry County.

It was called a "shotgun house," which has a narrow rectangular shape, about twelve feet wide, with rooms placed back-to-back, no hallways, and doors at each end. This was the most popular house layout in the South from the Civil War through the 1920s. The shotgun house was a sign of poverty at the time, but in some cities today (New Orleans, in particular), they are very popular with urban, young, middle- and upper-middle-class economic groups.

Our house consisted of three rooms: a living room with a bed in it, another room with two beds, and a kitchen. I was the youngest of the five children, and slept with my two brothers, Edgar and Lloyd. My two sisters shared the other bed in that room, and my mother and father slept in the living room. The heater in the living room ravenously devoured the wood that we brought in from the woodpile in the afternoon, but gave pitifully little warmth in exchange. The toilet was inconveniently reached by a path; the pungent odors too often reached the kitchen when the wind was blowing in the wrong direction.

Rather than having a beautiful grass lawn—fertilized, watered, and carefully manicured—Momma intentionally kept our yard bare of grass. Chickens ran free all around the house, so one of our chores was to sweep the yard regularly to keep it clean—particularly free of the chicken droppings. Momma was as insistent on having a clean yard as having a clean house.

We children spent as much time as possible playing outdoors. The gravel pit near the house was a favorite place. It was a magical place for children. Huge sandbanks to slide down; pond after pond, left by man and his machines gathering sand and gravel for highways and houses; turtles peeking out of the waters; an occasional snake lurking around the edge;

fish striking just enough to make you think they were in abundance, a thought discredited after a couple of luckless hours seeking to catch them. All of this could whisk hours from you before you knew they were gone.

Each year, as we moved through winter wearing heavy, high-top brogan shoes, we couldn't wait till we could go barefoot and play at the gravel pit. In 1975, I wrote a book entitled *Barefoot Days of the Soul*. I used "Barefoot Day" as my symbol for the promise of the gospel: "If the Son [Jesus] sets you free, you will be free indeed" (John 8:36). I had reflected and written about barefoot days one summer when our family had spent some vacation time with my parents in Mississippi. I played a lot with the children at the gravel pit that summer because, more than any other, that place linked me to my childhood.

Memories of my childhood came alive that summer, and I wrote the following reflective words.

> I'm not sure when it came,
>> mid-April, early May,
>> never later I'm sure.
> Barefoot Day!
>> Feet unbound.
>> Toes unloosed.
> Violets were the signal.
> These tiny fragile purple flowers
>> were the convincing sign
>> necessary for Momma to give
>> the word:
>> Shoes off!
> We would begin the search
>> early in March,
>> but that was usually futile.
> Yet
>> the anticipation was exciting.

Bringing water from the spring
    or carrying wood from the hill
    was an arduous task
    all winter long.
But when the sun grew warmer
    and the days longer,
    the path to the spring was
    inviting,
    and fetching water took twice as long.
Our eyes scanned the ground,
    looking for that purple face
    peeking through the
    moss
    or leaves.
When we could produce one,
    one tiny violet as proof of spring,
    barefoot days
    had come![2]

The days of cold rain, sleet, frost, and sometimes snow—the drab, dreary, cloudy days of winter—were gone. The exhilaration of spring— the warm sun thawing the ground, bringing bud and bulbs to life, coloring the grass green, making the sand warm—announced: Barefoot Day!

In my adult years, and now a minister of the gospel, nothing in my experience was more suggestive of the freedom Jesus offers. But then, it was the innocence of childhood, and the simplicity that poverty called for: playing with a homemade truck (a board for the body, a tin can for the cab, and jelly jar tops for wheels); games played with buttons on squares penciled on a cardboard box; climbing trees and wading in streams; fishing and swimming in the same water holes.

The clean yard was perfect for marking off a hopscotch pattern with the point of a hoe that was used to chop grass out of the vegetable rows in the garden. It was also a great place to play marbles. I didn't know any boy who didn't have a tobacco sack filled with his marbles. We were always ready. All we needed was a circle drawn in the middle of the yard, deciding how many were going to play (never any more than six, preferably three or four, but a couple would be just fine). We all had our favorite "shooter" and sometimes we would spend a good bit of time trying to negotiate a trade for a shooter your friend seemed to be effective with. We would decide whether we were going to play for keeps, meaning you kept all the marbles you knocked out of the circle; or for fun, meaning you won the game by knocking the most marbles out of the circle, but retrieved your marbles when the game was over.

I was never a good shooter in marbles. I couldn't get the knack of gripping my shooter firmly enough to shoot it strongly and, at the same time, control its direction. But I was good at playing jacks.

Though most of the time we played jacks on the floor in the living room, there were places in our front yard were the surfaces were firm enough for bouncing the ball and playing jacks there . . . which we often did in the late spring and summer. I would never play with anyone but my brother and sister at home, because boys playing jacks were called "sissies." My brother Lloyd almost always beat me at marbles, but I beat him at jacks. My sister Lois, Lloyd's twin, always beat us both.

Did I say poverty? We didn't know we were poor. We were not on welfare; Momma always sought to make that clear. The case she was intent on making was that no one in our family received a welfare check. We did occasionally receive what was called "commodities," primarily butter and cheese, and occasionally flour. I wondered why these things were designated commodities. And I didn't understand why Momma did not even want to acknowledge that we had gotten some butter on the day commodities were distributed. For Momma, and maybe for Daddy, there was a kind of shame connected with this kind of assistance.

I hear it all the time—*people are poor because they just have no personal responsibility.* A statement like that won't make it far with me. I know about a father who was totally responsible, but earned so little working at back-breaking jobs that a bit of welfare butter and cheese now and then enhanced our meager daily diet.

Our staple food included dried lima beans four or five times a week, with cornbread at every meal except breakfast. Sunday dinners were always a fond celebration with a chicken killed from our yard. My oldest sibling, a girl, was eight years old when I was born, then a boy, then twins who were two years older than me. It took me a long time to be willing to catch the chicken and wring its neck, which they seemed always gleeful about doing.

Until we got electricity, our lighting was with coal oil lamps. We called it "coal oil" then; now it's known as kerosene. I haven't been near kerosene in years, but I would recognize the smell in any setting. A gallon coal oil can was as much a part of our functional needs as the frying pan. I haven't seen such a can in years (everything is plastic now), but I see it clearly in my mind: round, about eight inches in diameter, with a wire handle run through a round, wooden spiral by which you held it. The spout was small, making it easy to fill the lamps. The little spout had a screw-on cap, and we were constantly warned, "Don't forget to put the cap back on!"

We always kept coal oil on hand. It served our lighting needs, and occasionally, when we couldn't get a fire started in the heater, we would pour just a bit of coal oil on the wood to make it start burning quickly.

We had three lamps and one lantern. I suppose we didn't have a flashlight because I can't remember ever using one during those years; we used the lantern at night to go to the outdoor toilet or to the barn. The lamps would be moved from room to room as needed. We had to adjust the height of the wick just right to prevent smoking that would smut the glass globe. Even with careful use, the fragile glass globe had to be washed two or three times weekly. In order to have light, we had to read and do our homework at the kitchen table. That's also where most of our fussing and fighting broke out.

Demer, where I was born, was once the biggest town in Neshoba County. The town was named for Elias Demer, a member of the United States House of Representatives from Pennsylvania who was persuaded by Adam Byrd, a congressman from Philadelphia, Mississippi, to open a lumber manufacturing plant in Neshoba County because of the vast acreage of virgin forest there. The land on which Demer was to be built was a portion of that territory ceded to the United States government in 1830 by the Choctaw Indians in the Treaty of Dancing Rabbit Creek. This treaty was the first of its kind under the Indian Removal Act, which allowed the president to negotiate with Indian tribes living within the boundaries of the existing states to voluntarily exchange their lands for unorganized territory west of the Mississippi River. How voluntary the exchanges were has been debated ever since, and is still a part of the shame in our history.

In our family lore, we claim Choctaw blood ran strong in my Grandma Polly, my father's mother, and my Grandma Liza, my mother's mother. My brother Lloyd had portraits of these two grandmothers painted from old photographs. None of the family can find the photos, but the portraits are in our kitchen, and I see them every morning when I make coffee. The images are captivating; both captured when they were old. They leave no doubt that we are close to that claim of native Choctaw blood.

They are dressed in common, everyday, handmade clothes, and it is obvious neither had the means to wear store-bought dresses. I don't believe I ever saw either of them without an apron on. The other identifying parcel of dress was their bonnet; neither went outside, winter or summer, without their handmade bonnet. The only thing elegant about the paintings is the character of each woman. Though both are about the same age at the time, Grandma Polly's hair is steel black, while Grandma Liza's (her name was Eliza, but we shortened it to Liza) hair was grey.

If you want to visit Demer today, there is nothing to find. What you can find, though, is the Pearl River Resort in Neshoba County. It is a

Native American–run resort located just a few miles from Philadelphia, in Choctaw, an unincorporated community and American Indian reservation. The reservation is owned and operated by the Mississippi Band of Choctaw Indians, the only federally recognized Indian tribe in Mississippi.

On their centuries-old homeland, the Indians gather each July for the annual Choctaw Indian Fair, where they celebrate their vibrant culture. The tribe is ten thousand members strong and Choctaw lands cover more than thirty-five thousand acres in ten different counties in Mississippi. Though deeply traditionally rooted, the Choctaw people elected a female tribal chief in October 2011. Because of our Choctaw connection, our two daughters, Kim and Kerry, rejoice in thinking that there is a barrier-breaking kinship that runs in our family.

People in the area will talk to you excitedly about the Choctaw and the Neshoba County Fair, but you will be hard put to find anyone to tell you anything about Demer. It's well-nigh impossible to get directions to where it is, or where it might have been. I tried. In the mid 1960s, in the midst of the civil rights upheavals, I decided to move to California. I had never visited my birthplace. For some reason that may speak of our grounding in the land, I wanted to see where I was born before I left the state.

The population of my birthplace is unknown today because the boundaries are unknown. It is, or was, on the present-day southern limits of Philadelphia, Mississippi. Philadelphia today has a population of seventy-five hundred and is the county seat of Neshoba County. When I was born, Demer was a thriving lumber mill community much larger than Philadelphia.

But try to find it today! News writer Jack Bertram described the effort this way: "Take the turn off the southwest corner of the city square, motor down Range Road a short distance, a drive measured as easily in heart-beats as miles, and no sign will be found announcing Demer. No markers, directional or historical or otherwise."[3]

So I had to use my imagination. I knew that in the early and mid-1900s, at the time of my birth, Demer had its mills, and hundreds of wood-framed mill hand houses, one in which I was born. There was a school, a church, a hotel, a depot, and a doctor. The doctor was not present for my birth, as had been the case for the birth of my siblings.

Happy Hollow was the name given to the housing area for the five hundred workers at the Demer lumber mill, one of which was my father. In my twenties, I became interested in my family history because I felt cheated by poverty and cultural and educational deprivation; in my cynicism I wondered how such a place could be called "happy." It took me too long to appropriate the fact that happiness and joy are not dependent upon external conditions.

The lumber industry was thriving in Demer during that time. Before my father was trained as a welder and worked in the shipbuilding industry, during and after World War II, he was a logger and then a stump wood worker. When I mention "stump wood" in telling my story, peoples' faces turn into a question mark. I have to do a little explaining. It was a part of the turpentine industry and there was a time, especially in parts of the South, when it was thriving.

In the United States the tree known as the longleaf pine once covered as much as 90 million acres. That is what brought the thriving lumber business to Demer. But due to clear-cutting, that vast pine tree resource was reduced by as much as 95 to 97 percent. The trees grew very large (up to 150 feet tall), taking 100 to 150 years to mature and could live up to five hundred years. The wood was prized and the undisciplined clear-cutting resulted in hundreds of thousands of stumps. The stumps left behind from the clear-cutting were resinous, did not rot, and eventually became fatwood. This ushered in a new stump wood industry, which flourished for many years.

Industrial uses for fatwood include production of turpentine. When fatwood is cooked down in a fire kiln, the heavier resin product that results is pine tar. The steam that vaporizes from this process is turned into a liquid that becomes turpentine.

Another use of fatwood is in the production of dynamite. I grew up hearing the word "Hercules." I didn't know that was the Roman name for the Greek divine hero, famous for his strength and his far-ranging adventures. The Romans adapted this Greek hero's iconography and myths for their literature.

Growing up in rural Mississippi, with the educational and cultural limitations of my childhood, I was not prepared to take note of *Hercules*, the 1997 animated musical. But I knew the name Hercules; it was the plant in Hattiesburg, Mississippi, at which truckloads of stumps were dumped daily, coming from the work of laborers like my father. One of the products of that plant was an explosive, and so the plant was aptly named Hercules.

During its heyday, the plant was one of the city's biggest employers, with more than fourteen hundred workers. February 26, 2010, was a sad day for the area when this long-standing plant announced that it would be closing its doors for good at the end of the year. The plant then employed only twenty-one workers.

For many years no stumps had been hauled to that plant to make explosives; it was then making paper-sizing products for use in tissue paper.

I am constantly awed at the wonder of God's creative activity, and chief in his creation, humankind. I am as awed as the psalmist's expression of wonder:

> When I consider your heavens, the work of your fingers, the moon and the stars, which you have set in place, what is mankind that you are mindful of them, human beings that you care for them? You made them a little lower than the angels and crowned them with glory and honor. You made them rulers over the works of your hands; you put everything under their feet: all flocks and herds, and the animals of the wild, the birds of the sky, and the fish of the sea, all that swim the paths of the seas. LORD, our Lord, how majestic is your name in all the earth! (Ps. 8:3–9)

In my father's work pattern, I see the pattern of God's creative investment in humankind. The closing of Hercules was a kind of period at the end of the sentence of his labor pattern as a logger and stump wood worker. Demer no longer exists because the lumber industry ceased to thrive. Hercules was closed because stump wood sources had diminished. But life goes on, and worker needs and patterns evolve. Though miniscule in comparison, Hercules continued. I know nothing about what they were doing when they announced they were going to close, but their work with paper was obviously based on the fact that wet strength additives ensure that when the paper becomes wet, it retains its strength. This is especially important in tissue paper. So, creative minds found a way to transition from explosive chemicals that come from wood products to chemicals used in paper, the combination of which results in construction of a strengthening network. Tell me we couldn't beat our swords into ploughshares and our spears into pruning hooks if we had the will.

Though for years we survived from the meager earnings of my father in the stump woods, that's not what I knew as important back then. Fatwood was also called "lighter wood" or "light wood." Knowing this now, I know why we called the kindling we used for starting a fire "lightered." It was a made-up word; I knew how to say it, but didn't know how to spell it, because I have never seen it written before, and it's not in the dictionary.

It was after years of being asked, "What are you saying? 'Lightered?' What is that?" and not being able to talk sensibly about it that I researched the whole issue and came up with this information. Fatwood contains huge amounts of terpene, which is highly flammable, thus it was and is used as kindling to start fires. Even when wet, it lights and is a hot enough temperature to set larger pieces of wood on fire. I'm told that in Louisiana fatwood is known as "rich lighter." I've carried too many armloads of it to be able to call it anything but "lightered."

Upward Mobility

Upward and downward mobility are terms used often in talking about Christian discipleship. Jesus was always referring to himself as the sent One. More than forty times in John's gospel alone he mentions the importance of being sent by the Father. God had to have someone on earth to represent him, so he sent Jesus. Jesus represented the Father who sent him; as Christians we represent Jesus who sends us.

In his letter to the church in Philippi, Paul wrote one of the most beautiful descriptions of Jesus we have in Scripture:

> Let the same mind be in you that was in Christ Jesus, who, though he was in the form of God, did not regard equality with God as something to be exploited, but emptied himself, taking the form of a slave, being born in human likeness. And being found in human form, he humbled himself and became obedient to the point of death—even death on a cross. (Phil. 2:5–8 NRSV)

Not only is this a vivid description of Jesus; it is a call to us. Jesus is a servant, and he leaves little doubt that it is a servant style to which he calls us.

I preach and teach a lot about that, and I have to be careful, especially when I deal with what we designate upward mobility. Upward mobility is the capacity or facility for rising to a higher social or economic position. The dynamic is the movement from one social level to a higher one (upward mobility) or to a lower one (downward mobility) as by changing jobs or marrying. It was in the mid-1940s that these designations came into popular usage.

We can talk negatively and positively about them. We preachers usually call for the negative dynamic, downward, because of the pervasive power of consumerism and the distorted desires of people for more and more things that really don't matter, that we really don't need.

It is easy to make the case that Jesus' lifestyle is one of downward, not of upward mobility. A friend of mine, J. D. Walt, director of Seedbed, created a kind of sound-bite description of the Christian way under the rubric: *down is the way up.* I don't argue against that because Jesus was very clear about what it meant to follow him: "Whoever wants to become great among you must be your servant, . . . just as the Son of Man did not come be served, but to serve" (Matt. 20:26, 28). Not only does Jesus call us to this lifestyle, he gives us life through this style: "Whoever finds their life will lose it, and whoever loses their life for my sake will find it" (Matt. 10:39).

Yet, upward mobility is one of those blessings that we should treasure, and one of the marks of our economic system at its best. Our family was happy in a three-room shotgun house, without indoor plumbing and electricity, but we were far better off when my daddy became a welder in the shipyard, rather than a stump woods worker. He was able to save enough money to build a small cinderblock three-bedroom house with indoor plumbing and electricity. Coal oil lamps became oddities. We bought one in an antique store years later as a nostalgic reminder. We had a fireplace, but we were not dependent upon it for our heating; electricity powered the furnace. We no longer had to depend on lightered to kindle a fire, or tote heavy buckets of water from a spring.

But not having to smell coal oil or carry firewood or tote water from a spring did not spare me from desiring more upward mobility. Those desires expressed themselves in crippling ways in my life.

When I moved beyond the confines of Perry County, a new kind of depression, other than the economic one in which we had lived, came over me. Travel, college, and seminary provided me with windows through which I looked out upon a bright, rich world. But when I looked out the rear window of my past, I saw a dull, deprived world. I felt that as a child I had been cheated. I became resentful and bitter. Thoughts of the past put a rancid taste in my mouth.

At the very beginning of history, the story of humankind, our story, is acted out, not only in Adam and Eve, but also in their sons, Cain and Abel. There is a lesson even in their names. Cain means, "I have gotten a man" (Gen. 4:1 KJV). Thus Eve, the proud mother, suggests that this son will bear the dignity of being the firstborn, and that for her, he is to be the quintessence of power and strength. "Abel," on the other hand, means something like "nothingness," or "frailty." The elder, from the very beginning, thus overshadows the younger brother. Abel is destined to play second fiddle. He is the representative of those who get the short end of the stick.

That's the way I had experienced life. There are those who are born with a silver spoon in their mouth, and there are those for whom the cry of hunger never ceases because poverty robs them of the very sustenance of life. My cry was not for physical food, but to be accepted and valued. I fallaciously thought I had to prove myself in order to be accepted and belong. Cain, as a name and symbol, speaks of the firstborn and more: *the blessed ones* or the ones we think are blessed, the ones who seemingly have everything, and easily find themselves in the center of things. That's the way I saw it throughout my early years (especially my teenage years).

The way it expressed itself in my life was an almost paralyzing shame that grew into resentment about my family, my circumstances, and myself. There is a difference between shame and embarrassment. Reflecting, it is clear that embarrassing experiences, known only to me, were the sparks that ignited the fires of shame.

I remember vividly an experience that had such a depth of embarrassment that I still feel a bit of embarrassment today. I also get in touch with the distorted shame that fired my depression for too many years.

It was a two-day experience as a guest in the home of strangers. I was attending a conference for members of local high school organizations that had to do with academic achievement. A psychologist might have fun exploring why I can't remember the name of the society of which I was a part that took me, with three others, from our school to the conference.

The conference was in McComb, Mississippi. McComb is located in Pike County, one hundred miles from our little town. I was so excited. That may have been the only time I have ever visited McComb, but years later, in my first years of ministry, I knew about it in another way.

During the 1960s, McComb and nearby areas were the site of extreme violence by the [Ku Klux Klan] KKK and other opponents to the Civil Rights Movement. In 1961, it was the location of [Student Nonviolent Coordinating Committee] SNCC's first voter registration project in the state, which was quickly met with violence and intimidation by authorities and local KKK. Fifteen-year-old Brenda Travis was expelled from high school for being in a sit-in at an all-white luncheon-ette and ordering a hamburger; she was sentenced to a year in a juvenile facility. In addition to physical attacks on activists, Herbert Lee, a member of the [National Association for the Advancement of Colored People] NAACP, was murdered in front of witnesses in nearby Liberty, Mississippi by a state representative E. H. Hurst, who was exoner-ated by an all-white coroner's jury. More than 100 black high school students in McComb were arrested in 1961 for protesting his murder. After severe beatings of staff, SNCC pulled out of the region in early 1962, moving north in Mississippi to work in slightly less dangerous conditions. In January 1964, Louis Allen was murdered in Liberty, Mississippi; a witness to Lee's murder, he had been suspected of talking to Department of Justice officials about it.[4]

The song "We'll Never Turn Back" was related to the 1961 events in the McComb area, Amite and Pike Counties. One verse said:

> We have hung our heads and cried
> Cried for those like Lee who died
> Died for you, and died for me
> Died for the cause of equality
> But we'll never turn back
> No, we'll never turn back
> Until we've all been freed
> and we have equality.[5]

The population of McComb is more than thirteen thousand today, but back then it was far less. No one, certainly not a teenager, would ever have contemplated that dark blot on McComb's history. I could not have imagined that an African American girl, Brenda Travis, would play such a significant role in one of the most significant movements of the twentieth century. That was not even a thought in our minds. But for a fifteen-year-old, living two miles out of a town of eight hundred, it was exciting to travel anywhere.

It was a regional conference and the students in the society in McComb hosted us out-of-towners in their homes. I immediately knew my host family was wealthy. The house was elegantly furnished. The room I shared with my host student was upstairs (along with his sister's room) and I was told there were two bathrooms, one for the mother and father in what was a new term for me, "the master bedroom." My family had gotten indoor plumbing only a few years before, and our bathroom served my mother and father and three children. (Two of the five children were no longer at home.) I wasn't used to the luxury of a bathroom shared only by one other person.

At dinner (they called it that; at my house, we called the evening meal "supper"), the table was elegantly set with china and sterling silver. At home, there was no china and none of our dishes matched. We used tin forks and spoons, not sterling silver. I made it just fine with the knife and fork, but had already picked up my corn on the cob to take my first bite when I became aware that everyone at the table was looking at me. I had not noted at my setting a small utensil I had never seen before, a "corn holder," which everyone else had inserted into either end of their corn on the cob, and were holding it without burning their fingers. Whether I made the right decision then or not is questionable. I tried not to acknowledge my embarrassment. I felt it would draw more attention to try to use the holders than to continue as though I was completely unaware of my failure to use the strange, tiny sword-like things beside the second fork at the side of my plate.

I was a quick learner. I was wondering now about the second fork, but I would wait and see what they did with theirs and follow suit.

I didn't think then about the difference between embarrassment and shame. I know my embarrassment was painful. And it didn't end with dinner. The room I shared with my host had twin beds, one for each of us. I had never imagined having a bed to myself. Until my older brother had recently left home, we were three in the bed. I was happy to be sharing a bed with only one. When Tom undressed and began to put on his pajamas, I was embarrassed because I had no pajamas. I had never worn pajamas.

I didn't know it then, but the kind of embarrassment I was experiencing accumulated and moved from being incidental to pervasive. It regularly punctuated my life and turned into shame. I was ashamed of where I lived, ashamed of my father's work, ashamed of the fact that I had grown up without indoor plumbing. I have often wondered if my mother and father were ever aware of the depths of my feelings; and, if they were, how much pain that must have caused them.

I am still haunted by the question: When I grew up and eventually dealt with my distorted shame, did I witness clearly to them that my life was full of meaning, and that their love and sacrifice for me and our family was a huge shaping power in my life?

I wish I had confessed to them how I had allowed my past to become a source of shame so wildly that it had become a hound of hell with which I constantly did battle. When not fighting it, I was running from it, or ignoring and denying it, trying desperately to repress it. I wrote about that, which had become an emotional life-and-death struggle, in my book *Dancing at My Funeral*. I'm sure my mother never read it, and I doubt if my father did.

Years later, soon after our move to California in 1964, I joined a small group of pastors who met biweekly with Dr. Everett Shostrom, a psychologist who was writing a book entitled *Man the Manipulator*. "Ev" was a disciple of Abraham Maslow, who was a leading voice in the humanistic psychology movement, which was most talked about, and had the most impact on the psychological thinking of those days. "Self-actualization" was the term Maslow used as the operative word for the growth of an individual toward the fulfillment of our highest needs.

Many ministers, myself among them, were impressed with this new movement, thinking it gave us a lot of help in dealing with the pastoral needs of our congregations. We asked Ev to mentor us in this discipline and he agreed. I doubt if his willingness to do so was completely altruistic. He was writing his book, which contrasted manipulation to actualization, and we could be a test group and discussion partners. So every week, he would read a portion of what he had written, and we would respond and discuss.

This group experience was the primary stimulus for a life-changing decision. It became apparent that I would either move to slay the beast, my hound of hell, or he would devour me. I was not completely naive. From the temporary successes I had experienced over the years, I recognized that I couldn't rescue myself in one fell swoop; it would be an ongoing process. Nor could I win the battle with my own resources. I was wrestling with principalities and powers, and could win only in partnership with Christ, through the power of the Holy Spirit.

I took a two-day retreat in the mountains, alone with myself and the hound of hell, open to Christ and dependent upon him. I began with a confession that was the backdrop against all my reflecting and praying. I was allowing my past to unnerve me as a child is terrorized by shadows on a bedroom wall. The struggle was impacting my ministry and my marriage, and was blocking my wholeness journey.

This is the way I told a part of the story of that retreat in *Dancing at My Funeral*:

Although my purpose was clear, I attempted to shield myself that first day by engaging in "busy" activities. I cleaned the cabin and filled potholes in the road. Slowly, I became able to throw off my everyday compulsions and inhibitions. I ran through tall grass, waded in a cold stream, skipped rocks across a crystal pool nestled under a powerful waterfall. I wafted leaves off a cliff and watched them float to a new resting place.

I was a tow-headed boy again—barefoot, shirtless. Memories of hours spent alone on a creek bank waiting for a fish to take my bait floated in. Being alone *then* hadn't been painful, I reflected. Why *now*?

I was becoming more at peace with myself, and finally I found courage to throw myself into the task.

It was then that those two days really became *mine*. I remembered, reflected, prayed. I cried, screamed, kicked rocks, and pounded on my pillow. At other times, I recited poetry aloud or sang. All the while I was recollecting, sorting out, throwing away, keeping.

It happened the second night. It was cold and I hugged the fire-place. It was also near Christmas. Perhaps it was those connections that conjured up this relic of my past, the roadside café. It appeared as I was myself driving down a desolate road. I went inside. The customers and waitresses all sat lifeless, like wax figures in a museum. I looked into their empty faces. Meanwhile, I was pained by the unbearable silence of the place.

There was a click of a coin and the whirring of machinery, and out of the jukebox came that loud, twanging voice singing, "Old Pappy Time Is a' Pickin' My Pocket."[6]

This reference to the café and the song was a flashback to an actual experience I talked about earlier in my book *Dancing at My Funeral*. I was driving from Mississippi to Georgia during the Christmas season, became exhausted, and stopped at a truck stop. Loneliness always seems more pervasive to me in places like that. And there's always a jukebox with song after song, telling of hurt, heartbreak, loss of hope . . . and always, always, *loneliness*. It was there in that place that night I first heard the song, "Ole Pappy Time Is a' Pickin' My Pocket."

The song haunted my mind back then, and now, in the retreat, it was back again to pronounce the indictment I had brought on myself by the way I had been dealing with my past. For the first time, I saw that my past had power to undo me because I myself was energizing it. The lesson I received from the tableau was that my past was *back there*, frozen in time as were those figures in the roadside café. The past couldn't hurt me unless I *let* it hurt me.

I had achieved what I had come to the mountains to accomplish: to deal with my history and to purge my mind and cleanse my soul. I had stopped dead in my tracks and I had turned and faced that hound of hell. To my delight, I discovered that he had stopped too. He didn't go away, but he didn't unnerve me any longer.[7]

CHAPTER TWO

Baptismal Waters

I don't know where Thompson Creek originates, but it is somewhere in southwestern Wayne County, a neighboring county to Perry. It meanders through Perry County into Leaf River in Forest County. Leaf joins Chickasawhay River, which becomes a principal tributary of the Pascagoula River, which flows to the Gulf of Mexico.

No one doubts the importance of water, but for a poor country boy, growing up in Mississippi, it was especially important. Until I was eleven, we children had to carry water from natural springs about two hundred yards from the house, or draw water from a well drilled in our front yard much later. According to our age and strength, the five of us shared the task of carrying water, which was required for daily drinking and cooking. On "wash days," once a week, the task was especially demanding because of the water required to fill the wash-pot in which dirty clothes were boiled in lye soap.

When my wife, Jerry, was pregnant with our first child, Kim, we were visiting my parents. I had never heard the story before, but sitting at the kitchen table where most of our family conversation took place, I heard it for the first time. Momma was excited about the fact that Jerry was going to have our first baby, and was sharing about her own experience. Being a city girl, Jerry's eyes grew bigger and bigger as Momma told about having no water in the house and having to carry water from the spring. With her only child, Irma, in one arm and a two-gallon bucket of water carried by the other, she climbed the hill from the spring, and later that day gave birth, at home, to my brother Edgar.

Friday was usually wash day. All the dirty clothes for the week, from a family of five children, would be gathered to wash. This washing required time, attention, and diligence. It would take place outside in the big, black wash-pot. Most rural families (without electricity) used this kind of pot. It was shaped as a kind of half-ball, with short legs attached to the curved bottom. During the school year, immediately after getting home from school on Thursday afternoon, we would tote water from the spring, fill the black pot, and gather lightered and other wood from the woodpile so Momma could set a fire beneath and around the pot early the next morning.

The white clothes, including sheets and pillowcases, were washed first, then the colored clothes together in a second washing. Sometimes, when the items were thought not to need boiling, they would be washed in a tub, using lye soap and a tin-wedged scrub board. After the items had been soaked, the strong soap would be rubbed on each item in turn, then rubbed up and down on the scrub board to get the dirt out. If the washing was in the black wash-pot over a boiling fire, we would use an old broom stick to poke up and down, and stir the items in order for the boiling water to get the dirt out. Once the pieces were deemed clean, Momma wrung them by hand, rinsed them in a separate tub with clean water, and hung them on the clothesline. Sometimes, in cold winter, the clothes would come so close to freezing that they would become stiff and look like dummies hanging on the line.

In spring, summer, and fall, and in the winter when it was not freezing cold, there was nothing like the smell and the fresh feel of clothes dried in the sunshine and breeze. Going to bed half naked on a freshly washed sheet, dried in the sun, was an indescribable delight. While the weekly clothes washing usually came on Friday, during the school year, as children, our bathing came on Saturday. Water would be boiled on the wood-burning stove in the kitchen, enough hot water to make warm a half-filled galvanized wash tub (the largest tub for domestic use). The tub would be set up near the stove so that, coming out of the tub, we would stay warm as we dried off.

Thinking about how little money my father made as a laborer during those years, I have often wondered how he saved the money to have a well drilled. Within itself, that's a witness to the importance of water. We children were happy when we got that well in our front yard. The water task was made easier; no more toting water from the spring. With a rope and a pulley we would lower a cylinder-shaped bucket into the well. The bucket had a valve that opened to fill with water, and then closed when the bucket was drawn up. The largest well bucket we ever had held about three gallons of water. So we could draw water once and fill the two buckets that went into the kitchen for cooking and drinking use, and the one bucket that set on a shelf on the front porch, ready for a drink anytime one was thirsty.

I can't remember the family ever having a camera back then, and we don't have many photographs from our growing-up years. Among the few pictures we do have is of the entire family at the well in the front yard. Momma and Daddy are seated in front of the well in two rocking chairs, brought out from the porch, and the children are standing around behind them. It is the only picture we have of the entire family when we children were young.

I have wondered why the well was put in the front yard. Would it not have been more convenient in the back, near the kitchen, and near the place where outdoor clothes washing took place? Again, it does say something about the importance of water; I wonder if Daddy might have wanted people to see it, to know that his family had a water well, and no longer had to carry water from a spring away from the house.

Water was especially important to us children. It was in the branches and creeks of Perry County that we had most of our recreation . . . swimming and fishing. We spent a lot of time in the branch a half-mile from our house catching crawfish. This was a sport that really defines what play ought to be. Because of the hot summer and lack of rain, the branch would almost go dry. But where there was a bit of water we could usually find crawfish. We didn't have anything to do with the crawfish we caught; we just caught them, put them in a jar, and later put them back in the water. Play is really play when it is purposeless in terms of meaning or accomplishment; it is doing nothing in a joyful way. We pronounced the name of creatures we were catching as though their name was spelled "craw" fish, not "crey" fish.

Now and then when I'm doing nothing and forgetting the meaning of play, I try to use my doing nothing purposefully. Those who know me know how purpose driven I am. That has been a huge issue with me: growing up in poverty with limited cultural, economic, and educational opportunities, I have been driven by a neurotic need to prove myself. That has made me a workaholic. Now and then when I fall into the snare of using my doing nothing purposefully, I wonder about the different names we give flowing streams of water. What determines whether they are brooks, streams, creeks, branches, or rivers?

The second stanza of one of my favorite hymns, "How Great Thou Art," goes, "When through the woods and forest glades I wander / And hear the birds sing sweetly in the trees; / When I look down from lofty mountain grandeur / And hear the brook and feel the gentle breeze."[1]

I don't know whether *brook* is a more poetic word than *creek*; it must be. I don't know a poem that refers to a creek, but there are many that mention brooks. I don't know a stream of water in Mississippi that is called a brook, but we have lots of creeks, and we have branches. Not having firsthand experience with brooks, I sought to get some distinction and this is what I found. A stream is a small flow of water that is full all year round. It may be small enough to ford without getting wet, or it could be up to four feet across. A brook is a larger stream; up to twelve feet across. A branch is probably a local term used to describe a stream, like a creek, only much smaller. The label doesn't give you any guidance as to the volume of water flowing through it. None of this tells me why we had nothing we called a *brook* in Mississippi.

Long Branch is where we spent endless hours. When the water in it was not plentiful, we caught crawfish. But there was plenty of time in the summer when we fished and swam in it. Our swimming was restricted to one portion we called our "swimming hole." Many times we would spend an hour or two fishing in the hole, but when the fish ceased biting, or we grew weary of waiting for a bite, swimming became more inviting. When there were no girls with us, which was usually the case, it was clothes off and into the water.

I never had a swimsuit until we moved to Chickasaw, Alabama, when my father worked as a welder in the shipyards there during World War II. Daddy didn't want us going to school in the city, but we moved there for a summer and soon discovered Eight Mile Creek, which had good swimming places. Unlike Long Branch, we couldn't swim naked; there were too many people around. My oldest sister, Irma, had a job and she bought my brother Lloyd and me our first bathing suits. (We didn't call them swim "trunks.")

But Thompson Creek was much more than the provider of endless happy times of fishing and swimming. Thompson Creek was my baptismal waters. It was there, on a warm Sunday afternoon, that Brother Wiley Grissom immersed me in cold flowing waters with those anointing words: "I baptize you in the name of the Father, and the Son, and the Holy Spirit."

Brother Grissom, a John the Baptist kind of guy, was the pastor of Eastside Baptist Church, which was about two hundred yards up the road from our house. He was a fifth-grade-educated preacher, with no formal theological training, but he was a powerful preacher. Years later, at age sixty, I became president of Asbury Theological Seminary, a graduate theological school training young men and women for ministry. In that setting, with that responsibility, I often thought of Brother Grissom.

Memory of him kept me aware of the fact that *calling* and *anointing* are as important (ultimately, maybe more important) as education.

Like John the Baptist, every Sunday he called us to repentance. He had no hesitancy in naming sin for what it is . . . a destructive power in our lives over which only the Holy Spirit can give us control. He was in the style and with basically the same theological perspective of all the religion I had experienced.

My mother was a professing Christian; my father was not. During my early years, we lived miles out in the country, never near a church, so we attended only spasmodically. The church we attended now and then was Dykes Chapel Baptist Church. I still don't understand the language, and I'm sure they didn't. A church and a chapel are not the same, whether you are using the word to designate a building or talking about the nature of the congregation that gathers. But that wasn't an issue for me or anybody in that community. It was the most visible church in a six-mile radius and the only church building I remember in the community. I heard it referred to as a "Hardshell Baptist" congregation, but no one ever seemed to agree on what that meant. Apparently it had to do with rigidity of doctrine and conduct. Everything about it seemed stern to me. My hunch is, it was referred to as "hardshell" more often by those outside the church, rather than members of the congregation. The pastor was present and preached only once a month.

My religious exposure came from many directions: traveling preachers who would mount the front porch of a farm house and preach to anyone who had heard the word-of-mouth news that he was going to be there. They gathered around in the yard, most of the listeners standing. There were ten-day revivals under a brush arbor constructed just for the revival when the crops had been planted, or when the harvest was over . . . once-a-year events, that may have been more a social gathering than a religious one. My momma used to say you could expect two or three babies born out of wedlock, nine months after those revivals. Holiness preachers who had little standing or recognition, but far more than a little passion and commitment, would preach for repentance and commitment. They were called "holiness," rather than the current language "charismatic."

I don't know how such haphazard expressions of church got to me, but they obviously did. I was a preteen and my exposure to it all was certainly limited. Though my mother was a Christian, and read the Bible, we were not a practicing Christian family that read the Bible together or attended church regularly. My father's father, Lewis, was an uneducated Free Will Baptist preacher who had to walk or ride a horse to all his preaching engagements. Though I heard stories about him, which came primarily from my mother, I never knew him. I regret that, and I especially regret not engaging my father in talking about his father.

Grandpa Lewis's brother, my great-uncle Wiley Dunnam, also became a preacher late in life. I heard him preach two or three times at Dykes Chapel, even after we moved out of the community; and one time as an adult, at a funeral. I didn't like what I heard, either when I was young or when I was an adult. He was a stereotypical hardshell preacher.

Though Brother Grissom was a John the Baptist type, his strong evangelical message was flavored with a kind of winsome expression of care and concern. I always knew he was against sin . . . and he often named the sins he felt were most common and destructive. I also knew he was certain of God's judgment, and to die without Christ would mean eternal separation from God. Yet, I did not hear his preaching the way I had heard other preachers. Their sternness and judgment was so pronounced that they seemed a bit happy that I might spend eternity in hell. But not so with Brother Grissom. His invitations at the close of every sermon were never the pleading, on-going calling, with an invitation hymn, that I thought would never stop. Most of the time it was a matter-of-fact, "If you are separated from God, feel a need for a relationship with Christ, know that you are guilty of sin, and are willing to repent and accept the forgiveness of Christ, come!"

There was both urgency and compassion in his call. And one Sunday I responded to his invitation. I walked down the aisle at the close of a

Sunday-morning worship service at Eastside Baptist Church, publicly professed my belief and faith in Jesus Christ as my Savior, and made a commitment, pledging to willfully allow him to be Lord of my life. I'm not even sure what language was used. I knew very little and, in retrospect, all my previous experience was not what I really wanted . . . and, in fact, even then, mystery of mystery, I knew Christianity was far more than what I had heard about. I think I responded to what I thought *might be* in terms of my own life if I committed myself to Christ. And that's what I did.

I was thirteen, and would you believe, my father, who was then forty, came down the aisle following me to make his profession of faith in Christ too.

The next Sunday afternoon, faithful Christians from our Eastside Baptist Church gathered on the banks of Thompson Creek about three miles from the church. I don't remember if there were other folks baptized that day because I have always celebrated the fact that my father followed me in baptism, though Brother Grissom baptized him first.

I can't tell you how many people I have baptized since that time, saying more than Brother Grissom said at my baptism. There was little ritual in Eastside Baptist Church. He did ask me if I repented of my sins and if I trusted Christ for salvation . . . that was about it.

In the United Methodist Church we baptize in a lot of different ways . . . by pouring, by sprinkling, and by immersion. Though pouring or sprinkling are not nearly as dramatic as immersion, we make far more of the whole event of baptism than Brother Grissom did. Our liturgy for the sacrament of baptism begins with an explanatory affirmation: "Brothers and sisters in Christ: Through the Sacrament of Baptism we are initiated into Christ's holy church. We are incorporated into God's mighty acts of salvation and given new birth through water and the Spirit. All this is God's gift, offered to us without price."[2]

In our preaching and teaching, we talk about how we receive our identity from others, from the expectations of friends and colleagues, from the labels society puts upon us, and from the influence of family.

But in becoming a Christian, we receive a new identity. We no longer allow others to tell us who we are. Christ now claims us and instructs us. A Christian is a new person, one who has "put on Christ." Baptism celebrates becoming that new identity.

That's the reason, at the beginning of our church's ritual, the candidates for baptism respond to a part of the service labeled "Renunciation of Sin and Profession of Faith." That liturgy begins with putting off the old, renouncing sin and the evil powers of the world, and pledging our loyalty to Christ. It is after that renunciation and profession, and after the entire congregation pledges to support and nurture in the faith the persons being baptized, and they corporately profess their faith through the historic Apostles' Creed, that the pastor says a prayer blessing the water in which the person is to be baptized.

I knew very little about the depth of what I was doing at age thirteen. I did know that it was the beginning of a journey and baptism was the high-water mark that signaled the beginning of the journey. Brother Grissom knew Thompson Creek was baptismal water, though he did not bless the water as I do, with the powerful prayer that states the place water has played in our salvation story.

Eternal Father: when nothing existed but chaos, you swept across the dark waters and brought forth light. In the days of Noah you saved those on the ark through water. After the flood you set in the clouds a rainbow. When you saw your people as slaves in Egypt, you led them to freedom through the sea. Their children you brought through the Jordan to the land which you promised.

In the fullness of time you sent Jesus, nurtured in the water of a womb. He was baptized by John and anointed by your Spirit. He called his disciples to share in the baptism of his death and resurrection and to make disciples of all nations.

Pour out your Holy Spirit, to bless this gift of water and those who receive it, to wash away their sin and clothe them in righteousness throughout their lives, that, dying and being raised with Christ, they may share in his final victory.[3]

What we United Methodists believe is so important that we are constantly calling people to remember their baptism. We take this position because it makes no difference whether you were baptized as an adult or as a child, we all start on a journey at baptism, a journey we label "going on to salvation." For the child, the journey begins in the nurturing community of the church, where persons learn they are loved by God and what that means. At some time later the child will hear the "Come!" like I heard from Brother Grissom: come to make his or her personal profession of faith, taking responsibility, accepting Christ as Savior and Lord.

Most often, this is during adolescence, at the time when the person begins to take responsibility for his or her own decisions. In retrospect, that is what was happening with me. I was not nurtured in the faith by the church. I had little Sunday church experience. But somehow, by God's grace, I must have felt I had to take responsibility for my own relationship to Christ, so like most people who are Christian, I made that decision as an early teen.

You have heard people say, "I was baptized Methodist," or, "I was baptized Presbyterian," which could mean that in baptism they got their identity papers and that was the end of it. But again, baptism is not the end. It is the beginning of a lifelong journey of faith. Though I knew something of great significance was happening at my baptism, I could never have imagined the meaning and richness of the journey I was beginning, and that that journey would take me far from Perry County, around the world.

Though my mother and father are long since gone on to be with the Lord, I still visit Richton, Mississippi, with some degree of regularity. My only living sibling, Lois, is there. To visit her I have to travel about two miles out of the little town, and cross a bridge that spans Thompson Creek. As I do, I thank God for Momma and Daddy and Brother Grissom and I praise God for my baptismal waters.

CHAPTER THREE

I Have Set My Face like Flint

My first memories of childhood were in what our family called the "Lafe Davis Place." I never knew Lafe Davis, but I have assumed through the years he was a wealthy man. He owned a lot of farm and timber land and a number of tenant houses. We were not tenant farmers (Daddy was a logger then), but we rented one of those tenant houses.

What I remember most about it was it was never warm enough in the winter and always too hot in the summer. I was almost two when we moved there, and I'm sure I slept with Momma and Daddy until I was about three, when I began to sleep with my two brothers. I can still feel the heaviness of the quilts Momma piled upon us three boys during the cold winter months. Once in bed, and the covers piled on, there was no moving!

The house was constructed of unfinished lumber; with no inside sealing, the wind didn't have to work hard to get to us. In fact, year round we had to set the coal oil lamps in certain places, lest they be blown out by invading wind.

There was a huge pasture in front and woods behind the house, multiple trees to climb, and a freshwater spring from which we got our water. Below the spring we dammed off the flow from the spring to create a play hole, for we were forbidden to play in the spring itself.

The house was located almost a half mile from the road where the bus picked us up for school. Mississippi has never been known for her commitment to education, but I didn't know that. Mulberry School, in Perry County, was the first I ever attended. It was called an elementary school, grades one through eight, but also had a primer class, which we now call kindergarten.

I don't know how it was allowed, but I spent most of my primer year, at age five, seated beside my seventh-grade sister, Irma. I'm sure it was not as much as I remember, but for a five-year-old who was always smaller than others his age, that is what I remember, and what we remember is what counts. Maybe the teacher, who had primer students through third graders to teach, was ahead of the time. She knew that my exposure in those upper classes would be more meaningful than the little attention I would receive from her. And maybe it was that start that led teachers later to promote me from the third to the fifth grade.

Denim overalls were our normal dress. Because denim is so long-lasting, I was more often than not wearing hand-me-downs. That meant nothing to me until about the sixth grade, when I became ashamed that everyone knew I was wearing overalls my older brother had outgrown.

Cleanliness was next to godliness for Momma, so every day when we got home from school we had to change into play/work clothes for the rest of the day. The difference was primarily their age, and the fact the play/work clothes probably were patched here and there. Also, it made the school clothes last longer. Most of the time we could wear a pair of overalls a week without them being washed.

I can't remember ever having a conversation with my parents about going to college. That just wasn't a part of who we were. No one in either of their families had ever gone to college; in fact, to my knowledge, no one had ever finished high school. I don't know when it became so clear, but by the time I finished high school, there was no question I was going to college . . . though I had no idea what I was going to study. I was convinced that a college education was my ticket out of poverty, and what I painfully perceived as a deprived and oppressive culture.

I was a serious student, and my teachers considered me smart. Miss Olga Cliffton, my high school English teacher, inspired me most. She introduced me to great literature and poetry. Other students laughed, but I took the challenge when she assigned a portion of the prologue to Geoffrey Chaucer's *The Canterbury Tales* for us to memorize:

> When that Averylle with his shoures soote
> The droughte of March / hath perced to the roote
> And bathed every veyne in swich lycour
> Of which vertu engendred is the flour.[1]

I memorized those four lines in my Southern expression of Old English, and even now, I get a laugh from my children by quoting it, though I have long since lost even a hint of right pronunciation.

We had no books in our home. We didn't have the money to subscribe to magazines. In fact, during my adolescent years we didn't read a weekly, much less a daily, newspaper. I don't remember reading a book until I was in high school. We had only the Bible to read. Yet, I saw it read only occasionally. Neither my mother nor my father went to high school; my mother read very little, my father, in later years, read the newspaper habitually.

But Miss Cliffton inspired me to read. The first book I ever purchased in college, apart from my textbooks, was a volume of Robert Burns's poetry. I could read him much easier than Chaucer. Because of a memorization assignment from Miss Cliffton, Burns's words that begin, "O wad some Pow'r the giftie gie us," are a part of the wisdom that has shaped my life. A modern paraphrase of those lines is,

> Oh, that God would give us the very smallest of gifts;
> To be able to see ourselves as others see us!
> It would save us from many mistakes and foolish thoughts.

We would change the way we look and gesture
and to how and what we apply our time and attention.[2]

I've often wondered about Miss Cliffton's private life . . . how happy she
was. She was unmarried, lived with and cared for her elderly mother, and
poured her life into teaching. She was a proud graduate of Blue Mountain
College, a private Baptist college for women, in Mississippi. She was an
ardent Baptist and that often came out in her teaching. Even so, I always
felt her education was more important than her religion.

More important than anything, Miss Cliffton's affirmation of me
and my gifts, and her cultivation of my appreciation for words, style
of writing, and the power of expression, contributed immensely to my
ministry of writing.

Our school term in Richton was eight months. After graduation from
high school at age sixteen (my birthday was later in August), I wanted to
get to college as soon as possible. Though we never talked about it, I knew
my father could not afford to pay my tuition, but I had almost four months
to work before the fall quarter of college began. I could not earn enough
in that time to take me through a year, but enough to pay initial tuition.
I would work part-time and get my education. So, off to Mississippi
Southern College (now University of Southern Mississippi), I went in the
fall of 1951.

The call to preach was a vague stirring in my mind. It had begun two
summers earlier when I participated in a three-day youth retreat. One of
the worship services was on the banks of Lake Lynn, a small lake near
where we lived. The preacher, David McKeithen, the pastor of the Richton
Methodist Church, got into a small jon boat, rowed out about forty
feet, stood in the boat, and preached. I was frightened because I could
not imagine him being able to stand in the boat and preach without it
capsizing. The preaching I had been exposed to would not allow a preacher
to stand *still* anywhere; they were always moving about, shouting, dramatically waving their arms and slapping the Bible, or pounding the pulpit.

But that was not the case with this preaching. It was not loud shouting, punctuated by body movement, but thoughtful and well-stated. There was passion, but it was not expressed so much with emotion as with his conviction about what he was saying. There was no question about it; he was calling us to discipleship, to faithfully follow Jesus. It was invitational; low-key, but challenging.

He suggested that Christ may be calling some of us into full-time Christian service, maybe to be a pastor or to go to the mission field. He made it clear, though, that every one of us was called to be Christian *full-time*, while some may have a full-time profession within the church. This was a new thought to me. Unable to sleep that night, I thought about what that would look like for me; but more, whether the Lord was calling me. From that night on, the thought never seemed far from my mind.

This preacher was unlike any preacher I had known. He was young and very much at home with youth. He was educated, and education was a very big issue for me. I had begun to attend the Methodist Church primarily because of the youth group and being impressed with the pastor. Though I felt like an outsider (I was not a member of the church; the other youth lived in town, I lived in the country), as I became more involved in the group, I had more opportunity to observe the pastor because he spent a good bit of time with the group, and I began to wonder what his life was really like. I found myself thinking, *I think I'd like to be like him.*

Those thoughts were sketchy and I shared them with no one. I was intent on finishing high school and going to college. My four-month summer job after high school was at a gravel pit, which was about a mile beyond our house on the Eastside Baptist Church Road, and near Lake Lynn where the preacher had grabbed my mind. I walked to work every morning. I was a handy man, doing whatever needed to be done and what the boss man thought I could do. One task was a responsible one. Gravel was loaded on freight cars, and when loading was taking place, the car would have to be moved three times to evenly distribute the gravel in it.

My job was to sit on top of the car and signal the engineer when to stop. That wasn't as easy as it might seem. Breaking a freight car takes more time than breaking an automobile, so I had to give the engineer the signal at just the right time, otherwise the car would not be evenly loaded.

Other than the freight car breaking job, most of the tasks I performed alone, so I had plenty of time to think and dream. The call to preach became a bit more clamoring. Though I did not share this with anyone, by the time I got to college, the calling pervaded my thoughts.

My feelings of not measuring up and not being culturally fit remained dominant, and kept me from being centered in thinking about what I might do with my life. The demon of embarrassment that had turned into shame about my life situation was always a mocking presence. I remember the one suit, one white dress shirt, and one tie with which I went to college. There were only two stores in Richton that sold clothing, and only one of them sold *dress clothes*. My father did not own a suit, but he purchased this one for me, and it was the least expensive one we could find in Richton. It was the first suit and tie I ever owned. The occasion for the purchase was the high school senior class play. I was cast as the father of two teenagers, and I had to wear a suit, appropriate for the character's age.

No matter how imaginative you may be, unless you have been subjected to severe, crushing embarrassment and cruel out-of-placeness, you can't imagine how I felt the second week of college when I arrived at a fraternity rush party in my drab, light blue, middle-aged attire. Amid that snappily dressed male crowd, I stood out like a person in a tuxedo wearing tennis shoes.

I was trying to cope with my crazy emotional situational battle, so despite feelings of miserable out-of-placeness, I stuck with the fraternity rush process, and got a bid to one of the three leading fraternities on campus. After a couple of months, I dropped out. The feelings of not belonging were too great. Yet, here is the irony: I had proven something; I *could* be a fraternity man! That pattern of empty proving was to demand too much energy for too many years. I wallowed in the destructive trough of believing that I had to prove myself, to prove I was worthy of being loved and accepted. The conversion was slow and painful; it took years to claim the fact that to love and accept on the basis of worthiness is not worthy of being called love and acceptance.

Poet Francis Thompson experienced the "Hound of Heaven," the incessant love of God following him. My life is a vivid witness to that same experience; God has not only followed, he has gone before me with extravagant love. But, for more years than I can number, there was another hound barking in the deep recesses of my mind, and I could almost feel his biting at my heels. His presence threatened to reveal who I really was—a limited, underdeveloped, uncultured, unsophisticated exile from rural Mississippi. Internally, I began minimizing the progress that I had made; I came to feel that the only difference between *then* and *now* was now I was wearing shoes and brushing my teeth with a store-bought toothbrush rather than a small branch from a sweet gum tree.

Though my feelings of being deprived and cheated were real in high school, I had made a place for myself, and no one knew my internal battle. How convincingly we can hide inmost raging feelings. I was as popular as anyone else. I was president of the senior class. For the sake of honesty, and maybe to give you cause to doubt the importance of that, I confess there were only sixteen in the class. I had the second highest grade average. I was on both the basketball and the football teams; though I never made first team, I played enough to earn a jacket and a letter in both sports. I was small and I think the coach knew I needed the affirmation, so he put me in the game now and then.

All of that belongingness faded in college; I was in a totally new environment. So I'm sure this new life station, and my fraternity out-of-placeness had something to do with my dropping out of college after two quarters. Money also had something to do with it; but the big reason was my struggle with the call, which was growing more intense and becoming more clamorous in my mind and heart. Yet, I still had no thought of sharing it with anyone.

During my last year in high school, I had become a regular in the Methodist youth group. The pastor must have sensed more than I thought, because he began to suggest books I might want to read, loaning them to me from his library. I never felt any pressure, or any thought that he might be leading me into the ministry. I asked him a lot of questions about doctrine and church governance. He paid attention, gave me time, invited me into his home, and I became a small part of his family.

I'm not sure of the timing, but I remember my thoughts. *What if I do become a minister?* I loved Brother Grissom, and continue to thank God for his preaching me into the Christian faith, but I could not imagine myself being a preacher at a church like Eastside Baptist Church. *If I do become a preacher,* I thought, *perhaps it should be in the Methodist Church.* I remembered how impressed I was in the worship service when everyone was invited to come to the Lord's Table for Holy Communion. I had never experienced that before. I found myself thinking about how much I heard the preacher talking about grace, and his preaching was never argumentative. In the sermons I had heard, the preacher seemed always to be in a battle about something; not so with David McKeithen. Add to it all, he was educated. Sometime in the midst of all those thoughts, I became a Methodist; I joined the Richton Methodist Church.

When I dropped out of college, I had not yet talked with anyone about the possibility of becoming a minister. My oldest brother, Edgar, was married and living in Mobile, Alabama, and he said I could live with him and find a job there. My first job was as a server at a drive-in restaurant. Until this day, because of that experience, I tip waiters at drive-in restaurants more than others. It was not an easy job, and I didn't make much money. I didn't go to work until 11:00 a.m., so I could spend my mornings looking for another job.

I had to wear my only suit for the interview for the job I got: a salesperson at Burt's, a women's shoe store. A coat and tie were required for daily work, so I had to borrow money from Edgar to buy two dress shirts, a second tie, a pair of dress trousers, and a blazer.

I worked only two months, my mind in turmoil as I wrestled with what was becoming more clamorous, what I perceived to be God's call. Edgar didn't charge me any rent, but I did pay my clothing loan back. I had saved enough money to pay my tuition, so I headed back to Richton to do whatever I needed to return to college, and to make clearer my call and how to pursue it.

Coming Clean and Being Specific: The Power of Words

We may say it brashly when we are verbally assaulted, "Sticks and stones may break my bones, but words will never hurt me." But our verbosity is a lie, and our assaulter knows it. Words can and do hurt. There is power in words. There's a marvelous positive expression of this in the Old Testament book of Job. One of his four friends, Eliphaz, is about to confront Job with what he perceives as sin, but genuinely wants to be a comforter. So he says to Job, "Your words have supported those who were stumbling, and you have made firm the feeble knees" (Job 4:4 NRSV). Moffatt translates it, "Your words have kept men on their feet, the weak-kneed you have nerved." Words can hurt, but they can also encourage and comfort.

One of the most amazing powers of words is that they make things real. Verbalizing something gives it a reality that is not there until the word is spoken. That's the way it was with my wrestling with, and finally making the decision to give myself to, a life of preaching. After the notion tumbled around in my mind in muddled confusion for months, with weeks when I could think of nothing else, I simply said to David McKeithen, "I think I'm being called to preach."

David had a wry, telling smile; it was one of the most beautiful things about him. But his smile that day was more telling than it could have ever

been before. "I know," he said, "I've just been waiting for you to acknowledge it."

Those words gave solid substance to my struggle, and when David
asked, "Are you going to answer?" and I said yes, my calling became *real*.

It was a lot like what happened four years later. I knew I loved Jerry. I
knew I wanted to marry her. In fact, I knew I was going to marry her. But
I went through some of the same process: struggle, muddled confusion,
lack of clarity about willingness and timing. I was four years older, and
she was only eighteen years old and less than a year out of high school. But
when I nailed it down, spoke the words, and sounded the question clearly,
a *reality* came that made everything else just a matter of *working it out*.

When I said yes to God, through David, the trajectory of my life was
set. Years later, in my devotional Bible study, I found the way to express
it in all its certainty. "Because the Sovereign LORD helps me, I will not be
disgraced. Therefore have I set my face like flint, and I know I will not be
put to shame" (Isa. 50:7). Flint is a hard, quartz-like substance, often used
to start fires. It is rigid and not easily destroyed. Setting your face like flint
means determination. You can be as passionate as you are determined.
When you are determined, you refuse to give up; you set your face like
flint. People who have dreams overcome obstacles because they want to
see their dreams fulfilled. I was determined; my face was set like flint, and
I got in a huge hurry, moving on with my calling.

In fact, I became too hurried. I missed a lot of educational and social
development opportunities because I was too single-minded. I was *called*
and I wanted to preach.

I received my local preacher's license in June of 1952 at age seventeen.
This was not ordination, but simply the acknowledgment that I had been
examined by an official body and approved to preach in the Methodist
Church. Steps to ordination were very demanding, including graduate
theological education. But this license was a *first step*, and I still have the
original certificate.

My father in the ministry, David McKeithen, acted wisely. He started immediately sending me out to preach. This was frightening and challenging. The first ongoing assignment from David was to go each Sunday for about three months to preach in a rural community to a congregation of twenty to twenty-five. It was more a family church than anything more. Uncle Walt was the patriarch. We had a piano in the small sanctuary, but he also played the fiddle. Almost every Sunday, he and his two daughters would provide special music accompanied by the fiddle, and when the volunteer pianist was not there to accompany congregational singing, he would do so with the fiddle.

Uncle Walt made it clear that he didn't favor preachers who had too many notes and didn't simply "preach the Bible." He would remain in the chancel (I didn't know that word then, the pulpit area of the church) with his fiddle, until I had announced my text, read the Scripture lesson, and prayed. He would then move down to the first bench (that's what we called them, not pews), sit by a window (this was summertime), and spit out his tobacco juice regularly.

I tried to take his spitting as an "amen," but that didn't help. What did help was his concern about preaching style: I had to become less dependent upon my notes. From the beginning, because of my uncertainty and insecurity, I have always written full manuscripts of my sermons. I have continued that through the years, and many of the books I have written have come from those full-sermon manuscripts. But my concern about Uncle Walt's approval drove me to be so familiar with my sermon text that I didn't have to be too dependent upon the manuscript.

While my passion to preach was raging, national passions were exploding into war. The Cold War followed World War II, and the struggle between communism and democracy took center stage. Korea had been under the domination of Japan. Now that Japan was defeated, Korea was divided by the 38th parallel between the victors, the United States and Russia. North of the 38th parallel was communism; south of the parallel, democracy. The American leadership saw their role in this war as the ultimate defeat of worldwide communism.

The war was relatively short, but exceptionally bloody. It began in June of 1950 when seventy-five thousand North Korean People's Army soldiers poured across the 38th parallel. Responding as South Korea's primary ally, within a month American soldiers had become fully engaged in the war. It finally came to an end in July of 1953. Almost forty thousand Americans died in action, more than one hundred thousand were wounded, with approximately 5 million soldier and civilian fatalities. Today, North and South Korea are still divided and tension continues to keep citizens in South Korea on edge. Interestingly, the church in South Korea has been one of the most dynamic in the world during the past seventy-five years.

During war, uncertainty prevails. The draft was a dim threat, but the war was nothing but dim. I considered the whole notion of "conscientious objection," but never had to make that choice. In the midst of it all, I was invited to teach in a country school. Difficult to believe, even now, I had only a year of college, and my major was, up until that time, journalism. Primarily because of the war, young people, especially young men, were scarce in Perry County. Teachers for country public schools were especially scarce. The principal of Mulberry School, where I had started to school as a five-year-old, convinced me that teaching fifth and sixth grades would serve my country well, since it seemed as though I would not be going into the army.

The way I saw it, I could teach for eight months, preach every Sunday, and save money for school. Even now, I'm not sure how strategic that was. What I don't know and what bothers me most in retrospect is *how I did it*, that is, how I taught. Poor children! I made it; I don't know how they did.

By the end of that year, I was in the Methodist preaching system. I had been licensed to preach and had preached almost every week during that eight months of teaching. I was in the process of ordination. I was on the list with the district superintendent seeking an *appointment*. That's what we call it in the Methodist Church. The place where a minister serves is called his or her appointment, or charge.

When there are not enough ordained persons to serve all the congregations, licensed local preachers are appointed. According to where one is in the ordination process, and in relation to the Annual Conference, one may not only preach and lead funeral services, one may perform weddings and serve Holy Communion.

In June of 1953, two months short of being nineteen years old, I was appointed to the McLain Charge. This charge had three congregations, one in McLain (the lead congregation on the charge), one in Beaumont, and one in Leaf. I jokingly tell people I did so well that first year, the district superintendent gave me a fourth church the next year, in a small community in Green County. In our ministry system, having one congregation is the ultimate professional status. More than one church on a charge is usually called a "circuit." The more congregations on a circuit, the lower the status.

Much of the appointment-making is simply dependent upon circumstances. That first year, 1953, I was initially assigned to the Waynesboro Circuit, which had seven congregations. That was to be my appointment and it lasted less than two weeks. I never had the chance to even visit. My appointment was changed to McLain. My friends thought I had gotten a huge promotion, from seven churches to three, in ten days' time!

A house, called a parsonage, is usually provided for ministers in the Methodist system. The McLain Charge had a three-bedroom parsonage into which I moved in the summer of '53. I started back to college that summer. Two other ministerial students from Alabama, Jon Couey and Lamar Brown, rented rooms together with me in a house in Hattiesburg close to the college. I lived there during the week, but on Friday afternoon I would head out for McLain to spend the weekend. I would visit as many church members as I could, especially those who were ill, and would preach in two of the churches every Sunday, and in the third church twice each month. At different times during the year, we would have special teaching services on Wednesday nights. Special events and revival services would be scheduled around my school schedule.

Do I hear you wondering, even saying aloud to yourself, "That's not a normal life for a nineteen/twenty-year-old"? You are right. There was nothing normal about it: a nineteen-year-old preaching the funeral of a seventy-year-old; a fifty-five-year-old telling his twenty-year-old pastor that his marriage of thirty years was ending; a sixteen-year-old girl being courageous enough to tell her twenty-year-old pastor that she is pregnant, and neither her boyfriend nor her parents know it; a congregation primarily of rural folks, listening to a sermon of a twenty-year-old, who is working out his own theology about war, because he has been inspired by a great preacher who is a pacifist.

No, not normal; strange, unusual, nothing you would think of as regular in the day-to-day living of a twenty-year-old preacher. But mystery of mysteries, God's grace is powerful when expressed in whatever ways possible. Two of the biggest lessons I learned during those years were: one, pretension is deadly. I did not have to know everything; people will accept your limitations if you are humble enough to admit them; and two, if I was going to err, I needed to err on the side of grace.

There was not much time, but young folks, no matter what they are doing and how busy they are, find time for dating. To be sure, it had a close connection with the Wesley Foundation on the campus and my work in the church, but there was dating, though there was nothing that came close to looking like a normal college dating life. Looking back, I don't know how it could have happened, but during those two years, there were three young women with whom, at different times, I had a special relationship. Under more normal circumstances, any one of them may have been a person I would have considered marrying.

I had been majoring in journalism, but when the die was cast and my preaching direction was clear, I changed my major to religion and philosophy. I also took as many psychology courses as possible. Dr. John

Nau, a Lutheran pastor, was my major professor who challenged me to be a more serious student. But this challenge had to wait to be actualized. Unfortunately, I considered college something I had to get through as quickly as possible. Preparing my weekly sermon had first priority on my time. I was never secure enough to wait until Friday or Saturday to do that preparation. Even now, I cringe when I hear a preacher talk about preparing his Sunday sermon on Saturday.

It was not until seminary that the life of the mind became a serious consideration for me. I came to the painful reality that I had cheated myself during my college years.

The Wesley Foundation was the campus ministry that sought to serve Methodist students. Sam Barefield, director from 1950 to 1957, had more influence on me than any other person in the college. He introduced me to the broader world of Methodism through national student conferences and guests he brought to the campus. It was years before I had any national leadership roles in the church, but I was challenged to that possibility at a national Methodist Student Movement Conference at the University of Kansas in 1953. The theme of the conference was "Christ Transforming Culture," and a college student gave one of the plenary addresses. I was moved by his passion, and astounded at his brilliance. I saw in him much of what I longed for, but was missing in my life. I was convicted of my failure in my college years, and determined that somehow I would make up for it.

That young man was Jameson Jones, who became an outstanding leader in the Methodist Church, the dean of two different seminaries, and gave two sons to the church: one now a bishop, the other having served as dean of Duke Divinity School, where his father had once served. Jameson died at fifty-three, having served less than two years as dean at Duke. His personal and professional life challenged everyone around him, but his challenge to me was in that one address at the student conference in 1953.

Two other persons who spoke at that conference continued to impact my life. Ralph Sockman, for many years minister of Christ Church in New York City, was one; I read every sermon of his I could get my hands on.

The other, Dr. Albert Outler, is one of the most significant John Wesley scholars in church history and a primary figure in the ecumenical movement of the twentieth century. Outler referred to John Wesley's theological methods as the Wesleyan Quadrilateral: Scripture, church tradition, reason, and personal experience. This explanation of Wesley is common throughout Methodism and has caused much of the confusion and turmoil we have had related to the issue of pluralism. Using the quadrilateral, Outler was key in shaping the theological statement for the United Methodist Church. This "new" church was the union of the Methodist Church and the Evangelical United Brethren Church. The statement and the quadrilateral began debate over theological pluralism, which has plagued the church since. Much to his sorrow, which he later confessed, the quadrilateral added to United Methodism's growing confusion over doctrine.

Though I followed Dr. Outler as he led the community of scholars who sought to make the works of John Wesley available to all, I did not have a personal relationship with him. I do remember a delightful experience. Years later, I became a member of the executive committee of the World Methodist Council. In 1978, my wife, Jerry, and I, with the executive committee, attended the celebration of the reopening of Wesley's Chapel in London. The chapel had been opened in 1778 and remained in continuous use by Methodists until structural problems forced it to close in the early 1970s. It was repaired and reopened on November 1, 1978, its two hundredth anniversary, in the presence of Queen Elizabeth II.

It was an historic occasion for Methodists from around the world. As a part of the celebration there was a royal reception with the queen. We were in a festive hall, with a symphony orchestra playing, all waiting for Her Majesty's arrival. Since Joe Hale, general secretary of the World Methodist Council, his wife, Mary, and Dr. Kenneth Greet, president of the council, and his wife were to be the first to greet the queen, Mary asked Jerry to care for her young son Jeff while they were engaged.

The excitement was at high pitch. When would we ever be in an audience with the queen? I've witnessed only few similar experiences, filled with such eager anticipation; an air of wistful expectancy was palatable. Jerry and Jeff were standing beside our dear friend, Bishop Lawi Imathiu, from Kenya. Patience not being my strong suit, I had moved over near the refreshment area; there might be a chance I would get a quick cup of coffee. Jerry was intent on making sure that Jeff would get a close-up view of the queen. To Jerry's amazement, the queen stopped directly in front of Bishop Imathiu. She had been told of Lawi's leadership as a member of the parliament of Kenya, which had once been a part of the British Commonwealth. While I was away, hoping for a cup of coffee, Jerry was elbow-to-elbow with Lawi as he was presented to the queen.

I assume Dr. Outler was doing the same thing I was, because we were together as we marveled at the elation. He had to speak loudly as the excitement rose; I strained to hear him say, "As those who for two hundred years have championed democratic institutions, we are quite beside ourselves, aren't we?"

Through the years, I listened for his wry humor and his incisive theological arguments as I became involved in the theological tension of a church of great diversity. As for Jeff, on return home, he told his teacher that his most exciting experience was finding a frog in Hyde Park.

Apart from Sam Barefield's personal influence, he opened my mind and heart to two of the pressing issues of the day: war and civil rights. He invited Dr. Henry Hitt Crane, senior pastor of Central Methodist Church in Detroit, to be one of the Religious Emphasis Week speakers. That church had

long been known as a "Peace and Justice" church. In 1830, Sheriff Thomas S. Knapp, who was a member of Central, resigned rather than carry out a hanging on the commons right outside the church.

Members joined a throng so horrified by the hanging that they threw the flogging post into the river and demanded an end to capital punishment in Michigan. That was the last execution in Michigan, which became the first English-speaking territory in the world to abolish the death penalty.[3]

Sam would not allow a witness like that to go unnoticed, and he wanted us students to be exposed to that dimension of the gospel.

In the tradition of that kind of social witness,

Dr. Crane, senior pastor from 1938 to 1958, was a pacifist in both World Wars I and II. He was summoned to both Sen. Joseph McCarthy's committee and the House Unamerican Activities Committee, accused of being a communist. His successor, Dr. James H. Laird was hung in effigy for his opposition to the Vietnam War.[4]

I knew nothing of the history of the church, or Crane's history. I experienced his courage as he passionately and convincingly shared his message. The most turmoil we experienced on campus came as a result. The Korean War had been raging and patriotism was celebrated. One of the professors, a retired military man (I believe, a navy admiral), publicly took issue with Crane and made pacifism a campus-wide issue. Sam received the negative brunt of the administration's effort to deal with the turbulence. I saw in Sam the kind of quiet confidence essential for leadership in times of turmoil and strife, but also I have been "nearly a pacifist" through the years, beginning in part during those college years.

It was not until December 1, 1955, when Rosa Parks, after an exhausting day at work, refused to give up her bus seat to white passengers in Montgomery, Alabama, that the civil rights movement and Dr. Martin Luther King Jr. began to get national public attention. Sam knew the struggle was only beginning, and he began to confront us with the issue and call us to witness and leadership.

One of the persons he introduced us to was P. D. East, the editor of the *Petal Paper*. Petal was a little town, just across the river from Hattiesburg, on Highway 42, just twenty miles beyond which was my town, Richton. P. D. was always happy to come to our Wesley Foundation gatherings. Though he was not a believer, he had the strong conviction that the church had to lead the way through the darkness that enshrouded our Southern culture.

He had no intention of ending up where he was as a crusader against racism and our Mississippi closed society. He built his little daily newspaper into two thousand subscribers and was making a good living. But he told us about how he just got sick of the daily hypocrisies; cunning laws to stop blacks from voting; the humiliation of black leaders who would be invited to meetings called by whites, but then told they couldn't stay because according to Mississippi state law, whites and blacks could not be in the same room together.

To challenge us soon-to-be-ordained ministers of the gospel, he told us of being in his office one Sunday morning . . . and there he'd take a long pause, then make a digging remark about not being in church because he would be with the same people who were crushing the souls of black people. As that remark would settle in our minds and grab our hearts, he would say in his distinctive, deliberate drawl, "I felt that if I didn't say something about what was stuck in my craw, I'd explode." What was stuck in his craw was the fact that, rather than loving and caring during those turbulent times of racial discrimination and upheaval, the church was, at times, actively involved in the oppression of and discrimination against black people.

It was this kind of witness that Sam made available to us in the Wesley Foundation that began to shape us even more than we realized. Whether overtly conscious of it or not, we had to deal with the nightmare of the soul of a man like P. D., who was seeking to pull himself out of the swamp of deep-seated prejudice that had seemed a natural way of life, and in doing so he was hazarding his livelihood and even his life.

P. D. was one of the persons some of us turned to for enlightenment and counsel when we returned from seminary and became actively engaged in ministry in that closed society he was so courageously challenging.

A few years ago, at least fifty years after the fact, a person who had been a young member in the McLain Methodist Church where I was preaching during those college years of being influenced by Sam and guests like P. D., reminded me of a sermon I had preached. He even remembered the title of the sermon, "Behold the Dreamer Cometh." He told me I had based the sermon on the story of Joseph, the dreamer, who was sold into slavery by his brothers, and that I had used it to talk about civil rights. Civil rights was a low-key subject then and I'm sure that is the reason I had only two or three people challenge my preaching.

That would not be the case ten years later, in the mid-sixties, after seminary, when I had returned to Mississippi and was involved in the civil rights movement, which was becoming more and more turbulent, with riots taking place at Ole Miss, and civil rights workers being killed all over the state.

CHAPTER FOUR

Calling Confirmed

I don't know how it is with you, but I can recall occasions when a text of Scripture grabbed my imagination, gripped my mind, burrowed its way into my soul, and became a part of my being. In many instances, I can relive the setting when that happened and it energizes me.

Such an occasion was Senior Recognition Day at Candler School of Theology, Emory University, 1958, and I was graduating. The dean had invited Dow Kirkpatrick to speak at our service. Dow was at his best, and that was great! His text was 2 Corinthians 4:1–6:

> Therefore, since through God's mercy we have this ministry, we do not lose heart. Rather, we have renounced secret and shameful ways; we do not use deception, nor do we distort the word of God. On the contrary, by setting forth the truth plainly we commend ourselves to everyone's conscience in the sight of God. And even if our gospel is veiled, it is veiled to those who are perishing. The god of this age has blinded the minds of unbelievers, so that they cannot see the light of the gospel that displays the glory of Christ, who is the image of God. For what we preach is not ourselves, but Jesus Christ as Lord, and ourselves as your servants for Jesus' sake. For God, who said, "Let light shine out of darkness," made his light shine in our hearts to give us the light of the knowledge of God's glory displayed in the face of Christ.

Dow told a story I have never forgotten. It came out of the World Methodist Conference, which met in Oxford in 1951. The high point of that program was the service held in St. Mary's Church, the university church, commemorating the life and ministry of John and Charles Wesley. There was only one man alive at that time that was the *right* man to preach on such an occasion. He was John Scott Lidgett, then more than ninety years old.

During his lifetime, he was often referred to as the greatest Methodist since John Wesley. He was an author, preacher, theologian, and reformer. He remembered his mother sharing her memories of having heard John Wesley preach. Lidgett was then in good health, but without much strength. His doctors decided that if he would conserve his strength, he might preach that evening. So, they brought him to Oxford on the train and put him in a hotel to rest. When the time came, they dressed him in his preaching robe and brought him to the church in a taxi. They took the pulpit chair out to the car, sat him in it, and carried him into the church. He didn't stand all during the service until time to preach. New life seemed to come to him. He preached for thirty minutes—vigorously. Then, just as he invited the congregation to join in prayer, he swooned and collapsed, every ounce of energy having gone from him.

Many of the congregation undoubtedly thought they were witnessing the passing of this great man. He was carried from the church in an ambulance back to his hotel room, where a doctor was waiting. His friends gathered around and kept vigil. The report is that about two in the morning, he roused, opened his eyes, looked around, and said, "Preaching always did take something out of me."

Well, it does. And it should. My calling to preach was confirmed that day at Candler School of Theology. For me that day was one of those Mount Tabor experiences, one of those occasions when God allows us to see a portion of his glory and, in the ecstasy of that experience, lays his claim upon our lives, and we are never quite the same again.

I am sure I had read that Scripture passage before, but it never hit me as it did that day. It penetrated to the deepest core of my being and has been a part of me ever since. I rehearse the message often.

Whatever ministry I have, and have had, is "through God's mercy." Keeping that in mind, I keep perspective and I "do not lose heart." I know that we have the treasure of the gospel "in jars of clay to show that this all-surpassing power is from God and not from us" (2 Cor. 4:7). Not all the time, but most of the time, I have been able to confess: "We are hard pressed on every side, but not crushed; perplexed, but not in despair; persecuted, but not abandoned; struck down, but not destroyed" (2 Cor. 4:8–9). After all these years, I believe more passionately than ever, "therefore I have spoken" (2 Cor. 4:13). I "know that the one who raised the Lord Jesus from the dead will also raise us with Jesus and present us . . . to himself. All this is . . . so that the grace that is reaching more and more people may cause thanksgiving to overflow to the glory of God" (2 Cor. 4:14–15).

I knew little about theology schools, so I did the most natural thing a person would do: I went to the school my father in the ministry, David McKeithen, had attended. So there I was, at Emory University.

As in college, so in seminary, I had to work in order to live and pay for my education. As in college, so in seminary, my passion for preaching trumped everything else. I was not willing to even sacrifice the short term best I could offer in preaching for what I was really there for: a long-term issue, a part of which was cultivating the life of the mind. Paul's confession, "Woe to me if I do not preach the gospel," (1 Cor. 9:16) had me in a kind of slavish, but joyful bondage. Everything else took second place to my sermon preparation.

I took all the classes in homiletics (the art of preparing and delivering a sermon) available. Dr. G. Ray Jordan, the primary homiletics professor, had written *You Can Preach*, the text for his basic course in preaching. I spent three years in seminary, trying to prove him right! I'm certain Dr. Jordan, deep down, wished he had been born in Scotland, because he thought the Scot preachers were the best in the world, and he wanted to be one. He even tried to affect a Scottish accent.

I was never tempted to try to speak like a Scot, but was challenged by the Scot preachers. One of them particularly, James S. Stewart, has had my loyal attention for years. He was renowned both as preacher and New Testament scholar. He was chosen to deliver the Lyman Beecher Lectures at Yale (our nation's premier lectures on preaching), and I have read those lectures—published in his book *Heralds of God*—numerous times over the years. I sought to incarnate the core of his message: the man and the message had to be in harmony. Belief had to be supported by thought. The listener had to sense that the proclaimer believed what he was preaching. During my first years of ministry in Mississippi, James Stewart became important in my understanding of the New Testament, and in my theological thinking. His book on St. Paul, *A Man in Christ*, became one of two books that has been most influential in shaping my theology.

Though I took all his courses, Dr. Jordan was not my favorite professor. My two favorites were Dr. Claude Thompson, who taught theology, and Dean William R. Cannon, who taught church history and theology. One of my most memorable classroom experiences was with Dean Cannon. It was in my first semester. Ever a theologian, one of his first lectures in church history was about the incarnation, the core doctrine of the Christian faith. He closed that lecture with G. K. Chesterton's poem, "The House of Christmas."

> There fared a mother driven forth
> Out of an inn to roam;
> In the place where she was homeless
> All men are at home.
> The crazy stable close at hand,
> With shaking timber and shifting sand,
> Grew a stronger thing to abide and stand,
> Than the square stones of Rome.
>
> For men are homesick in their homes,
> And strangers under the sun,
> And they lay on their heads in a foreign land
> Whenever the day is done.

Here we have battle and blazing eyes,
And chance and honour and high surprise,
But our homes are under miraculous skies
Where the yule tale was begun.

A Child in a foul stable,
Where the beasts feed and foam;
Only where He was homeless
Are you and I at home;
We have hands that fashion and heads that know,
But our hearts we lost—how long ago!
In a place no chart nor ship can show
Under the sky's dome.

This world is wild as an old wives' tale,
And strange the plain things are,
The earth is enough and the air is enough
For our wonder and our war;
But our rest is as far as the fire-drake swings
And our peace is put in impossible things
Where clashed and thundered unthinkable wings
Round an incredible star.

To an open house in the evening
Home shall men come,
To an older place than Eden
And a taller town than Rome.
To the end of the way of the wandering star,
To the things that cannot be and that are,
To the place where God was homeless
And all men are at home.

Along with the whole class, I was spellbound. As the dean left the
room, we sat for minutes in silence. No literature class in college had

introduced me to Chesterton. I had never heard the poem before, but I memorized it before the semester ended, and I doubt if a Christmas has passed since that I have not found the occasion to quote it. Put that poem together with a part of Dow's text at my Senior Recognition Day and you have enough to go on in thinking about the incredibility of the gospel, especially the incarnation.

I would have never thought then that I would one day have a friendly relationship with Dean Cannon. He was elected a bishop of the church, and became a leader in the World Methodist Council. Years later, I became the chair of World Methodist Evangelism of the World Methodist Council, so we were together in meetings around the world. Alone with him and Dr. Thomas Oden, I shared in calling together the persons who founded the Confessing Movement of the United Methodist Church.

Bishop Cannon wanted me to be a bishop. He was on the edge of anger when I refused to be nominated by my conference to stand for election. He was visibly irritated when we were together, after I accepted the presidency of Asbury Seminary, because he felt I was choosing that ministry track over the episcopacy. We were together on an occasion a year before his death. As we reflected on the state of the church and our concern, he surprised me by bringing up the subject of my not being a bishop, and assured me that perhaps I had made the wise choice.

Because I had to work in order to live and go to school, I chose what I thought was the very best opportunity available. Along with a fellow student, Eldon Smith, I was privileged to lead in planting a Methodist congregation in Southeast Atlanta. Our first task was to go from door to door in the neighborhoods close to the property on which a church building would be erected. We would share our faith, announce that a congregation was being born, and that a church was going to be established. We would keep careful notes on where we thought persons were on their spiritual journeys, and the level of their degree of interest in being a part of a new congregation, in order to follow up and eventually have gatherings with folks interested in the new church venture.

We now have an expansive literature on church planting. Seminaries teach how-to courses, as well as the theology behind the enterprise. Well-developed sociological and spiritual surveys have been designed. Many Annual Conferences have professionally developed programs of selecting and training church planters; but this was not so back then. We had no specific training, or resources, so we did it by the seat of our pants, the soles of our shoes, our knees in prayer, and the Holy Spirit.

Eldon and I worked together for a year, then the district superintendent declared it a pastoral appointment, and I was assigned! I served as the pastor until my graduation from seminary in 1958.

I take credit in influencing the name of the church: Aldersgate Methodist Church. The name itself was a ready opening to teach and preach the Bible and doctrine with a Wesleyan accent. I was a convert to Methodism, and believed deeply that the Methodist/Wesleyan faith and way, with its pronounced emphasis on grace, was the clearest and most faithful understanding of the gospel. So much of what I had experienced in the religion of rural Mississippi was negative, restrictive, spirit-dulling, self-depreciating, and hemmed-in. The Methodist emphasis on grace for *all* was liberating and freedom-giving. Yet, it was clear, demanding, and challenging, expressed in four strong convictions: (1) all people *need* to be saved; (2) all people *can* be saved; (3) all people can *know* they are saved; and (4) all people can be saved *to the uttermost.*

The Methodist movement was born in large part out of an experience John Wesley had in a prayer meeting on Aldersgate Street in London. We need to rehearse that story often.

Wesley had struggled for years, yearning desperately for the assurance of salvation. He had even come to America as an Anglican priest missionary, but returned to England, committed but miserable, knowing something was missing in his personal Christian experience. He confessed his lack of faith and growing misery to Peter Böhler, a Moravian friend, who counseled him, "Preach faith till you have it. And then because you have it, you will preach faith."

John acted on the advice. . . . [yet] found himself crying out, "Lord, help my unbelief!" However, he felt dull within and little motivated even to pray for his own salvation. On this day, May 24, 1738 he opened his Bible at about five in the morning and came across these words, "There are given unto us exceeding great and precious promises, even that ye should be partakers of the divine nature." He read similar words in other places.

That evening, he went reluctantly to a meeting in Aldersgate. Someone read from Luther's *Preface to the Epistle to Romans.* About 8:45 p.m. "while he was describing the change which God works in the heart through faith in Christ, I felt my heart strangely warmed. I felt I did trust in Christ, Christ alone for salvation; and an assurance was given me that He had taken away my sins, even mine, and saved me from the law of sin and death."[1]

In our very name, at Aldersgate Methodist Church in Southeast Atlanta, we had a ready entre to teaching and preaching the core of the Methodist faith and way: personal salvation and assurance, which leads to personal and social holiness . . . all grace, and all for all!

The congregation grew into a dynamic fellowship, and the membership was proud to share a part of Wesley's experiences as descriptive of theirs in relationship to our fellowship: "there I felt my heart strangely warmed." In a changing neighborhood, probably with inadequate leadership to meet that challenge, the congregation has long since been disbanded. The building is now occupied by another faith community, but every year, usually the first Sunday in August, twenty to thirty persons who were a part of the original group gather for fellowship and prayer. They live all over the Atlanta metro area, attend many different churches, but they stay in touch with each other, and they meet face-to-face to remember more than fifty years ago when "their hearts were strangely warmed."

These people not only meet annually, they share in other ways. There is an e-mail list through which they communicate. A person who was a teen during those first years of Aldersgate posted one of those recent e-mails. He was informing the people of the condition of his brother who was seriously ill, in fact, near death, and was calling for prayer.

This communication caused me to look at the list. There were five people who were young teenagers during those first Aldersgate years, along with the lady who was their teacher/leader. There was the preteen granddaughter of the layperson who had inspired the planting of the church. Her mother, who was a single mom, faithfully brought her daughter to church and Sunday school every Sunday, and was also on the list. There was also a couple, at the time recently married and starting their life together in the church, on the list. What a witness to the influence of the church from generation to generation!

The most significant thing that happened to me during those three years in seminary was that I met Jerry, the person I have loved and been married to for sixty years. Many ministers have married persons in their congregations, but few, if any, quite like this.

Jerry's entire family—her parents, Gerald and Lora Morris, along with her sister, Dianne, and her brother, Randy—all became some of the charter members of the congregation, and some of the most active participants. Gerald and Lora testified that their relationship that led to marriage began when she fell down the steps of the Grant Park Methodist Church into his arms, following a meeting of the Epworth League (the youth fellowship of the church). They were now professing Christians, but not a part of, or active in, any church. They made sure their two oldest, Dianne and Jerry, were in Sunday school and church every Sunday. Because of other family members, and its location in the community, the church was Woodland Hills Baptist.

I'm not sure Dianne and Jerry had much choice in the matter, and maybe it was because they were happy to see their parents renewed in faith and excited about the church, but they, with their parents, were among our first members.

Dianne had finished her first year in college and Jerry was in her junior year of high school. Naturally because of our similar age, if I was to have any romantic attraction, it would be for Dianne . . . and so it was, for a brief season. We dated sporadically and casually. The truth is, I was dating the whole family, through being regularly in and out of their home as their young preacher, who was finding his way as a pastor, and seeking to lead them in an enterprise none of us knew much about . . . the founding of a new congregation. Those were some of the most exciting days of my life.

Who can describe how things like this happen? I certainly can't. As time went on, any romantic interest connected with the family shifted from Dianne to Jerry. That interest became serious, and after two years, we married on March 15, 1957. For a year, until I graduated from seminary in 1958, a young woman who had been known as an active participant in the youth group of the congregation, and a Sunday school teacher of the kindergarten class, was now the pastor's wife.

As with all stories, Jerry can tell it better than I. She tells it that she "encouraged" the relationship of Dianne and me, insisting to Dianne that she would make a great preacher's wife because she played the piano and prayed comfortably and well in public. She wryly suggests that she later discovered that I was looking for something *more* or *other* in a wife than one who could play the piano and pray well in public. She tries to put a spiritual spin on it by saying that she had misunderstood the Lord. He was not saying that "Maxie was for Dianne," but "Maxie was for me."

She goes on to say that the Lord made that clear to her on an all-day family outing to Lake Trahlyta in the North Georgia mountains. Two things happened. One, a number of us, including her father, had swum out to a platform in the middle of the lake. Jerry swims, but that is not her sport of choice. But she was not to be left out. She thought that if she couldn't make it, certainly her father would help her. She made it to within about twenty feet. I may have been the only one looking, but it was clear that she was not going to make it. So I became her "savior," jumping in and assisting her to the deck.

After about an hour of conversation, one by one persons began to swim back to the mainland, until only the two of us were left, and she had to confess that I would have to swim along with her in order for her to make it back.

The second thing happened on the drive home. Her father and mother and brother were in one car; Jerry and Dianne, with her college roommate, Betty Jo, were in my car. Jerry loves this part of the story, which she embellishes gloriously. Dianne was in the front seat with me. Jerry and Betty Jo were in the back. Dianne became ill and wilted, head-down on the passenger doorframe. We were trying, but I'm not sure how sympathetic we were to Dianne. The radio was on and Pat Boone began to sing, "I Almost Lost My Mind." I joined him singing, and soon Jerry was leaning up between Dianne and me, singing along with Pat and me, as poor Dianne suffered alone on the doorframe.

A lot of couples have what they label "our song," a particular song connected with their love life and their coming together as a couple. None would be as seemingly unfitting as ours. Interestingly, I still can quote the lyrics from memory, and I sing it aloud now and then, especially when I'm driving. And now and then, when we are driving, one of us will break out, singing, "When I lost my baby I almost lost my mind."

Jerry loves to say that my saving her from the lake, and this experience singing with me and Pat Boone, was God's word to her that the partnership he wanted was not Dianne and me, but the two of us. She would want everyone to know, however, that on Christmas Day, six months after our wedding, Dianne married Bill Leslie. They had been dating all along.

Jerry reminds those listening to her story that she and Dianne, with their mother, had always prayed for whom they would marry. It should not come as a surprise that not only have both been happily married for sixty years, each marriage has produced three children, an ordained minister in each. How's that for "Thy will be done"?

Aldersgate had no building at that point; we were meeting in the neighborhood elementary school. So we were married in Durham Chapel of the Candler School of Theology on March 15, 1957, by (you guessed it) David McKeithen, my father in the ministry.

We had decided to honeymoon at New Smyrna Beach in Florida. We could do nothing glamorous or exotic because I had no money. Jerry's family had vacationed there through the years. I had had no experience making reservations for lodging, so I gave that no thought, and undoubtedly we could find a place on the beach when we arrived there. We married in the evening, which meant we would not drive far from Atlanta before finding a place to spend the night.

Jerry also likes to tell about how, as teenagers, when the freeway system was being developed in Atlanta, and the motel movement started by Holiday Inn was gaining momentum, on some Sunday afternoons when they could have the one family car, she and Dianne would drive toward Florida, looking at the new motels that were being built, and talk about which one they would want to spend their first night of marriage in.

It was after 10:00 p.m. when we left the reception, driving toward Florida, with no plan or reservation for lodging. We were hardly on the way before I started trying to stop at a number of places to seek lodging. But Jerry was selective; she wanted to find the "most beautiful one," that maybe she and Dianne had seen. That went on endlessly, I thought, and we were far out of the city, and there were no motels to be seen. When Jerry tells the story, she reminds her listeners that, "Maxie never turns back; he keeps going." Finally, I'm sure with marked agitation not appropriate for your first few hours of marriage, I said emphatically, "We are stopping at the next motel, no matter what it looks like!"

We did, and there was nothing welcoming about it. In fact, Jerry says her heart sank when we entered the room; the lampshades were crooked and pictures on the wall were cheap prints, hung unevenly. The next morning when we left to go on our way to New Smyrna Beach, wanting to record the first night of our honeymoon, Jerry took out the camera, and there it was, the name of our first motel: Nubby's Truck Stop.

As the theology school grew, another chapel was built and Durham Chapel became a part of the library. The building in which it was located has now been replaced by another building, so the place where we were married is no more. Yet the covenant we made there is as strong today, sixty years later, as it was that evening. And memories like Lake Trahlyta and Pat Boone reflect the stuff that has made our life together so rich, rewarding, and pure, unvarnished *fun*. Fortunately, I haven't "lost my baby" and, for the most part, I haven't "lost my mind."

Partnership in Marriage and Ministry

I don't know when I became as certain as I am that love is decision and marriage is commitment. The flower of love burst into full blossom when Jerry and I became one in marriage. But love is a fragile thing, demanding a lot of attention. It must be watered with intentional honesty and fed with deliberate care, or else it will fade and lose its fragrance. Sadly, during the first years of our marriage, I didn't give our flower that kind of attention. I confessed in *Dancing at My Funeral*, "that at least once, I almost chopped the flower down. We had not been married but a few months and this was our first conflict. I wasn't prepared to recognize, much less to deal with the conflict."[2]

I had such distorted notions about what it meant to be a mature person, how to relate honestly, and how to express anger, without cutting another person down. More distorted was my illusion about ministers and ministry. I thought any chink in my armor of perfection meant unworthiness for my profession. I thought my marriage had to be a model!

With that distorted image squeezing in, there was no chance for healthy relational interchange. I needed to control my emotions, especially my temper, and none of that was present in Jerry. She had no preconceived thoughts about a preacher's image and certainly none about a preacher's wife. On one occasion, she honestly expressed herself. I responded calmly, which upset her all the more. Soon she was crying.

"This is outrageous," I said in a superior air that must have made her feel like dirt. I stalked out of the bedroom and went downstairs, calling over my shoulder, "When you are ready to discuss this calmly like an adult, I'll be in my study!"

It took me a long time to come to the awareness that an emotional chunk of Jerry died that day, and also a chunk of our relationship. I was not alive enough to sense the pain, but Jerry was and she felt it.

It's too bad that I didn't know then what we have learned together now. Few marriages are as effective as they ought to be. There is too much pretension; too many couples settle for mediocrity in relationship and live together on a starvation diet when they could be feasting upon a banquet of joy and fulfillment.

I can't recount a time line of our development, but I did discover that marriages that have withered through neglect or deliberate stupid actions (such as my cutting her off that day early in our marriage) can be brought to life again. Three dynamics contributed to our developing an exciting partnership in marriage and ministry. One, we had marriage faithfully modeled by our parents. The expressions of love and faithfulness in the marriages of our parents were totally different from each other, but what was present in both was unquestioned commitment and faithfulness.

Two, we discovered the fact that love is a decision. To be sure there is romance, emotion, deeply shared physical feelings including sex, but the love that makes a lasting, fulfilling marriage is the *decision* to love. Every day we make a decision to love, no matter what, whether we feel like it or not. And often we don't!

Marriage is more than feelings. The feelings of courtship are different than feelings of later married life. Our feelings at this stage of our life are quite different than when we were in our forties. Married love is a decision. As our marriages mature, we become more aware of who we are and this generates apartness as well as togetherness.

Feelings are important, of course. But we don't pledge to love according to our feelings. We pledge to love "for better or worse, for richer or poorer, in sickness and in health." As we decide to love, we find an at-homeness with each other that frees us to share our deepest desires and disappointments.

The third dynamic that helped forge our partnership in marriage and ministry was commitment. The decision to love gets marriage headed toward life and meaning; commitment provides the necessary power for getting there.

The commitment is to the institution of marriage, yes; but more important, to our mate in marriage. Our commitment to marriage and to each other was thoroughly grounded in our commitment to Christ.

There is a sense in which this commitment demanded more of Jerry than of me. Early on she did not have the immediate satisfaction of shared ministry because that had to develop as our ministry expressions developed. Without that immediate payoff, she had to willingly leave her family in Georgia as a twenty-year-old, and go to Mississippi, not only being challenged by a new way of life as a minister's wife, but without her immediate family for support. Then we moved from Mississippi to California, and continued a life of moving here and there to fulfill what we have felt was God's call, all possibly and sometimes simply endured because of deliberate commitment to Christ, to each other, and to partnership in marriage and ministry.

One experience will affirm this truth dramatically. We were three years in ministry back in Mississippi, when I got a call from a judge. I knew his concern for a sixteen-year-old who was attending our church. He was being reared by a single mom who was emotionally unstable. I knew the mom; I had sought to help and had counseled with her on three or four occasions. The conditions were getting desperate and the judge was feeling the young man might need to be taken from the home. But where would he go?

The judge was not talking as an official of the court, but as a concerned person, and I've always wondered if his shocking idea had not originated with the mom. The shocker: "I wonder if he might live with you?"

I knew Freddy. He was an outstanding young man, a bright student, popular in school and in our youth group, who deserved whatever good could be done. I thought about it all day before I even felt like sharing it with Jerry. I was open, but she would be the one who bore the greatest burden. I had no mind or will to try to convince her that we should do this.

We had a two-year-old daughter, Kim, and were expecting another baby. We lived in a small, twelve-hundred-square-foot parsonage with three bedrooms and one bath. We were planting a new congregation that could afford only a small salary. All the rational odds were against taking in a teenage boy.

I didn't even get to the point of asking her to consider what we might do. She was ahead of me in her generous thoughts, and suggested that we should at least see if he would be happy living with us.

We did not adopt Fred, but he became our new sixteen-year-old son, and lived in our home until he went to college and we moved to California. He worked, but we supported him as much as possible and he spent his summers with us during college. Though too old to be our son, he is that . . . a son by choice and decision. Only with Jerry's commitment to our partnership in marriage and ministry could this have happened.

It is abundantly clear to me that our life and ministry has been possible because of this shared commitment to partnership. I will have failed in the rest of the story if this partnership is not transparently recorded.

CHAPTER FIVE

Back to Mississippi, for a Season

The pattern of a Methodist minister's service is set. Most people spend their ministry life as a part of what is called an Annual Conference. The nomenclature is strange to an outsider. Annual Conference designates a geographical area, many times defined by state geographical lines, in which there are a number of Methodist churches, bound together in mission and ministry, with a bishop as the spiritual and temporal leader.

The Annual Conference is the organizing center around which local churches and clergy have their institutional identity and life. The Annual Conference is divided into districts with an administrative leader, called a district superintendent.

An ordained pastor is a member of an Annual Conference. Our governance is connectional, a part of which means clergy are appointed to local congregations by the bishop of the Annual Conference. Local congregations do not call ministers, though the congregation is a part of the decision process. Individual clergy are a part of an itinerancy system, meaning they are committed to go wherever they are needed to respond to the mission of the whole church. The system made great practical sense in the early days of our nation as we sought to share the faith and establish the church wherever there were people. Ministers had to go where the people were. An itinerate ministry was the most systematic way of doing that most effectively. This made Methodism the most dominant Protestant expression in the early part of our country. In the years following the Revolutionary War, one out of every five persons in the nation was a Methodist.

Though radically altered in many ways, the system of itinerancy is still in place. The bishop, with the district superintendents, determine the placement of the clergy. Today, it works out practically that ordained ministers itinerate within the geographical bounds of an Annual Conference. So, in a normal pattern of ministry in the United Methodist Church, I would have spent all my ministry life in the Mississippi Annual Conference.

I was a part of, and committed to, the system, and that is the way I thought it would be. There was never a question about whether I would return to Mississippi after my theological training in Georgia. And though there was a lot of wondering, there was no questioning: I would be assigned by the bishop to serve somewhere.

I was appointed to Gautier Methodist Church, on the Mississippi Gulf Coast, with the additional responsibility of planting a new congregation across the river in Pascagoula. In my less-cynical moments, I like to think that the decision of the bishop and superintendent was based on my experience of planting a church in Atlanta. The strength and the weakness of the system played out rather dramatically in this, my first appointment.

I was excited and on fire, ready to take my place in the band of Wesley's preachers who were serving the kingdom in Mississippi. Jerry and I had been married for only fifteen months. She shared my excitement, but not my confidence. She knew when we married that I was, in the old language of itinerancy, a "traveling preacher," and would have to go wherever I was sent. But young love and romance have a way of accepting ideas without dealing with the reality of their meaning. She knew that we would always be living in whatever house (called a "parsonage") the church provided, and that we would not own our furniture since furnishing came with the house. What that would look like for us had not yet been tested.

We had gotten off to a good start in Atlanta. When we were married, the church rented a two-bedroom apartment in a new complex for the parsonage, and furnished it both adequately and beautifully. It was located about two miles from her parents. Who would not think this kind of life as a pastor couple would be okay?

We owned a few things, so we had to rent a small U-Haul trailer to move to our new appointment, but when we got there we couldn't move in. There was no furniture. Our friend Jerry Furr was pastor of Leggett Memorial Methodist Church in Biloxi, twenty-five miles from Gautier. He and his wife, Marlene, invited us to move in with them. We accepted their invitation and parked our U-Haul in their yard. My excitement was being dampened, and Jerry began to face a reality she had not yet considered.

In 1958, Gautier was a small sleepy village; today it is a growing suburb of Pascagoula with more than eighteen thousand residents in beautiful new homes as well as the stately old ones that have been there for more than a hundred years. The church was small like the community, with less than a hundred members. Very seldom were there more than fifty in worship on Sunday. There were a few more than that our first Sunday because they were surprised to have a new, young pastor. Their surprise was anything but joyful and therein was a problem. They were gracious, but guarded in their welcome. I preached as best I could and they listened, as best they could. As we closed the service, a layperson came forward, obviously intent on speaking. The congregation were not as surprised as I; they seemed to know what was coming. He let me know that he was speaking for ten men and he said something like this: "Preacher, we don't know you, so we have nothing against you, but we want you to know we have been done wrong, and we are leaving the church."

I was shocked. No course in seminary had taught me how to deal with that kind of situation. But there was more. I had learned some of the story and understood some of their reasoning. They had not been talked to about a potential change in pastoral leadership. The pastor I was succeeding was a *local* pastor who served the church part-time, and worked in the shipyard in Pascagoula. He was obviously doing a good job and was loved by the congregation. Without consultation, they were now to welcome a young seminary graduate who would live in their parsonage, serve as their pastor, but would have the major responsibility of planting a congregation in another community. I could understand how they would feel they were being used.

Their pastor had owned his own furniture and had moved. The parsonage was empty, with no furnishings, and the new pastor was there without furniture, but in the Methodist way, the promise was a furnished home in which to live. Responsible people had dropped a lot of balls, communication was dormant, and trust was now on its deathbed.

In many Methodist churches the women take responsibility for the parsonage. Such must have been the case there, because the president of the Women's Society of Christian Service got the floor, following the announcement of the men that they were leaving the church. She minced no words. The new pastor and the congregation could not count on the women providing furniture. They had no money to do so.

Then another surprise took place, which gave Jerry and me a positive emotional change of pace. A young man, the son of the president of the Women's Society, rose from a pew in the middle of the sanctuary. Obviously surprising his mother, he said, "Momma, you know I am going off to college. I'd like for the preacher to have my bedroom furniture. I won't be needing it." The mood change was palatable and Jerry and I knew that the hurt and anger had nothing to do with us. We were as much victims as they were.

Twenty-five years later, I was preaching revival services in the Methodist Church in Corinth, Mississippi. A young woman lingered after one of the services to speak to me. She said, "I bring you greetings from my father, Andy Bond. He is sorry he could not come. He said to tell you he was the guy who offered you his bedroom furniture in Gautier years ago. He has followed the course of your ministry, and wanted me to thank you for him." What a charming witness to the church as family connected across time and space.

I don't know why, but we never got his bedroom furniture. His gesture, though, was monumental for us. Nor do I remember how, but the house was soon furnished. It was not the most comfortable or beautiful parsonage we have had in our ministry, but it is the most memorable. When we saw it the first time, driving up pulling our U-Haul, there were flowerpots on the porch, but the flowers in them were long since dead for lack of water. Portions of the curtains in one of the living room windows were hanging limply on the outside because the widows had been closed without pulling them in. It was not a Whistler look (crisp white curtains blowing in the gentle breeze coming through an open window), but a look of desolation, and not an inviting picture!

It was bungalow style, with a porch across the front. They referred to it as "the old railroad house." I learned it had been owned by the railroad, and used for an employee. The church had purchased and moved it to the site, next door to the church. The original house had no bathroom, so one was added. How it happened could never be explained, but the added bathroom was not on the level of the rest of the house. In fact, the bathroom itself was on two levels. You stepped up into a kind of entryway, and had to take a couple of steps before stepping down into the bathroom itself, where there was a tub, a sink and a toilet on yet another level. You had to be careful that you did not bump your head when you opened the door and stepped up into the room. When we had guests, we had fun explaining bathroom use, urging them to be careful because it was *split-level*.

After a bumpy start with the congregation, we developed warm pastoral relationships and some special personal friendships. But there were more learnings that came quickly. I immediately plunged into the possibility of a new congregation in the Bayou Casotte area of Pascagoula, spending hours calling on the few people who were living there, and trying to find out from the city leadership about the population and commercial projections. In those days we had no sophisticated help in the church-planting enterprise; we found our way as we stumbled along. It took only a couple of months for me to conclude that we were four or five years early in trying to establish a congregation in that area. The population would come someday, but it was not yet there.

We were spending a lot of time with Marlene and Jerry Furr in Biloxi during those first months. Jerry was my listener, hearing all my pains about the Gautier congregation and all my reservations about the possibility of a new church plant. Against my reticence, he finally insisted that we must share my concerns with the bishop. The district superintendent was new on the job, with no background on the situation and no invest-ment in the enterprise, so we felt we were not violating protocol. To Jerry, protocol was not as significant an issue as it was to me. He knew and had a friendly relationship with the bishop. The bishop had ordained me, but I did not know him. Jerry made the appointment and I shared the story as I had experienced it, and my thoughts about the future. Though I'm sure the bishop got more input, he obviously trusted my thinking. Within a couple of months we were no longer seeking to plant a congregation in Bayou Casotte, Pascagoula, but in Bayou View, Gulfport.

I later learned that in the Gulfport area many, including the previous district superintendent, knew that this was the prime location for a new church plant. Also, as early as 1953, First Methodist Church of Gulfport had acquired land in anticipation of a new church for residents of the new Bayou View area of the city.

For the year we lived in Gautier, I preached every Sunday to that small congregation and served them pastorally, but I spent a lot of time in Gulfport, visiting people and recruiting the band of people that would the next year be chartered as a new congregation of which I would serve as pastor.

Despite the rocky beginning, our year in Gautier was rich and rewarding. Nine of the ten men who had left in the beginning had returned to the church. Though a happy turn of events, I have thought often about the one who did not return, having learned that he was a bootlegger. If I had stayed with that congregation, would I have continued to seek him as the "one lost sheep out of the one hundred" about which Jesus talked in his parable?

It did not take long for a sense of identity and community to develop that made our common life and worship meaningful. Our closest neighbors were two African American families across the road and about a hundred yards from the church. One was an elderly lady who lived alone; the other, a couple who always had extended family in and out. They were active in their congregation, one of the historic black Methodist denominations. Remember, this was 1958 in Mississippi, and churches were deliberately and formally segregated. It was always meaningful when one of our members would drive by, see Jerry and me on the porch visiting with our neighbors, and later indicate they had seen us there and raise a question or express puzzlement. I never felt there was anything dramatic about it, but it was a quiet witness.

In the spring before we moved to Gulfport, we were driving to Atlanta to visit Jerry's parents. We had an auto accident near Greenville, Alabama. The Stabler Clinic, staffed by four doctors (a father and his three sons), took care of us in an excellent way. One of the doctors, though not a plastic surgeon, sewed an almost completely severed ear back into place, leaving only a slight trace that somewhere along the way something had happened to my ear. The ear was the least concern. I was hospitalized for more than a month with a fractured skull. The churches of the town rallied to our support, providing a place for Jerry to stay so she could be with me daily. High on the list of meaningful support was a financial contribution that came from the congregation of our African American neighbors in Gautier. It was not a big amount, but it was huge in terms of their resources and its meaning to us.

Twenty persons from the Bayou View area in Gulfport met every week in 1958, planning and praying for a new church. These persons were among the first members of the congregation when it was officially organized. One hundred and forty-five people were present at the first worship service on November 23, 1958; eighty-two were received into membership. That service was held in a Quonset hut.

The fellowship hall, the church's first building, was completed in nine weeks. Billy Guild, our architect, and Roy Anderson, our contractor, and their families became members of the church. The Easter Sunday service was held in the new building with four hundred in attendance. Charter membership was closed that day with 205. I was still working in both places, Gautier and Gulfport. At the June 1959 session of the Annual Conference, I was appointed full-time pastor of the new congregation, now named Trinity Methodist. In three years, we grew to 450 members and on Palm Sunday, April 15, 1962, we entered our new sanctuary. At that time in the history of the Mississippi Annual Conference, Trinity Church was a model of fast growth.

A Mentor in Prayer

Years later, during my years of ministry at the Upper Room, I did a filmed conversation with Archbishop Anthony Bloom, the Russian Orthodox Church leader who had written so helpfully about a life of prayer. When I questioned him about ordinary persons, living the contemplative life of prayer in the everyday world, he used an image that I have remembered all these years. He said a Christian should be like a sheepdog. When the shepherd wants the dog to do something, the dog lies down at the shepherd's feet, looks intently into the shepherd's eyes, and listens without budging until he has understood clearly the mind of his master; then he jumps to his feet and runs out to do it. Another characteristic, which is no less important, is that at no moment does the dog cease wagging its tail.

This is a picture of joyful obedience, which I seek to at least hint at in my daily life. The prayer dimension of it began in a serious way during my years at Trinity Church, in those first years out of seminary. Nettie Beeson, who practiced contemplative prayer as Anthony Bloom described it, was a member of the congregation. She became my chief mentor in prayer. She was a widow in her early seventies when she became one of the charter members of the congregation. No one was more excited and committed.

From the very beginning, as a member of the leadership team, she was always calling us to prayer, reminding us that the enterprise on which we were embarking could be successful only if we were empowered by the Holy Spirit, and that empowerment came primarily through prayer. I know she knew I was limited both in my understanding and practice of prayer. Though it never came through as a criticism, she challenged and inspired me to read and explore the broad expanses of the practice of prayer. She had financial resources, which enabled us to bring some of the giant teachers of prayer to our congregation: Frank Laubach, Estelle Carver, Louise Eggleston, Tom Carruth, and others.

While I count those contacts and relationships some of the most significant growth encounters of my life, I began to do a stupid thing. Even in this area so crucial to our lives as Christ-followers, I allowed my neurotic notion that I had to prove myself to hinder my growth in prayer. I began to compare my prayer life to the prayer life of these persons— measuring myself by their stature. And you know where I came out: a pygmy. This led to false humility and self-depreciation. For many years, I would find myself cowering back in prayer, thinking, *Who am I to pretend such boldness in prayer?*

Along the way, I have discovered that when I am authentically humble, when I see my weakness in its proper light, I can acknowledge my weakness without self-depreciation. This gives me boldness. I don't apologize for my weakness, either in the area of prayer or in any other area, but glory in that weakness, knowing that recognized and acknowledged need is the one condition necessary to appropriate the power of Christ. It is when we are weak that his strength is ours; when we are inadequate we can depend upon his adequacy. It is when we know we are without power, that we can appropriate the power that is available to all of us. And so, I remember the word of Jesus that I have only to have faith no bigger than a grain of mustard seed to move the mountains in my life, and to share in the intercession that will move the mountains in the lives of others and in the world.

The Launching of a Writer's Life

Another senior woman in the Trinity congregation significantly shaped the direction of my ministry. Clara Mae Sells was also in her seventies. She was a retired Methodist deaconess.

Deaconess movements developed in many Protestant churches in the late 1800s as laypersons began working with people not reached by pastors or existing agencies of the church. Though late coming, it was realized that women were an untapped resource for ministry. The notion spread in the denominations related to the Wesleyan revival. In the United Methodist Church today, deaconesses and home missioners are laywomen and laymen who have been called by God to full-time vocation in ministries of love, justice, and service.

Clara Mae had been an early adopter of this lay ministry pattern as a deaconess, and had taught English and literature in small mission schools for fifty years. She encouraged me in my writing and preaching, and launched my writer's life.

One day she showed up at my office with an armload of the weekly articles I wrote for the *Daily Herald,* Gulfport's daily newspaper. The newspaper had a religion page in every Saturday edition. I was bold in thinking this was a way to communicate the Christian message, so I volunteered to write a weekly column and they accepted my offer. I had been writing these for a couple of years, when Clara Mae came with what she thought were the best, and suggested that we needed to publish them as a devotional book.

I was game, but had no idea what to do or how to do it. She volunteered to organize them in some formal way and to suggest any editorial work I needed to do. My weekly column in the paper was entitled Channels of Challenge. Three weeks later she came back with the reflections organized as daily readings for eight weeks, each week with one theme. The title? You guessed it: *Channels of Challenge*. The eight weekly themes were: the giver of challenges, the challenge of self, the challenge of others, the challenge of choice, the challenge of adversity, the challenge of daily living, the challenge of social concerns, and the grace to meet challenges.

There is nothing quite like publishing your first book. If you publish more, the first one, in all probability, is not going to be your most important one . . . and certainly this is my case. But still, there is nothing quite like having the first one come from the press. Women writer friends have told me it's something like having your first child. But apart from that excitement, I was affirmed by the fact that Dr. G. Ray Jordan, my homiletics professor, wrote the introduction and Dr. E. Stanley Jones, a primary shaper of my spiritual and theological life, wrote an endorsement.

It takes a lot of time from the point a manuscript is accepted to the time it is actually published. So, Clara Mae didn't live to see the book in print, but it is dedicated to her memory and to Nettie Beeson, who challenged me to greater heights of prayer and devotion. More than thirty books have followed that first.

I am an avid fan of the *Peanuts* cartoon. The artist, Charles Schulz, is a marvelous, practical lay theologian. My sermons and writings are punctuated here and there with one of his cartoons, which I believe gives light and meaning to the message I am trying to communicate. After *Channels of Challenge* was accepted for publication, I realized that some of the columns I had written for the newspaper were based on *Peanuts* cartoons. I began to write more reflections on *Peanuts* that I thought communicated a particular Christian message. *Wouldn't that be a great devotional book*, I thought. When I had finished enough of those and had organized them into a format similar to *Channels of Challenge*, I couldn't muster the courage to submit them to a publisher. I didn't think Abingdon Press, which was publishing *Channels of Challenge*, would consider it when that book was not yet off the press, and so I tucked the manuscript into a desk drawer.

But I couldn't forget it. Sometime later, I got the nerve to send it to the publisher that was then publishing some of Schulz's work. Within two weeks, I had a letter from the publisher, expressing excitement, and promising to send me a contract, but they would have to contact Mr. Schulz first. Can you imagine my exhilaration? I was ecstatic . . . for two weeks! Then another letter came. "Sorry, Mr. Schulz says no to our request for permission because he has given permission for another book, *The Gospel According to Peanuts*." That author, Robert Short, became a kind of official Christian commentator on *Peanuts*. My book would not have been comparable, but if I had not procrastinated, it might have been my second book. The lesson I have lived by since that happened: keep writing and don't procrastinate.

Not only did my serious life of prayer and my budding writing career begin in Gulfport, our family grew there. Two of our three children, daughters Kim and Kerry, were born in Gulfport. Also, in fear and trembling, we took a sixteen-year-old, Fred Davis, into our home. He has been a part of our family ever since. Each year, the three days after Christmas, we have a family time. Kim, with her husband, John Reisman, and their children, Nathan, Maggie, and Hannah; Kerry, with her husband, Jason Peeples, and their son, Jacob; and our son, Kevin, are there. And joining them is our chosen son, Fred, along with his two sons: Roger, his wife, Joy, and their children, Grace and Clayton; Rick and his wife, Wyeth, with their children, Elliot, Carlyle, and Oliver.

CHAPTER SIX

Back to My
Baptismal Waters

W ater is a life-giving gift. It is life-giving for all of nature. We can't live without water.

In the Christian faith, water plays a significant role in the expression of God's intervention in history and in our personal lives. It has a long association with God's saving deeds. Water flowed from the rock as God's gift to Old Testament people. The water of the Red Sea was divided to liberate God's people from slavery. Jesus was baptized in the waters of the Jordan, and heard the Father's affirmation, "This is my Son, whom I love; with him I am well pleased" (Matt. 3:17). He came walking on the water to calm the storm on the Sea of Galilee. Ritual washings were required for the Jewish people before entering the temple.

Almost all Christian denominations practice baptism as the act of initiation into the Christian faith. Roman Catholics, as they enter the church, dip their fingers in the font with holy water, and make the sign of the cross, often touching their forehead with the water. As a sacramental act, they repeat this ritual on leaving the church.

Most Methodists don't remember their baptism, because they were baptized as infants or small children. As I shared earlier, I was baptized as a teenager by immersion in the cold waters of Thompson Creek, and I remember it . . . vividly. I return often in my mind to those baptismal waters. Thompson Creek was my Jordan River.

A lot of mystery surrounds this signal event of baptism in our Christian journey. It is a powerful symbol, but it is more. To be sure, we are called to remember it and stay aware of God's grace, but it's more. When I came out of those waters of Thompson Creek, I knew in my heart of hearts that God had mysteriously worked something wonderful in my life. Through the years, scriptural affirmations about baptism not only have inspired me, they have shaped my understanding of the Christian way.

> And Peter said to them, "Repent and be baptized every one of you in the name of Jesus Christ for the forgiveness of your sins, and you will receive the gift of the Holy Spirit. For the promise is for you and for your children and for all who are far off, everyone whom the Lord our God calls to himself." (Acts 2:38–39 ESV)

> "Do you not know that all of us who have been baptized into Christ Jesus were baptized into his death? We were buried therefore with him by baptism into death, in order that, just as Christ was raised from the dead by the glory of the Father, we too might walk in newness of life. For if we have been united with him in a death like his, we shall certainly be united with him in a resurrection like his." (Rom. 6:3–5 ESV)

> "For as many of you as were baptized into Christ have put on Christ." (Gal. 3:27 ESV)

I talk about this here because it was at this time in my ministry, back in Mississippi, following my theological training, that another significant event took place at Thompson Creek, an event that ushered in a kind of baptism of fire.

Even during our courtship, Jerry and I would dream of having a getaway place, which would be our own private retreat. In the Methodist system, we knew we would live in parsonages, homes provided by congregations for their pastoral leadership. It was a necessary and practical policy, because in the Methodist itinerate system clergy move from place to place to serve the missional needs of the church. There was even a short period in our history when ministers stayed no longer than four years in one place.

Jerry and I even dreamed of the dishes we would have in our lodge. More than dreaming, we came across some dishes we thought would fit beautifully in our someday lodge. We purchased two mugs for our coffee, and a tiny mug, symbolizing that we were going to have children in our getaway place.

So, it was a romantic notion: we would have our own place. It would not be too practical; it would have to be in a beautiful setting, and the setting itself would have to be peaceful and life-giving. Though we had to pinch pennies to live during those first years of ministry, it did not limit our dreaming. Soon after our move to Gautier, we discovered Belle Fountain Beach, an isolated two-mile stretch of beautiful white sand beach on the Mississippi Sound. A section of it was being developed for homes. The part that had been laid out into small lots was a slice of land between the water of the sound and a wetland swamp. There was a plethora of wildlife from alligators to foxes. Though we were not birders, it was a paradise of birds that fed our love of nature.

Our economic situation may have had something to do with it, but we fell in love with the smallest and least expensive lot. It was priced at $2,200; we could buy it, but there was no way we could borrow enough money to build on it, so we gave it up . . . yet that didn't dampen our dreaming. We even named the place we would have built on it Tanglewood.

The dreaming later became a reality. We took the risk and borrowed $2,500 to buy seven acres of land that bordered a ten-acre lake, near the home place where I spent my teenage years. It was a few miles from Thompson Creek and even closer to the church in which I was converted. Though already beautifully wooded, Jerry and I planted two thousand pine trees during the six months we owned it. It felt good to be land-owners, and we looked forward to our place on that land.

Yes, it was only for six months. A cloud on the deed was discovered, and the ownership of the person from whom I purchased it was being questioned. I got a taste of being intimidated by political influence and money. I wish I had had the nerve and the money to pay an attorney to clarify the cloud. The person who claimed ownership was a wealthy leader in the community, and I didn't challenge him. (Sadly, he was the leading lay person in the Methodist church, and I'm sure that clouded my thinking.) In a tangle of disappointment, I gave up the land, got my money back, paid off the loan I had borrowed to purchase it, and continued to dream.

In 1961, our dreaming was realized in a concrete way. We joined our friends, Paul and Nancy Sanders, and purchased a fish camp. That's what the owners called it, but it became far more than that for us. We named it Hidden Haven.

Remember my baptismal waters about which I shared earlier, Thompson Creek. Its meandering through Perry County from its source in southwestern Wayne County brought it to a few miles from Eastside Baptist Church, making it an ideal place for the church to baptize new Christians. It meanders on beyond my baptismal site, making its way into Leaf River, two miles northeast of Beaumont. In that journey, it passes a half-mile east of Richton, continues south a few miles, paralleling Highway 15. About six miles south of Richton, it flows under a wooden bridge on the Hintonville Road, at which point our dream of a getaway retreat became a reality.

Just beyond that Hintonville Road bridge, on your right, is a driveway and a gate which, if you don't know they are there, you'll miss. The narrow driveway, wide enough only for one car, is lined with large trees with low-hanging branches, some of which brush the top and the side of your car as you pass along. The gate opens to nine acres of land, bordered on the right by the creek, and defined by a big bend of the creek at the back of the property. In that bend was the fish camp, invisible from the road and bridge because of the thick woods. It became for us Hidden Haven, about which we had dreamed. It is difficult to resist talking about the providence of God, and God's blessing when I think and write of this.

Although I had grown up a few miles away, and the property was owned by a family I knew, I had known nothing of the hideaway until I went there on a spiritual-life retreat in college. The wooden cabin sat atop twelve-foot creosote wood pilings to protect it from flooding. It was divided into three sections: a great room and kitchen, flanked on either side by bunkrooms equipped to sleep twenty people altogether. There was also a large, welcoming screened porch on the front.

Hidden Haven was only about eighty miles from Gulfport, so it was easy to spend our off days there. It was *hidden*, but it was also a *haven*, which we needed. Our congregation had grown rapidly, and the pace of leadership was demanding. But more demanding and mentally and emotionally draining was the civil rights furor that was raging and becoming more intense and violent.

Not only was Mississippi the nation's poorest state, it was also, as the late historian C. Vann Woodward once put it, "the most profoundly isolated from national life and opinion." Some saw it as a closed society resembling a police state. Following the assassination of civil rights leader Medgar Evers in 1963, the NAACP's Roy Wilkins concluded that no state had "a record that approaches that of Mississippi in inhumanity, murder, brutality, and racial hatred. It is absolutely at the bottom of the list."[1]

My congregation was flavored by a few military and civil service people from other sections of the country, working at Eglin Air Force Base, making my situation a bit different from that of most of my pastor friends across the state. Even with this out-of-state population presence, tensions still ran high as I sought to be faithful to the gospel in my preaching and teaching. As is so often the case, our suffering— emotional, relational, physical, or spiritual—shapes us more than our feelings of well-being and success. That was true of this period in our life. Though our church was looked on by the system as exceedingly successful, I felt emptiness at the heart of what outwardly appeared to be a dynamic Christian fellowship. I could not evade the fact that the fellowship of the congregation was not a lot unlike the fellowship of the Rotary Club.

In my pastoral leadership, I placed a strong emphasis on prayer and small-group sharing. It was in my small prayer/share group that I received the most spiritual strength. At one season in that group life, we studied a book by E. Stanley Jones, *In Christ*. It was one of the two books that have most shaped my theology and spiritual formation. The other book, *A Man in Christ*, by the outstanding New Testament scholar and preacher, James Stewart, whom I mentioned in chapter 4, is a study of the life of Paul and his understanding of Christian discipleship as living *a life in Christ*. A sign of the personal impact of those two books is witnessed to throughout my life in my preaching and writing, and specifically in two books I wrote: *Alive in Christ: The Dynamic Process of Spiritual Formation* and *The Workbook on Being Alive in Christ*.

We sometimes think, with some justification, that there has been little change in civil rights, but we are forgetting the past: the denial of voter rights, the gross inequalities in education, severe poverty, and discrimination in housing, employment, and social life. As I reflect, I find it difficult to believe that my black Methodist minister friend in Gulfport, Henry Clay, was never in our home for a meal. We were together in our churches and when we would meet together with the mayor to try to secure paving or lights for the streets in the black section of the city, but not in our homes. That kind of social expression was out of the picture in those days, and neither Henry nor I felt that was the place we wanted to protest, or make our witness. In the midst of the church pray-in protests, we never had visitors at Trinity Church. Henry said he put our church off-limits for the pray-ins because he did not want to create or add more problems for me, given my commitment and the work he and I were doing together.

Henry was the pastor of St. Mark's Methodist Church. Due to the compromise that came with the union of the Northern and Southern Methodist churches in 1938, St. Mark's and Henry were a part of a non-geographical Central Jurisdiction, a judicatory made up only of African Americans. In order to get a union between the Northern and Southern Methodist Churches, segregation had to be guaranteed. The Central Jurisdiction was established basically as a denominational center for all black Methodists. So, though in the same city, and though the churches were both Methodist, Clay had a different bishop and district superintendent, and there was no programmatic or formal missional connection between us. Our coming together had nothing to do with normal denominational governance or structures; it was our commitment to racial equality and the common good of our city.

It is a telling commentary on the situation that Henry had a difficult time seeing the mayor alone, or with some of his black colleagues, but he and I together were never denied an appointment. Maybe that was because our church was known in the city for its rapid growth, or the middle- and upper-middle-class residential area we primarily served, or the many young civic leaders in our membership, or maybe because I was known through my weekly newspaper column.

I remember only once that I was in the mayor's office without Henry, so I am not sure how often he practiced this particular odd exercise. He had a small basket in the center of the conference table. Occasionally he would wad a piece of paper and, with deliberate form, pitch it into the basket as though it was a basketball. Though this could have been just a bazaar quirk, I have a notion that since he did not do that when I was alone with him (and I'm confident he did not do it with the school superintendent, or the county judge, or the president of the largest construction firm in the city), that he did it with Henry and me as a way of intimidation, or diminishing any thoughts of importance we might have.

We were in his office once to complain about the fact that he had not followed through on some promises he had made months before, to pave the streets and provide street lighting in the area of the city in which Henry's church was located. Henry was visibly upset and could not hide it. As he began to talk, the mayor began his quirky exercise with the paper and the basket. That upset Henry more. Though angry, he was civil in his confrontation. Had the mayor responded with more emotion, even anger, I think Henry would have felt more valued. Instead, passively, almost in a monotone voice, the mayor, with a slight glance up at Henry as he tossed a paper ball into the basket said, "Rev-ren, I think you have a complex."

Henry bolted upright from his chair, his full six feet, five inches towering over the seated mayor, "You are right, Mayor, I do have a complex, and you gave it to me!" He strode from the room, erect and proud, as I followed bewildered.

I am aware of how, especially during my early years of ministry, people with money, position, titles, or more education intimidated me. Even with that kind of awareness, as a person of white privilege, it is impossible to comprehend the oppressive intimidation experienced by persons like Henry. Though I think my being reared in poverty and limited educational and cultural circumstances has made me sensitive to the suffering of people, and that I sometimes feel a genuine kinship with the poor, any intimidation I have experienced is only a hint of what African Americans were suffering in Mississippi during those years.

In 1961, Henry invited me to an event at his church featuring some white missionaries to South Africa. He knew my interest in apartheid, and my admiration for Nelson Mandela, about whose courageous opposition to apartheid and his moral leadership we were beginning to hear. Along with a few other whites, I attended the meeting. When it was over, I came out of the church to find police cars with flashing lights everywhere. Word had gotten out of an integrated meeting at the church.

I went home, but at midnight Henry called to say the police chief had been in his home discussing the meeting and was insisting that, by morning, he was to provide names of all the white people who had attended. Henry would not give my name without my permission. I gave him permission and a few days later a representative of the mayor called for an appointment, and cautioned me of the dangers of attending meetings with "communists." This was a part of the closed society in the South: to accuse as communist those who did not agree with the status quo. I thought the warning was silly but I later learned of all the accusations of "communist" made against Martin Luther King and his friends. It was a tool of diversion and intimidation.

I have a file folder packed with stories, letters, and news articles, which provide a collage of the depth of the racial divide, the fallout of hatred, the estrangement and severing of relationships, the distorted, and oppressive dynamic of Mississippi's closed society.

One of those is a Drew Pearson column titled, "A Rabbi's Kindness Didn't Pay in Mississippi." It was written at Christmastime in 1964. The article begins:

> Christmas being the anniversary of a Jew born in Bethlehem nearly two thousand years ago, I write the story of a Jew who lives in Mississippi today. His name is Rabbi David Ben-Ami, of Temple B'Nai Israel in Hattiesburg, and his trials and tribulations began when he befriended ministers of other faiths and incurred the wrath of modern money changers.

The column has very special personal meaning. In the winter of 1963, Jerry and I, with our small children, Kim and Kerry, were driving from Gulfport, Mississippi, to my parents' home in Richton, about ninety miles away. We had left Gulfport following a church meeting where angry feelings about my involvement in and preaching about the racial situation were expressed. It was sleeting and the road was becoming icy on that unusually cold night. It was close to midnight out on a dark, lonely country highway. Then it happened. Our car simply stalled. Totally inept at anything mechanical, I was hopeless and I knew there wasn't much chance of anyone stopping to help us at that hour of the night. This was before cell phones.

The children were getting colder, and mine and Jerry's anxiety was rising by the minute as we desperately thought what we might do. Our desperation cut off any thoughtful consideration of possible options, and after what seemed an eternity, a car came to a screeching halt beside us.

I told the driver that our car had stalled and I had no explanation for it. It simply would not start. Without asking any further questions, the stranger asked where we would like for him to take us. Obviously that assurance gave us peace enough to remember that friends lived in a town about fifteen miles away. We had no way of calling them, so the stranger helped us transfer the luggage to his car, and went out of his way to take us to our friend's home where we spent the night.

The man's accent was different from mine. He obviously was not a Mississippian. I surmised that he was Jewish, and his warm ministry of care reminded me of another Jew, and the story he told about a good Samaritan. He was Jewish, and his name was David Ben-Ami, Rabbi of Temple B'Nai Israel in Hattiesburg.

It was this man about which Drew Person wrote his newspaper article. His troubles began when he befriended ministers of other faiths. The Rabbi visited pastors who had been thrown in jail for demonstrating against racial injustice. He befriended a white Presbyterian minister who had been involved in this struggle for equality, and he had assisted in distributing turkeys to needy Mississippi families of all races. Rabbi Ben-Ami's congregation was upset and had asked him to leave. The article is in my file as a vivid reminder of what it was like in those days.

Conflict and confrontation across the state spread and became more and more intense. Voter registration projects, efforts of blacks to get into the University of Mississippi, federal condemnation of segregated public schools, and widespread establishment of private Christian schools became explosive acts across the state.

The pressure kept building as the civil rights movement became more expressive and expansive. At a time when I was spiritually, emotionally, and physically worn out, and about to throw in the towel, Tom Carruth, a Methodist minister who later became one of my primary mentors in prayer, convinced me to attend an E. Stanley Jones Christian ashram. As indicated earlier, I had been strengthened by Jones's book, *In Christ*, and knew about his work as a missionary evangelist in India. He had been especially effective in bridging the chasm between Hinduism and Christianity, and reaching intellectuals. He wrote a book that informed the modern missionary enterprise, *The Christ of the Indian Road*.

The holy men of India had their ashrams, places apart, to which people would go and spend time under their tutelage. Jones took this model as a foundation for the Christian ashram. He felt the need for a spiritual base, a retreat for spiritual refreshment, where there could be in-depth study and reflection in the company of a close-knit group. He wanted to be accountable to others. And so in 1930, he and Ethel Turner, a British missionary, and Rev. Yunas Singh Sinha, an Indian pastor, started the first Christian ashram in India.

Later, stranded in the United States during World War II, while his family was obliged to remain in India, Brother Stanley transplanted the Christian ashram to the United States and Canada.

The model is a week-long experience of living together in community, daily worship and preaching, Bible study, common labor, prayer, and sharing. In this dynamic, Jones insisted that there was no holy man, no guru in the Christian ashram; Jesus was the Supreme Teacher, but everyone was a teacher and everyone was being taught. During the week, all titles are left behind. There are no reverends or doctors, or even mister, miss, or missus. Everyone is either brother or sister.

One of my colleagues, Gerald Trigg, was feeling similar spiritual needs and admired Jones as I did. After our worship services one Sunday, we left Gulfport and drove almost all night to Clearwater, Florida, for our week in the Christian ashram with Stanley Jones as our leader. The week began with the "Hour of the Open Heart," a time when persons shared their needs and hopes for the time together. It's amazing how quickly people can identify and relate when they lead in their sharing not from strength but from weakness and need. The feeling of belonging to each other becomes palatable and prayer is easily focused. Community is almost instantaneous. Transparent, honest conversation flowed spontaneously the following days. In such a community, worship and Bible study, physical chores that support community, and common meals take on inexplicable richness.

The ashram week closes with a healing service and the "Hour of the Overflowing Heart." I had shared with Brother Stanley during the week, and he knew my struggles and brokenness. When I went to the altar for healing prayer, he simply asked me, "Brother Maxie, do you want to be whole?" My response was more than a simple yes. It was that, but it was a YES response of my total being to Christ, in whom alone I knew I could fulfill the ministry to which he had called me.

I returned to Gulfport, not in weakness and defeat, but in strength and commitment, invigorated for the struggles I knew lay ahead. I wanted to share what I had experienced, and I immediately began to plan for Stanley Jones to lead an ashram for us in Mississippi. I took no note of the fact that Brother Stanley's radical commitment to the Christian faith and the vision of an inclusive kingdom of God often led to his being called a communist. His accusers were also offended at his insistence on racial inclusivity at his Christian ashrams. An essential principle of the Christian ashram was that races and classes come together on the basis of complete equality.

My passion to share what had meant so much to me numbed me to possible misinterpretation of what I was seeking to do. With the support of Jerry Trigg and others, I scheduled Stanley Jones to come to Mississippi for a week-long Christian ashram. I'm sure he agreed to come as an act of support and solidarity with our ministry and the struggles he knew we were having. I shared with my bishop, Marvin Franklin, my idea of Stanley Jones coming to our state. He was affirming, I'm sure because he knew only his name and worldwide reputation. We secured the use of the new Camp Wesley Pines Youth Camp in Gallman, Mississippi, printed our brochures, and excitedly advertised the event. But lo, while our bishop was out of the country in Asia, visiting Methodist mission sites, in the fall of 1962, the Conference Youth Camp Committee rescinded their agreement for the event to be held at Camp Wesley Pines. They argued that they had a gentleman's agreement, when rights to the land and lake had been secured, that they "would not promote integrated meetings in the camp until such time as the Mississippi Conference became an integrated church." They believed that we who were sponsoring the event were trying to "bring pressure" on the rest of the Annual Conference by having an integrated meeting. Their capstone claim was that such a move was "too explosive" at a time of "tense" conditions in the state just after the riots at the University of Mississippi, emanating from the efforts of a black student seeking enrollment.

I didn't surrender readily. We moved the event to Gulfside, the Central Jurisdiction (designated black) Conference Center, on the Gulf Coast in Waveland, Mississippi. Later, sadly and reluctantly, Brother Stanley and I agreed that opposition to the event was so intense it was not a good idea to proceed. I had one of the brochures framed, and for years it was on a shelf in my study, reminding me of a failed attempt to be faithful. Even today, on my desk, is a small framed picture of Brother Stanley, standing between Jerry and me, with each of us raising a hand with three fingers pointing upward, which is the Christian ashram greeting, "Jesus is Lord," also the original and foundational creed of Christianity.

A few months after cancelling this event, Brother Stanley and my friend Tom Carruth invited me to travel with them, as a youth speaker, to lead Christian ashrams in Scandinavia. I knew they didn't really need me, but they knew I needed the kind of affirmation that involvement with them would provide. Their action was a challenging characteristic of Christian leadership and what it means to mentor those who are coming after us. I have sought to follow that leading.

I knew it was time for a corporate witness, a witness to the church. Violence against blacks and black churches in Georgia made the news across the nation. I commented on that in my Channels of Challenge column in the Gulfport newspaper, then wrote, "At the University of Mississippi, the symbol of Christianity, a cross, was burned in the wake of state politicians threatening to go out of the business of education if a Negro was admitted to that institution." I warned, "In a day when we should be taking a stand on crucial issues, we dare not piddle with the insignificant. We dare not dabble with the unimportant and fail in the tremendous task to which we are called."

Many of my fellow ministers were feeling the same way, and I joined three of them to make our witness: Jerry Furr, Jerry Trigg, and Jim Waits. On Monday, October 15, 1962, we gathered at Hidden Haven, on the banks of Thompson Creek, my baptismal waters, none of us aware that what we were about would result in a baptism by fire.

Two weeks earlier, violence had occurred on the campus of the University of Mississippi on the night before James Meredith finally succeeded in registering as the first known African American student. The primary riot protesting the admission of a black person to the university had involved three thousand people, with three hundred federal marshals seeking to control them. These marshals, who endured thrown bricks, bottles, rocks, iron pipes, and Molotov cocktails, finally fired tear gas and smoke canisters into the crowd. When the smoke cleared the next morning, casualties numbered two dead and hundreds injured, including one hundred sixty marshals, twenty-eight of them wounded by gunfire.

This epitomized the violence that was boiling over throughout the state. We four were young and had no significant institutional voice. We had hoped that our bishop and other conference leaders would speak out in response to the rising tide of violent expressions of anger and inhumanity. The silence was deafening. Though accused of arrogance, we were responding in humility. We knew it was past time for some to say that not all white Mississippi Methodists would continue to live silently in the closed society that was taking its destructive toll on our state.

We began our meeting with prayer, not knowing what we should say, but knowing we had to say something. It was a time when remaining silent would have been irresponsible on our part, and we would be betraying the gospel we were committed to preaching.

The two largest newspapers were located in our state capital, Jackson. Nearly all of the Mississippi newspapers were owned by segregationists. The Hederman brothers, owners of the two Jackson newspapers, were more than your average run-of-the-mill segregationists; they were passionate. Every day these papers fed the population with vicious condemnations of those who were challenging what was termed "the Southern Way of Life." The White Citizens' Council and the Ku Klux Klan circulated harsh condemnations against anyone who dared question any aspect of the system committed to the closed society that we had become.

Burning in our minds were these vocal, vicious segregationist groups that were speaking everywhere, every day, and we wanted to condemn them. We resisted that desire, and decided we simply needed to express our conviction and commitment. We wanted to speak positively about what we believed. What resulted from our marathon sharing was a kind of manifesto of less than six hundred words, which we titled "Born of Conviction," with four main points:

One, freedom of the pulpit. Ministers were feeling severely restricted in what they could say. The closed society sought to shut down any atmosphere of free expression and responsible belief. In a day when the clearest, sanest, and most devoted voices needed to be heard, there were widespread threats against pastors who sought to be faithful in preaching the gospel.

Two, affirmation of faith and commitment to the official position of the Methodist Church that "God is Father of all people and races . . . all men are brothers" and "Our Lord Jesus Christ . . . permits no discrimination because of race, color, or creed."

Three, private schools for the sole purpose of preserving segregation were springing up everywhere, so we expressed our support for public schools and opposition to "the diversion of tax funds to the support of private or sectarian schools."

Four, we expressed our "unflinching opposition to Communism." We felt it essential to express this opposition because the White Citizens' Council and the Ku Klux Klan circulated literature all over the state declaring that the Communist Party was stirring up all the racial unrest in the South. Persons and groups who were seeking reform and racial reconciliation were all labeled "communist." (A copy of the statement is in the appendix.)

We had no hint of the gravity of what we were doing. It seemed so simple and rational. We were addressing our church, the Methodist Church. We secured the signatures of twenty-four other pastors, and the group was referred to from that point on as "the 28." The statement was printed in the *Mississippi Methodist Advocate* on January 2, 1963. Wire services immediately picked up the story and it made newspapers all over the nation, especially across the Southeast, and all hell broke loose. Every newspaper in Mississippi carried the story.

Joseph T. Reiff, professor of religion and chair of the religion department at Emory and Henry College has written a book with the same title as our statement: *Born of Conviction*. Dr. Reiff grew up in Mississippi, and writes from a personal, as well as a professional perspective. The larger theme of his book is white Methodists and Mississippi's closed society. Though an expansive exploration of religion and race in Mississippi's closed society, he structures his book around "the 28." He explores the theological and ethical understanding of the signers through an account of their experience before, during, and after the statement's publication.

I was in my office at the church on the morning of January 3. I heard a car screeching to a stop in the parking lot a short distance away. One of our most active members, a dear friend and the doctor who had delivered both our daughters, stormed into my office, threw a copy of the *Times-Picayune* (a New Orleans newspaper) down on the desk and shouted, "What the hell is this? I have never been so disappointed in my life!" He was shaking and his voice quivered, "No one has meant more to me spiritually than you, and now you do this. I can't even discuss it."

He turned and left, as though I had done some violence to him personally. He simply did not know what to do, and did not want to become violent himself. I followed him to his car, gave him a copy of the statement, urged him to read it, and to give me a chance to discuss it with him.

Beliefs and practices don't change easily. It doesn't take much hatred to hold us tenaciously. My friend read the statement and struggled with the issues we addressed against the backdrop of our close personal relationship. Two weeks later he came by the house on his way to the hospital. With tears in his eyes he asked for forgiveness. He had read and reread the statement, and though he recognized it as Christian conviction, he admitted he couldn't accept my position. A few weeks later, I preached a sermon on the evils of conformity and the call of God to be transformed and to make a commitment to him. Old patterns of thought and belief again raged up in my friend, and when someone asked, "Wasn't that a great sermon?" he responded, "Hell no! As far as I'm concerned he just tendered his resignation." That's the kind of emotional roller coaster most of the people in the congregation were on.

And Jerry? One can only imagine how a twenty-three-year-old with two babies, far away from her mother and father, seeking to express friendship, to witness, and to share in developing a congregation, felt on long nights when she knew what I was seeking to do. She readily affirms that she was sustained by Christ for this partnership in marriage and ministry.

"Born of Conviction" became an issue across the state. Because four of "the 28" were pastors on the Gulf Coast, not only the churches where they served, but the coast population became enmeshed in conversation. Two groups, other than people in my congregation, were openly supportive, the Unitarians and the Mennonites—especially the Mennonites.

At that time, Mississippi had only one small Mennonite congregation, Gulfhaven, located about five miles north of Gulfport. But there was also Camp Landon, near Gulfport, a part of the Mennonite Central Committee. It had been quietly serving the black community since 1945. The Mennonite Central Committee is an Anabaptist organization whose primary mission is peace-making. According to their website, they strive "to share God's love and compassion for all through relief, development and peace."[2] We fail to recognize, and we too easily forget, the unnamed, unsung, quiet witnesses, who in almost every inhumane and evil situation in our communities, stand bravely and firmly, reminding all who will pay attention, that there is a kingdom reality beyond which we are acknowledging.

My relationship was not with the Mennonite congregation, but with the persons who lived in and ran Camp Landon. They often worshiped with us; they knew and were supportive of the work Henry Clay and I sought to do in the black neighborhoods of Gulfport. My work was primarily interacting with the community political forces. They worked primarily with physical and material support, and with educational and recreational programs at their camp. As soon as "Born of Conviction" was out, they were at my door offering support and prayer.

I don't know where the Baptists, Episcopalians, Lutherans, Presbyterians, and a lot of Methodists were, but the Unitarians, and especially Mennonites, made the scene with prayer and encouragement.

I still can't quite accept Joseph T. Reiff's claim that our "Born of Conviction" statement could be called "the second-best-known white clergy statement in the Civil Rights era."[3] People who study and reflect on the era readily agree that the first-best-known was the "Good Friday Statement" issued by eight white Alabama clergy, pleading for a gradualist approach to race relations, to which Martin Luther King responded in his "Letter from a Birmingham Jail" in April 1963.

In chapter 4 of his book, Reiff compared the "Born of Conviction" statement to other statements made during that period of the civil rights movement to confirm the claim he made about the significance of the statement. He wrote:

> Though several other clergy groups issued public statements on race relations in the South during those years, most were ecumenical and included more signatures. Some southern ministers took a stand on the race issue in the 1950s and 1960s and often suffered as a result, but this is the story of 28 ministers of one denomination and one judicatory unit within that church who took a stand together in Mississippi, generally considered the most recalcitrant of Southern states, during the time when its resistance peaked.[4]

Within eighteen months of the signing of the document, eighteen of the twenty-eight signers had left Mississippi, two left later, and only eight continued their total ministry vocation in the state. In explanation of his use of *Born of Conviction* as the title of his book, Dr. Reiff explained that not only were the statement's signers motivated by deep convictions, but the responses to the statement and to the situation in which it emerged also reflected a wide variety of convictions: public or private support, angry rejection, or silent, tacit, sometimes conflicted approval of the segregated status quo. The phrase "born of conviction" is used in the book to refer to the statement itself, the complex set of events set in motion by its publication, and the larger contextual puzzle of which it is the central piece. He concluded that among all the statements made during that perilous period, "given the critical element of the context in which these statements were issued, there was arguably no Southern clergy statement that came at a more critical time than this one."[5]

I was one of the twenty who left.

CHAPTER SEVEN

California,
Here We Come!

Those days were tough. I have often wrestled in my conscience about having left Mississippi. After all these years, I find myself thinking, *if the church had been different ... if there had been leadership in the church that would have supported us young clergy who were seeking to be faithful ... if the church itself had not been impotent because of internal political and personality/leadership struggles . . . if I had felt any support from the bishop and conference leadership, even from my older minister friends, then I would have stayed*. But who knows?

While we may find meaning contemplating the what ifs, it is fruitful only if we do not get stuck in regret, but find the positive will and power to move forward, expressing whatever revelation we may have had from our contemplation.

The same thing is true with the if onlys. *If only* I had been more convincing and powerful in my preaching and teaching. *If only* I had engaged the public leadership more directly. *If only* my bishop and district superintendent had been less negative, if not supportive. *If only* I had been more strategic in engaging like-minded support. Again, it is easy to get stuck in regret and not learn from the *if only* reflections. The only right response to "if only" and "what if" is "no matter, this is where I am now, Lord, where are we to go?"—claiming that God's will is not going to take us where God's grace will not sustain us.

Though many of "the 28" were forced to leave their congregations, I was not. An organizing pastor of a congregation has a unique relationship to the people of that congregation. For many of them, he is the only pastor they have known, and their knowing him has come over a period of time in which they have shared a common venture, even sacrificed, to give birth to something new. There were numerous people who wanted me to stay, saying things like, "Mississippi needs people like you." My district superintendent couldn't understand why I had helped write the statement in the first place, making my signing it even worse. He and other supporters of the political controlling force of the conference were clear that I and other signers of the statement had ruined our future in Mississippi. Ron Bailey wrote an article for *Life* magazine which was never published. In his interview with me, I described my main concern about staying or leaving.

> How can I work within the framework of a closed society and improve it? How can I maintain the tenuous dialogue between myself and my congregation? I'm not afraid. Let people curse me. Let them threaten me. But if I go too far, then my people will not listen to me. Then I'm no longer an effective force and I'm lost to the cause.[1]

I was reappointed to Trinity Methodist Church for the 1963–64 conference year (June to May), though not everyone welcomed the appointment. Many of "the 28" had gone, and many of us who remained were struggling with what to do.

Bishop Gerald Kennedy was one of my heroes. He was the bishop of the Southern California–Arizona Conference. He was a powerful preacher and I would travel hundreds of miles to hear him preach whenever he came to our section of the country. He was on the cover of *Time* magazine on May 8, 1964. *Time* began its discussion of my hero with these words:

There are people in the pews, dollars in the collection plates, and 65 million Americans who claim to be Protestants. But the outwardly prosperous Christian churches are beset with inner anxiety. Ministers fear that their congregations are no more committed to the church than to the country club. Denominational leaders despair at the widespread lay unwillingness to recognize the race question as a moral issue.[2]

That was not simply an appropriate introduction for the article about Bishop Kennedy and his innovative, prophetic leadership, it was an accurate description of the culture and the church. I had read Kennedy's books, heard him preach, and a few weeks after the publication of "Born of Conviction," with some other signers of the statement, met him in New Orleans, where he was on a preaching mission. He not only was a model preacher, he represented a style of episcopal leadership in the church, refreshingly different from what we were experiencing in Mississippi. He graciously extended an invitation to come to his conference if I felt I had to leave Mississippi.

In addition to Bishop Kennedy, when the news of "the 28" spread across the nation, numerous people wrote or called to express support. Dow Kirkpatrick was among them. He had been a pastor in Atlanta during my seminary days and had preached the sermon on Senior Recognition Day that solidified my calling. (I spoke of this in chapter 4.) He had been a Protestant leader in the civil rights struggle there. He was now the senior minister of First Methodist Church in Evanston, Illinois. At that time, this church was nationally known for its social witness, and pastors who provided prophetic leadership for the whole church. Dow wrote, expressing support. Later, when news was spreading that some of "the 28" were being forced from their pulpit, he called to offer his support. When he learned that I was probably going to leave Mississippi, he offered me a position as his associate in the Evanston church.

The offer to start a new church in San Clemente, California, in Bishop Kennedy's area, trumped Dow's offer. I was more excited about planting and leading a new congregation than being an associate in an established one, and serving under Bishop Kennedy was icing on the cake. He officially requested Mississippi Bishop Franklin for my transfer to his conference, which became effective February 10, 1964.

Jerry does the best job of anyone I know in talking about the church as family. She began to experience that early in our marriage. Within fifteen months after our marriage, she had to leave her family in Atlanta and move to Mississippi. Even in the rocky start we had in Gautier, with a congregation that felt betrayed by the system, a season of not being able to move into the parsonage because there was no furniture, and ten men leaving the church, it was not long before there were people around us, loving and supporting us, seeking to meet our needs, and wanting us to feel at home. The young man who offered his bedroom furniture became a kind of symbol for the church being family for us.

We had two children while in Gulfport, Kim and Kerry. The doctor who delivered those babies did so without charge, and he and his wife became our dear friends. That's the reason I was so hurt, and he wept, when he couldn't understand and accept what I witnessed to in "Born of Conviction." That's the reason I wouldn't let him go with his anger and emotional response; I stayed with him in a way so that he knew his anger would not permanently separate us. Years later, when his teenage son became involved with drugs, he called me in California, simply to share his pain.

There was a bond of faith and love, despite the tension. Our months in the church from the time "Born of Conviction" was issued and the time we left, fourteen months later, were different from the previous four years: more honesty, less superficiality, more genuine expressions of love and acceptance without hiding sharp divisions in thinking. They had a reception following our final worship service, wanting to send us on our way with affirmation. There was food and fellowship, a lot of tears, but also a lot of laughter.

When it was time to go, we got into the car. Jerry was crying, Kim, our oldest, was confused, but climbed into the backseat on her own. Our doctor's wife, Doris, passed a tray of sandwiches to Jerry as I was backing out. We got a few blocks away; Jerry was still crying, and I pleaded, "Please, stop crying, see that the children are okay. We are on our way." When she looked into the backseat of the car to check on the children, she was shocked; we had left our youngest, Kerry, in the nursery back at the church. When we returned a gang of people were in the parking lot, laughing. They had found Kerry in the nursery, brought her out, and as we drove in, they held her high, all of them with broad smiles. Along with the young man who offered his bedroom furniture, that, too, became a metaphor for church and family . . . people caring for one another.

When Jerry tells the story, she puts it into personal perspective. She had left home and family in Atlanta to move to Mississippi; that was dramatic enough, but now we were going across the continent to California. Though we had the names of only two couples in San Clemente, she knew they would be family, and others would join them as we established the faith community there. To confirm that, she would name the two couples who would greet us there, the McCaslins and the Ahlmans, and then she would probably describe two other older couples, the Kleinwachters and the Woods, who became surrogate grandparents to our two daughters, and then to Kevin when he was born. He was delivered by a doctor who was also in the church and a close friend, as had been the case with our baby doctor back in Gulfport.

Unlike Gautier, we had a lovely, fully furnished home ready for us in San Clemente. The district superintendent, Ken Miller, had purchased it with conference monies. His wife, Evie, had chosen the furniture. The two of them became like parents to us, but before long, his style of leadership and his trust made me a full participant in the life of this new Annual Conference.

San Clemente, a city in Orange County, California, had a population of a bit less than sixteen thousand when we moved there. The population today is more than sixty-five thousand. San Clemente sits on the coast halfway between Los Angeles and San Diego. The city is called the

"Spanish Village by the Sea" because of its Spanish Colonial–styled architecture. The houses in the original part of the town are white with red tile roofs. In my years there, I never ceased to marvel at the beauty and abundance of Bougainvillea, the official city flower.

The town was founded primarily by Ole Hanson, former mayor of Seattle, who wanted to create a coastal Mediterranean-style resort town that would be a haven to Californians who were tired of the big city. It was that, in part, but far more residential than resort. Marine bases, south of the town, and freeways which made it easy to commute to work in upper Orange County and Los Angeles, all made population growth constant.

In 1969, an event occurred that accelerated the town's growth and the reputation of San Clemente. President Richard Nixon bought part of an estate owned by H. H. Cotton. Nixon named it "La Casa Pacifica," but others referred to it as the "Western White House." I never had the opportunity to preach to Mr. Nixon; he came to San Clemente after I moved to Anaheim. About two years before I moved and before he had purchased the place, I discovered it was not occupied, and I spent many late afternoons relaxing and reflecting in that lovely spot above the Pacific Ocean.

The Ahlmans and the McCaslins, the two couples whose names we were given, had originally expressed interest in a new Methodist church in San Clemente. They made it their mission to make us feel at home. Almost every Friday night, for at least the first three months, one or both couples would take us to dinner. Our favorite restaurant was the Anchor Inn. Though we had spent the last five years on the Mississippi Gulf Coast where seafood was plentiful, neither of us had ever eaten lobster thermidor, which became our favorite entrée. We still choose it when we can find it on a menu.

All great stories begin with a dream and someone who believes in it. Ken Miller, the district superintendent, was the dream leader for the church in San Clemente. He saw the need, and pursued it tenaciously. He planted the idea in the mind of Bishop Kennedy. Someone described it this way, "Ken asked the bishop to think and pray about it, and the bishop did what bishops do when they need to pray . . . he went on a cruise to Hawaii. On the trip he struck up a friendship with a nice couple, Dr. and Mrs. Ray Reeves. When he learned that the Reeves had property in San Clemente, he shared that he wanted to build a church there but he didn't have any land. As faith (not fate) would have it, Dr. Reeves said, 'I'll give you the property.'"

The founding pastor of a congregation plays a huge role in shaping the character of the church. Nettie Beeson's challenge and mentoring of me in prayer, along with the way the small prayer/share group of which I was a part at Trinity in Gulfport had ministered to me, were strong personal signals of how I would impact the shape of this new congregation. Also, there were a few ground-breaking church experiments across the country about which I had read that inspired me. One of them was the Church of the Savior in Washington, DC. Elizabeth O'Connor was a staff member of that church for more than forty years. Her writings poignantly and beautifully gave voice to the journey and spirit of the early years of the Church of the Savior community. I sought to incorporate the dynamic of the personal and social expressions of the gospel, which were so power-fully integrated and practiced in the Church of the Savior, into our new Christian community in San Clemente.

We had no church building; in fact, we had no church in any formal sense. Our first months were spent meeting people, getting to know the community, and having small gatherings in our home. In those gather-ings, I would cast the vision of a church that took seriously Wesley's commitment to personal and social holiness. Because of my experience in Gulfport, when it became obvious that the fellowship of the church was not significantly unlike the fellowship of a civic club, I was passionate in emphasizing a personal relationship with Christ and his call to disciple-ship which made Christians "a peculiar people" . . . a holy people, with a worldview distinctive from, and sometimes in conflict with the culture in which they live. This called for spiritual discipline and a commitment to personal holiness.

Social holiness is also called for in the Wesleyan faith and way. This means that our life together in the congregation is focused on holiness, but it also means that we are to act together in our witness and response to the social issues that violate human and community rights and wholeness.

In these small home gatherings we had the opportunity to teach the Bible, theology, and Christian discipleship in an informal family setting. We also had the opportunity to share our story. They soon learned of our civil rights involvement in Mississippi and had the opportunity, as we drank coffee and shared refreshments, to question us and hear our concerns. Knowing our story and what had led us to come to California made it obvious that we intended to build a congregation sensitive not only to civil rights but to all the issues that negatively impact the human family and that disregard the value of all God's creation.

Like other members of "the 28" who went to California, I was warmly welcomed by the larger church. They knew what had brought us there, though they thought it was far more than it really was, wanting to treat us as heroes, inviting us to speak in churches everywhere.

In March 1965, one year after I left Mississippi, Dr. Martin Luther King Jr. led the march of thousands of nonviolent protestors from Selma, Alabama, to the capitol in Montgomery; it was a five-day, fifty-four-mile march! Fifty years later, when I saw the magnificent film *Selma* that told that story, I wondered, *Had I been in Mississippi, rather than in California, would I have been a part of that march?*

Seeing that movie, I also recalled an evening in California back when King was planning the march. We were in a social gathering of pastors and their spouses; naturally, civil rights and the march were the subject of conversation. Two men were talking on the side and Jerry heard one of them say, "I think I'll go to Selma, for the march," then laughing, he concluded, "I may even get hurt and come home a hero."

Had I heard this, I could not have responded gracefully. There could be no hint of laughter or casualness to what was about to happen. I discovered that while my new friends in California were concerned and their concern was genuine, they did not begin to comprehend the complexity of the problem and the deeply rooted, ugly culture in which so many people were unconsciously trapped.

We had been in California only a year, but I had already concluded that liberal California was not exempt from what I had experienced in Mississippi. In fact, I confronted that issue in some of the speeches I made that year, saying,

> Though there was blatant inhumanity to man in Mississippi, there are subtle forces of hatred at work here in Southern California, whose destructive powers are being strongly felt. Therefore, though speaking specifically about the situation in Mississippi and my experiences there, let none think smugly that he is removed from involvement, or free from blame and guilt. The eruption of a racial crisis in one section of the country is a pointed finger at every person who has contributed to a system that has robbed a good portion of our population of their rights as citizens, and ... of their dignity as children of God.[3]

Five months after Selma, and in the season I was making my speeches, the Watts riot broke out in Los Angeles on August 11, raged for six days, and resulted in more than forty million dollars' worth of property damage. The rioting claimed the lives of thirty-four people, but there was also more than one thousand reported injuries. Before order was restored on August 17, police had made almost four thousand arrests. This was both the largest and costliest urban rebellion of the civil rights era. *Wow, what have I done?* I thought. Leaving Mississippi, had I jumped out of the frying pan into the fire?

When the riots broke out, our congregation was getting established, and we had recently moved into our first building. I knew the missional aspect of our calling was taking shape when some of our members visited Watts to express concern and offer support. We were fifty-five miles away, so it was not possible to be personally involved. Our people were impressed with a group within the community who were working with children, and needed a van to transport them about in that community in which there were so many facilities destroyed by the riots. In faith, one of the couples, Helen and Frances Line, guaranteed the payment on a new van. We parked it on the lawn of the church, and in three weeks we had the money to pay for it.

We began our worship life as a congregation on Easter Sunday 1964, in the Elk's Lodge. To get to our worship space in the building, we had to pass through the bar area, and the smell of the Saturday night parties was rather pronounced. It was a sense reminder that while worship may be a concentrated time away, it should never be away from life as life is.

On December 20, 1964, we broke ground for our new building. Our contractor, Ray McCaslin, was a charter member of the congregation and was committed to finishing the building as soon as possible, and he did so, in ten months.

The building is located on a dramatic site, the land Dr. Reeves committed to Bishop Kennedy on the Hawaii cruise. In our friendship with Dr. Reeves as we developed the congregation, he had increased his 5-acre gift to 11.2 acres. It is on a high point just off the freeway going south from Los Angeles to San Diego. As you come into the edge of the city, traveling south, you look to your left and you can't miss it. The original building was designed by the firm of Edward Durell Stone, an early proponent of modern architecture in the United States. One of his signal achievements was the John F. Kennedy Center for the Performing Arts in Washington, DC.

For a building to be used in a multipurpose way, it was beautiful. It was basically square, with covered porches on every side, taking advantage of views in every direction, ocean and mountains. We sought to be innovative and our worship was in the round. The experiment did not prove effective. It was an important lesson learned early on: innovation should not be the goal; we innovate to create and/or to enhance meaning. As our congregation grew, worship in the round simply did not work. We went back to a more traditional seating arrangement, but kept the pulpit as close to the people as possible.

The ceiling in the very center of the building was a pyramid of stained glass, with modern Christian symbols designed by Jerry. As a part of the design, she had the dove, representing the Holy Spirit, descending into the worship area. The studio that produced the windows reversed the direction of the dove, and had we installed it as they had fabricated it, the Holy Spirit would have been leaving rather than coming. We couldn't have that. We wanted the Spirit *coming* to empower us in order that we might *leave* worship to be the hands and feet of Jesus.

They corrected their mistake with a new window, and gave us the one that would not rightly fit the designed space. We have hauled that window everywhere we have moved since leaving California. We finally found what we thought was the final right place for it. We built a frame for it to be an outside stand-alone icon on the grounds of Rose Hill, the president's home at Asbury Seminary, where it is today. It made a section of the grounds of Rose Hill an outdoor chapel.

The van for Watts was a visible sign of the development of the congregation's missional DNA. We set a goal of giving 50 percent of our income, apart from our initial building costs, to mission. San Clemente is less than one hundred miles from Tijuana, Mexico. We formed ministry relationships with a congregation and mission groups in that city. But we didn't have to go to Tijuana to serve people from Mexico; they were all around us. Our most significant ministry to them was a program of teaching English as a second language. We used the Laubach Literacy teaching plan: *Each One Teach One.*

Frank Laubach was known around the world as a mystic . . . a person of prayer, as the "Apostle to the Illiterates" and as "Mr. Literacy" by *Time* magazine. I had been introduced to his writings by Nettie Beeson as she mentored me in prayer. In 1984, on what would have been his one hundredth birthday, the U.S. Post Office put his picture on a postage stamp, honoring him in their Great American series. He is the only missionary ever to be honored in this fashion.

Laubach created his "Each One Teach One" literacy program in the Philippines while working among Muslims. Today, more than sixty million people around the world have used his program to learn to read.

Though primarily a reading program, we used it as a way to teach English as a second language. Jerry was involved in the weekly classes in our church. Since the program is phonics based, the leader would not let Jerry teach the class that had to do with word endings (i.e., "ing"), because she said we Southerners never put the endings on our words.

Through the inspiration and generosity of Nettie Beeson, Laubach was one of the persons we were privileged to have with us in a prayer teaching conference at Trinity Church in Gulfport. In his presence I felt "more spiritual" myself. More than anyone else, for me his praying was the most intimate, personal talking with God I have ever known.

His book that meant most to me is *Letters by a Modern Mystic*, in which he shared insight from his experiments in prayer. After all these years, I remember how he began one of his letters:

> I climbed Signal Hill today, in back of my house—talking and listening to God—all the way up, all the way back, all the lovely half hour spent on the top. A few months ago, I was trying to write a chapter on the discovering of God. Now that I have discovered him, I find that it is a continuous discovery, and every day is rich with new aspects of him and his working. If I throw these mind-windows apart, and say, God, what shall we think of now? He always answered in a beautiful, tender way.[4]

I share this to illustrate the impact his teaching made on me. I have never been as much the mystic as I have longed to be, but his model of seeking a constant intimate relationship with God, and loving and acting on behalf of others by teaching them to read, has been my challenge.

Introduction to the World

The Vietnam War raged during my time in California. Historians have difficulty nailing down the date of the beginning of that war, but we know that it ended with the fall of Saigon on April 30, 1975. This war was fought between North Vietnam—supported by the Soviet Union, China, and other communist allies—and the government of South Vietnam—supported by the United States and other anti-communist allies. The United States' level of engagement varied through many years.

Though the Vietnam War was pervasive, even apart from it, the sixties were one of the most culturally revolutionary times in modern history. The Woodstock Festival was more than a three-day music festival. In our popular culture, Woodstock is seen as the launch event of the New Age movement in the 1960s and 1970s. The festival is widely considered to be the birthing grounds for a countercultural generation. During the sometimes-rainy weekend, thirty-two acts performed outdoors before an audience of four hundred thousand young people.

The New Age movement gained momentum as the civil rights movement continued to grow, and, along with the the United States government's military involvement in Vietnam, civil unrest was more and more pronounced. You could not be a faithful, thoughtful preacher during this time without acknowledging and responding to different theological and moral expressions flowing out of the New Age movement, and calls for justice implicit in the civil rights movement. The intensity of civil rights was as pronounced in California, but the issue was, in a sense, more close at hand in Mississippi because prejudice and injustice were more institutionalized. One of the big differences between my Mississippi and California experiences related to the more radical social and moral popular thinking emanating from Woodstock and the New Age movement. Traditional family values were being questioned, alternative lifestyles related to sexuality were being championed.

Throughout the 1960s, social tensions continued to develop concerning women's rights, the experimentation with psychoactive drugs, and challenges to authority. The "American Dream" began to be questioned and reinterpreted, hippie and other alternative lifestyles emerged, and the British Invasion, headlined by the Beatles, all intertwined to define a pronounced countercultural dynamic.

California, forever the trendsetter and the epicenter of cultural change, was tough and demanding for churches and church leadership; yet its openness gave opportunity for more freedom of expression and experimentation. It was a challenging time for a country boy from Mississippi who wanted to be relevant to the culture by being faithful to the gospel.

President Kennedy, as popular as he was, seemed impotent in handling the war. He was assassinated, and President Johnson, who succeeded him and led in significant social/civil change such as voter rights, felt forced not to seek reelection because the Vietnam War raged on.

Camp Pendleton is the major West Coast base of the U.S. Marine Corps, and was south of San Clemente. Not far away, San Diego was the home port of several aircraft carriers of the U.S. Navy, and the location of a large naval air station. Some of our most active member families were military, which made the Vietnam struggle a close-at-home reality.

Military personnel were in and out of our home, and some of them became family friends. Chuck Lee, a navy pilot who came from a divided family, became a close friend. His mother was a very active member of our congregation. I never knew his father, a high-ranking naval officer. Chuck had heard stories (from Jerry, of course) of my love for a 1954 MG sports car, which I drove back in Mississippi, but left behind with the move. He had a Triumph, a British sports car, and on one of his deployments left it with me to drive while he was away.

I do like cars, maybe not in the normal kind of way. I have owned only two new cars; having discovered early on that someone else can best pay for the huge first-year depreciation of any car, and that most cars have far more good life than the first couple of years many people drive them. I also concluded that if you are going to buy a used car, and if the family is going to have two cars, which became the case for us early on, one of them could be more than simply utilitarian. So, my first venture based on this philosophy was the 1954 MG British sports car, which I enjoyed for three years in Mississippi before moving to California. In California I had three different cars of this genre: one of the early Mustang convertibles (1965), a 1958 Porsche, and a 1963 190 SL Mercedes convertible. In all instances, except one, I sold the cars for more than I paid for them.

Chuck, who left his Triumph sports car with me, had flown enough military missions to be exempt from more, but (I believe to impress and please his father), he continued to fly, and was shot down on a mission in Vietnam.

The intensity of the war was up and down. At a low period in the conflict, mission leaders in our conference planned a mission visit, anticipating the end of the war and the need for the church's witness in the aftermath. Chuck's mother wanted to use insurance money from his death to do something for the children of Vietnam made orphans by the war. I borrowed $2,000 to participate in that visit, in part to investigate the possibility of some mission enterprise in memory of Chuck.

Two months before we were to go, the Tet Offensive broke out. North Vietnam attacked South Vietnam in a series of surprise military and civilian attacks. Needless to say, our mission trip was canceled.

The congregation shared my disappointment because the mission sensitivity of the congregation was at a high point. A few months later I received a letter from an accounting firm in San Clemente, informing me that an anonymous donor had deposited $2,500 with them for me to use to fund a mission trip, in place of the one that had been canceled. The donor had made it clear that he/she wanted me to see the world that I obviously cared about. Though the donor was never identified, Jerry and I have had fun contemplating who it might have been.

The $2,000 I had borrowed for the Vietnam mission trip was still in the bank, so we added it to the $2,500 and, with a bit more squeezed out of my small salary, planned what was to become one of the most transformative experiences of our lives.

Two priorities shaped the trip. One, Tanzania. John Hillstrom, a veterinarian lay person in the congregation, had felt the call and had gone to Tanzania as an agricultural missionary with the Board of Missions, to develop cattle and poultry growth. Our church was supporting him and his family and we wanted to visit them.

Two, India. Our congregation was supporting Dr. K. N. Nambudripad, an Indian neurosurgeon who served as head of the neurosurgery department in the Christian Medical College and Hospital in Ludhiana, India.

With our primary interests in Africa and India, our travel agent did a magnificent job in planning an around-the-world trip. Starting in California, he booked us through Hawaii (for sheer pleasure) and then Hong Kong. Our Board of Missions connected us with housing and educational work that was being done for refugees from Red China, and the "boat people," the teeming masses who had spent practically all their lives on sampans. The church and the government had done an outstanding job building apartment complexes for refugees from China and the boat people. Creative ministry was taking place on the rooftops of these apartment complexes. The Chinese minister who guided us on our visit was a refugee from China, barely escaping the communists fourteen years before. With government permission, the church transformed some of the rooftops into recreation areas, workshops, and classrooms. The school we visited was headed by a young woman, small in stature, but a giant in heart, a dynamo of dedicated energy. Her joy was contagious. A full-fledged kindergarten was in session. There was a sort of home economics group for young women meeting. There was vocational training and recreation for all ages.

It was just after Easter and the rooms were decorated on the Easter theme, and a big poster greeted us in one room: CHRIST IS ALIVE TODAY. Today was underlined, and I knew it was so. Even now, when I remember this experience, I can hear those little children singing in their language a tune known all over the world: "Jesus loves me this I know."

Jerry has kept the emotional impact of this experience before us with a painting that has been hanging somewhere in our home, wherever we have lived, for more than fifty years. A casual glance misses the core of the painting, a child asleep on a park bench. Jerry had seen this child the day after we had visited the rooftop school. The child asleep on the bench, though faintly outlined, is in the very center of the painting. In the background are the high-rise public houses; in the foreground are the sampans that have housed the people who now live in homes on shore. She titled the painting, "The Least of These . . ." The painting is a powerful reminder that the mission of the church is always to care for "the least of these," and to provide means for the underserved to move from where they are in desolate circumstances to a more secure place that contributes to their total well-being.

Our anonymous donor had impacted our lives on the first leg of our journey. Today, more than fifty years later, I believe that public education is the civil rights issue of the twenty-first century. As I am seeking to lead our congregation in caring for the least of these in Memphis, through public education, Jerry and I are in an endless line of compassion sweeping back to Jesus through those Christians in Hong Kong and that little girl on the park bench.

From Hong Kong, we were off to Thailand. Neither Jerry nor I had traveled much. My friend and roommate in seminary, Buford Dickinson, and I had hitchhiked through England and Scotland. Jerry and I had crossed into Mexico, across the border from San Diego. But this travel was dramatically different. I had never seen anything like Hong Kong, and now Bangkok and the exotic River Kwai. Golden palaces, floating markets, majestic porcelain-laid spires—all breathtaking.

Wat Pho, the Temple of the Reclining Buddha, may have been the most surprising, certainly the dramatic reminder that we were traveling in lands where Christianity was the minority religion, and what we represented was as foreign to the people as they were to us.

Though wide-eyed tourists who sought to take it all in, overwhelmed by the wonders we were seeing, our perspective was always flavored by the fact that we were on our way to India and our anticipated visit with a man whose story had thrilled and moved us deeply. Even the dazzling Taj Mahal in India did not divert us from what our hearts were set on, visiting Ludhiana Christian Medical College and Hospital, one of Asia's outstanding educational institutions. The motto is "Where hundreds are trained to heal millions." When we were there we were told that 2,416 well-qualified students had applied that year for the fifty-two places in the MD program.

Our original excitement about visiting there had been diminished a bit just before our journey commenced. We had received word from the director of the hospital that Dr. Nambudripad would not be there to greet us. An important family event was taking him away during the time we planned to be there. Yet, the itinerary was set; this was a once-in-a-lifetime trip and we would see the remarkable medical work being done, work that our little church in California had been supporting.

The temperature was 105 and we sweltered for two hours in endless lines that pressed the ticket windows of the main railway terminal in Delhi. We were finally at the right window, and were there for thirty minutes, seemingly because the ticket master wanted to impress us with the efficiency of the system. We had our tickets for Ludhiana. With great sighs of relief, we settled into our air-conditioned compartment of the Flying Mail, what was then one of the trains that made India so proud of her rail system.

Out the window of our compartment, the station was alive with people, and yet, we were alone. People with huge bundles lounged on the platforms. Entire families huddled together. Little children slept in other children's arms. The fortunate ones availed themselves to the wares of the vendors who were everywhere, peddling their drinks, sweets, and fruit. It was a strange world of brazen contrasts. Beggars moved in and out of the people. Though we couldn't understand what they said, their pitiful eyes and mournful voices made clear what they were seeking. Those on long journeys spread their bed rolls on the concrete platforms where they could find space and stretched weary bodies as they waited for their trains.

The journey from Delhi to Ludhiana is about six hours. In a small town along the way, the train had some sort of problem and we were stranded for about an hour. While there in our comfortable air-conditioned compartment, another train drew up beside us on an adjoining track, no more than five or six feet away. We learned it was a third-class train, with people packed in the cars; those with seats sat numbly or hunched up on all fours on wooded benches, and in many cases children not seated in parents' laps were on racks above the seats, older ones standing packed together in the aisles. Those who could were hanging out the window, seeking whatever bit of fresh air they could get—a painful picture of discomfort and misery.

We were feeling another kind of misery and discomfort, spirit and heart pain. A few feet away was a world of suffering totally removed from our experience. The temptation was to pull down the curtain and shut it out, but that would have added insult to the injury of people who stared at us from their miserable plight.

Our disappointment in not seeing Dr. Nambudripad was becoming more intense as we continued the journey. We had learned much about this man through the director of the hospital. He came from a family of scholars. His grandfather was one of the leading Sanskrit authorities in India. To their palatial home in Kerala, students would come to study this ancient classical language of India and Hinduism from the master. It was no wonder, then, that when Nambudripad was converted to Christianity, while studying in Britain, his family, steeped in the cultural, social, and religious beliefs and practices of Hinduism, disowned him, cutting him off from the family circle. Their reaction was so violent they had him incarcerated for a time in a mental institution.

But now he had become a neurosurgeon, brilliantly practicing his profession day in and day out, witnessing to his patients . . . and often, on off days, he would proclaim his faith, preaching in the public square. We were so sad we would not see him. The truth is, there was a kind of anger that fumed within. We were coming half way around the world to see him, and after all, our church had been paying his salary for two years. Couldn't his family time be scheduled differently?

The station at Ludhiana was almost as frightening as Delhi. Such strange sights and sounds and smells. We were caught in an avalanche of people. How would we ever make contact with whomever was there to meet us, if anyone was there? How dumb I was! It isn't difficult to spot a young, beautiful blonde white woman, accompanied by a not-too-much-darker man, loaded with the obvious paraphernalia of foreign travelers, no matter how big the crowd of Indians. We had taken only a few steps when a small fellow shyly inquired if we were the Dunnams. What relief. "I'm Nambudripad. Welcome to Ludhiana."

We couldn't believe it. He was there. Dr. Nambudripad! But he was so small, so shy, so soft-spoken. Was this our hero? His only distinctive mark was his white shirt and trousers, common apparel of a doctor. I later realized that even his dress was not distinctive. Many men in India wear white.

Well, I'm glad you are here, but I'm not sure there is going to be anything exciting about it, I thought. We had heard so many things about this brilliant doctor whose remarkable life was an inspiration to all who knew him. Was meeting him going to be so anticlimactic? *Here he was, such a non-distinctive, meek-looking fellow,* I thought. I was not spiritually sensitive enough to see it rightly: humility. I confess my thought: *I surely hoped he appreciated the effort his benefactors have gone to, just to see him.*

Our days in Ludhiana were filled; the atmosphere was alive. Things were happening. Results were so obvious, though the task was so monumental. From other staff members we heard more of the story of this unusual man, the sufferings he had experienced, the sacrifices he was making to serve, his brilliant teaching, his skill as a surgeon, the research he was doing, his preaching in the market place. I got the feeling that here was another Albert Schweitzer who had stayed with his own people.

It was Dr. Nambudripad who put us safely on the Flying Mail the third morning, as we headed back for Delhi. In his halting way, he thanked us for coming, for the support our church was providing, and with a firm handshake, he wished us Godspeed. We knew the depth of his sincerity. As the Flying Mail pulled slowly out of the station, we passed a third-class train. From our air-conditioned compartment we gazed again at poverty, misery, and suffering. This time our pain and heartbreak was more intense. The director of the hospital had told us that Dr. Nambudripad had been to Kerala before we arrived, and had returned just to be with us. He and his wife and three children had traveled that two thousand miles to be with his family on the occasion of a great wedding celebration. This was the first time he had been invited to participate in any family activity, since he had been ostracized eight years before. To be with us those two short days, he had returned by third-class train from Kerala. Soon after we boarded our train, he would join that poor mass of Indians in those stifling quarters to return to Kerala and rejoin his family celebration. But you can't ride an air-conditioned train when you are living on a two hundred dollars per month salary paid by the church of well-to-do, air-conditioned, coach-riding Americans.

There were to be two more big stops; Tanzania, which was one of the two destinations that were musts in our travel, and the Holy Land, which was a special plus, and easily included when you are going from India to Africa.

We've been to the Holy Land at least a half dozen times, and no visit has failed to be meaningful, giving vibrant life to Scripture, often providing special joy or offering unique challenges. Visits in recent years have been punctuated with questions intrinsic to the whole Middle East crisis and the plight of Israel.

That was not the case with the first visit. My engagement with the issues of the sixties, the Vietnam War, the cultural revolutions going on in the United States, and the intensifying civil rights struggle left little emotional or mental space for serious engagement with what was going on in the Holy Land. I suppose I was simply too young and not yet alive to the issues of the world to even consider what had happened in 1948 when Britain surrendered her mandate government of Palestine. This Mandate governance began in the mid-thirties when the Turks had been driven out, and Britain took over to protect Palestine until a free Palestinian government could be established.

Now, war-weary and unwilling to lose more young men to defend Palestine from the Zionist underground, Britain surrendered their Mandate governance, and the State of Israel was established.

We were in Israel in the spring of 1968, less than a year after the famous Six-Day War. Unaware of the historical circumstances preceding this event, with the rest of the world I confess, with some degree of shame, I was in awe of Israel's military success. Leading up to the Six-Day War in June of 1967, tensions were running high. In the Sinai Peninsula, the Egyptian forces had been mobilized along the Israeli border. Knowing this, and fearful of what Egypt was planning, Israel preemptively initiated a succession of airstrikes against Egyptian airfields on June 5, virtually destroying the entire Egyptian air force, with few Israeli losses. At the same time, the Israelis began a ground offensive into the Gaza Strip and through the northern and central routes of the Sinai. Egyptian leader Gamal Abdel Nasser, realizing defeat, commanded the evacuation of the Sinai.

In six days, Israel's scope of control tripled: they had won the Gaza Strip and the Sinai Peninsula (from Egypt), the West Bank and East Jerusalem (from Jordan), and the Golan Heights (from Syria). Arab forces had sustained losses of more than twenty thousand with Israel losing less than a thousand. The world was singing the praise of this "little David" nation that had confronted the giant "Goliath" and won.

But the West and the world outside the Middle East seemed to pay little attention to civilians displaced due to the war: 300,000 Palestinians left for the West Bank and about 100,000 Syrians became refugees. Also,

Jewish communities were being forced out around the Arab world with the hopes they would go to Israel.

When we visited Jerusalem, the result of the war was still being expressed. Houses near the Wailing Wall, formerly owned and occupied by Palestinians, many of them Christian, were being destroyed. In the following years, I learned more of the story.

In 1994, the World Methodist Council bestowed the Methodist World Peace Award on Elias Chacour, a Palestinian Christian, now a bishop of the Melkite Church, for his years of peace-making efforts. When he was a boy, not only were the land and orchards that had been in his family for generations taken by the Zionists, his entire village was destroyed. This unlawful confiscation of land and destruction of property happened throughout Galilee. It was on these lands that kibbutzim were established and Jews from America and European countries occupied them.

In 1948–49 tens of thousands of Palestinians (many of them Christian) were killed, and nearly one million forced into refugee camps. This kind of oppressive killing and forceful confiscation of land was not the story we knew in 1968. Even our travel agent, knowingly or not, was a part of championing the Zionist cause. As a part of our Holy Land visit, he booked us for two days in a kibbutz in Galilee. It was a marvelous experience, meeting young men and women from America and Europe, who were on a mission to transform the land and establish a nation. We could have become true believers, and for a long time were unquestioning supporters of Israel. Turning the wilderness into a garden was the story headlining the news coming out of the new State of Israel for decades. It was a true story, but without some of the chapters, including the massive funding that was coming from all over the world. The news of the holocaust and the Nazi cleansing of Germany created deep sympathy for the Jews. Add to that the distorted understanding of Jews and Christians that the land belonged to Israel by divine decree, and you had extravagant and unquestioned support of the Zionist dream of a Jewish state.

During that time period in our ministry, Jerry and I were drawn to the notion of living in an intentional community. The kibbutz experience fed that longing. The common caring and sharing was contagious to an outsider. Even to a casual observer, the affirmation, cultivation, and expression of individual gifts, and the commitment of all to work as work was needed was intriguing and inviting.

Then, and now, Galilee is our favorite section of the Holy Land. We purchased a painting at the kibbutz there when we visited in 1968 and that painting has been in our home for more than fifty years. It's a landscape looking across the Sea of Galilee to the Golan Heights. Jerry, particularly, connects the painting with her Holy Land experience. When we host groups on visits to the Holy Land, she always tells this story.

We were visiting the Garden Tomb, in Jerusalem, believed by many to be the garden and sepulcher of Joseph of Arimathea. It is an alternative site to the famous Church of the Holy Sepulcher as the place of the crucifixion and resurrection of Jesus. The interdenominational association that owns and manages the garden do not claim, nor could they ever prove, it is the precise place where Jesus was buried and was resurrected. When in Jerusalem, we always visit both the Church of the Holy Sepulcher and this beautiful garden place where you can see and experience several things that were there when Jesus died and which match the accounts in the four gospels.

We were sitting on a bench in the garden near the entrance of the tomb, relaxing and imagining not just what might have happened there, but seeking to absorb all that we were experiencing in the Holy Land, even questioning whether we might be missing something. We had no thought that we would ever have the opportunity to return, and we wanted to get the full impact and meaning of this most religiously significant setting in the world.

A guide came with a group of tourists to the entrance of the tomb. We were close enough to hear him as he talked about the tomb and made a plausible explanation of the possibility that this could be the actual cave in which Jesus was buried. But his word that was, for Jerry, the descriptive and transformative message of the entire trip: "Now you may go into the tomb and spend some time of reflection and prayer, but don't expect to find Jesus here. He rose from the dead and is alive in the world, and it is in the world that you must find him."

Jerry refers to that moment as her "Holy Land Experience." Indeed, we had seen Jesus in Hong Kong where families were being rescued from poverty and the misery of life on the sampans, and little children were being taught in schools on the rooftops of new housing for the poor. We had seen him in the hospital in Ludhiana, especially in the healing ministry and humility of Dr. Nambudripad. We knew we would see him in John and Gen Hillstrom when we arrived in Tanzania.

In the spring of 2012, I preached in the East Jerusalem Baptist Church. Alex Awad is the pastor. His brother, Bishara, was then the president of Bethlehem Bible College. They are among a forgotten people in the Middle East crisis: Palestinian Christians.

There were seven brothers and sisters in the family. The mother and father, devout Christians, taught them the ways of Christ. They were all together in the same house back in 1948. War had been raging all over the city, and then, one week, fighting was in their neighborhood and finally on their street. At sunset the fighting died down, and their father went outside to assess what was going on, and was killed in the crossfire between the Jordanian and Israeli armies.

The next morning, when shooting temporarily subsided, neighbors gathered in the small apartment. No priests or pastors were able to reach them. Neighborhood men had dug a grave in the courtyard behind the apartment building. Huda Awad, their mother, read words of comfort from the Bible. With tears streaming down their faces, the children joined their mother in reciting the Lord's Prayer, and the men carried the body to the makeshift grave.

Fierce fighting resumed that afternoon, but ended before dark. In the middle of the night a Jordanian soldier came and ordered the family to evacuate because they expected the Israeli army to return any moment. "We will let you know when it is safe to return," they promised. The Awad family left and never saw their home again.

The mother got a job nursing at twenty-five dollars per month but could not sustain the family. Bishara and Alex were placed in a home for children. Ironically, the home was next door to the building that later became the church where Alex was the pastor and I was the guest preacher. As he told me the story he pointed to the upstairs room where he and Bishara lived until they both, by the compassion of the Christian community, came to the United States to study.

Both Alex and Bishara returned to their homeland, despite the violence that characterized daily life. Bishara and his mother tried to visit his boyhood home, but it had been destroyed and a road built, so they couldn't find the exact location. After the 1967 war, his mother had written the mayor of Jerusalem, requesting permission to move her husband's bones, but the request was ignored. So there isn't even a grave-stone to mark and commemorate his father's existence.

What was not lost, however, was the gospel message and the strong Christian influence his mother and father had on Bishara and Alex. Both have become lights of love and reconciliation in this hate-filled land of the greatest Lover and Reconciler of all times. Bishara became a teacher and wanted to impart love and reconciliation to his students. He saw that the conflict between the Israelis and Palestinians was leaving deep scars on their children. Many had lost both parents, and many, separated from their parents during the 1967 war, did not know whether they were dead or alive. Anger and violent behavior characterized the school community. Bishara's message that he had learned from his parents—love God, love your neighbor, love your enemies—was not getting through to his students.

"Why Lord?" Bishara prayed. "Why are there no results? Why would you bring me back to my homeland and not use me?" In his book, *Light Force*, Brother Andrew tells Bishara's story:

The silence seemed to accuse him. He walked the halls past the rooms where the boys slept. Many of them tossed and turned fitfully, groaning or talking in their sleep. He wondered about their dreams, which no doubt reflected their private pains. Each of them had experienced harassment from Israeli soldiers . . . Feeling humiliated and power-less to do anything effective, many students had thrown stones at the soldiers and carried their defiance of authority over to the teachers at the school . . .

Bishara walked out the back door of the school . . . and stood under the night sky. It began to come clear. Emotions he had repressed for so long welled up in him. He blamed the Israelis for the death of his mother and father and the loss of his home in 1948, for the twelve years he had to live in an orphanage separated from his mother, for the years of exile in the United States. The hatred had festered, but now he recognized in himself the same hatred that was in the boys under his care. As it was destroying them, it was destroying him. Unless he conquered his own anger and bitterness, he could not help them.

Tears welled up in his eyes. How could he, a man who had given his life to Christ a dozen years before, who was committed to be an instrument of God in the Holy Land, help these young angry boys? There was only one answer. His voice broke the silence of the night: "Lord, I beg you. Forgive me for hating the Jews and for allowing that hatred to control my life."[5]

When I shared with Bishara and his brother Alex, I knew that with every ounce of his being, he had meant that prayer. The two of them are living it out as lights in the darkness. They may not be thinking this way, but they are demonstrating that intercession is not primarily a prayer a person prays, but something a person does. Through their intercessory lives they are providing "meeting" (*paga*, the meaning of intercession) for Palestinian Christians, Arab Muslims, Jews, and Messianic Jews. It is a slow, frustrating, painful process, but now and then reconciliation happens and light shines in the darkness.

Not only does the painting of the Golan Heights induce wonderful memories and call us to prayer, on the table in the part of our den where Jerry and I read Scripture and pray together almost every day, there is a marble plaque with this inscription, "Pray for the Peace of Jerusalem." Alex and Bishara are often in our prayers, as is Father Chacour and all the forgotten Christian Palestinians in this war-ravaged land.

Our last stop of that life-changing trip was Tanzania. I think it was through John Hillstrom that the cardinal root of Protestantism was really planted deep in my thinking and the way I have sought to minister. John took my preaching seriously. I never thought of him becoming a missionary, but he heard God's call. He had no formal theological training, but he studied Scripture, both privately and in groups at the church. The agricultural needs of Tanzania could be met by his training and talent, and in that he heard his call. That should be the way the normal Christian thinks: where the needs of the world and my talent and resources meet, there exists a call.

We spent three days with John and Gen, were inspired by the way they had adjusted to a completely different lifestyle and the way he related to the Tanzanians and they to him, and we were challenged to be more bold in preaching the gospel that includes at its heart the Great Commission:

> Then Jesus came to them and said, "All authority in heaven and on earth has been given to me. Therefore go and make disciples of all nations, baptizing them in the name of the Father and of the Son and of the Holy Spirit, and teaching them to obey everything I have commanded you. And surely I am with you always, to the very end of the age." (Matt. 28:18–20)

John died a too-early death, killed in an auto accident. He is buried in the soil of Tanzania, a land to which he had gone in response to the Great

Commission, because he was seeking to live the Great Commandment: "'Love the Lord your God with all your heart and with all your soul and with all your mind.' This is the first and greatest commandment. And the second is like it: 'Love your neighbor as yourself'" (Matt. 22:37–39).

A Questionable Move

I believe the most glaring limitation to the Methodist way of deploying preachers is the pattern of making appointments. The purpose of our system of itinerancy is to be able to place pastors in places where they are most desperately needed, and where their gifts are best suited. And that ideal is sometimes operative. But more often than not, from my observation, appointments are made according to salary and time served in a particular place. The outworking is that company men who are faithful and steady are moved every four or five years to a congregation a bit larger than the one they are in, with an increase in salary.

From my perspective, in retrospect, I should not have been moved from the new church we had planted in San Clemente, to a thriving, much larger suburban church in Anaheim. Five years was simply not adequate. I was young and not confident enough in the system to raise questions, nor mature enough to think clearly about what was best for the ministry of the whole church I'm sure the pride which is at the core of our original sin was also a factor. We had been very successful. The congregation had grown rapidly; we had built a wonderful building; I was being recognized not only in the conference but beyond. The church to which I was being appointed was three times larger, with a beautiful sanctuary, a pipe organ and outstanding choir, a large staff, including an associate minister and youth director, and as senior minister I would have a full-time secretary. Though I had a fruitful and meaningful ministry in West Anaheim Methodist Church, I believe the kingdom would have been best served if I had spent ten years, rather than five, in St. Andrew's by-the-Sea in San

Clemente. I know that Bishop Kennedy, and my dear friend, Ken Miller (my district superintendent), were affirming me and my leadership, and for that I was grateful.

Our son, Kevin, was born in San Clemente and occasionally claims to be a Californian. Those California years came at a special time in our family. Our move from San Clemente to Anaheim put us within a few miles of Disneyland. This was before Disney World in Orlando. We could see fireworks from our backyard, and visits to Disneyland were not once-in-a-lifetime for our children; we were there regularly, primarily because out-of-town visitors who came to see us also wanted to visit.

In those years, under the dynamic of Bishop Kennedy, Methodism was growing. West Anaheim Methodist Church, to which I was appointed, was a stellar example of church growth. It was less than twenty years old when I arrived, but had more than one thousand members. Two ministers had preceded me, so I was now serving a church that had some history. I had helped birth my previous three churches. Though relatively young in the context of all the churches of the conference, this church was established, and I had to fit into a history and an operational style.

Maxie at age eleven.

The Dunnam family around the well. Mother and father, Cora and Murdoc, are seated; standing left to right: Lloyd, Edgar, Lois, Irma, and Maxie.

A partner for the journey. Wedding in Durham Chapel, Candler School of Theology, Emory University, Atlanta, Georgia.
Off for our honeymoon, March 15, 1957.

Jerry and Maxie with two children, Kimberly Lynn and Kerry Leigh, and adopted son, teenager Fred Davis.

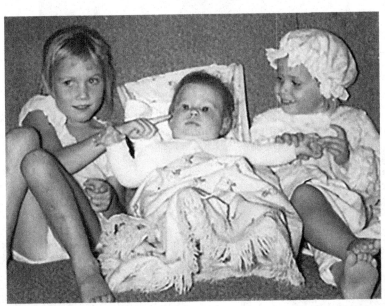

Three children: Kimberly Lynn, Gerald Kevin, and Kerry Leigh.

Kimberly Lynn, Fred Davis, Kerry Leigh, and Gerald Kevin.

Celebrating Jerry's seventy-fifth birthday with our children and their spouses, John and Kim Reisman, Kevin Dunnam, and Kerry and Jason Peeples.

Grandson Jacob Peeples.

Grandchildren Maggie, Nathan, and Hannah Reisman.

Having a conversation with my father in the Methodist Church and in ministry, David McKeithen.

E. Stanley Jones, missionary/evangelist, who served primarily in India, more than any other single person, shaped my theology. Our lifted hands is the Christian ashram greeting, with three fingers upward underscoring the earliest creed of the church, "Jesus is Lord!"

Aldersgate Methodist Church in Atlanta, Georgia. Few pastors have had the opportunity of planting a new congregation. I have had the rare privilege of planting three. This is the first, planted during my years as a student at Candler School of Theology, 1955–58.

Trinity Methodist Church, Gulfport, Mississippi. Planted as a part of my first assignment out of seminary, 1958.

St. Andrews-by-the-Sea Methodist Church, San Clemente, California. Planted in 1964 when I transferred from Mississippi to California, under the appointment of Bishop Gerald Kennedy.

Jerry and me at our last commencement of my presidency of Asbury Seminary.

Students presented us a reproduction of the stained glass in the prayer chapel of the Dunnam-Florida Campus of Asbury Seminary as we closed our last year as president of the seminary.

CHAPTER EIGHT

Becoming a World Christian

God's grace will not take us where his grace will not sustain us. Though this statement is my conviction, there have been occasions when I have doubted it. Even so, it has been proven true over and over in the way our ministry journey has played out.

We were having a great time in California. Our ministry was rewarding and, in my judgment, effective. Yet, both Jerry and I had deep longings to get *back home*. We were able to visit our parents only once a year, sometimes twice. Our children were growing up without knowing their grandparents or their cousins. So, we began to pray that some call might come from somewhere closer to home.

I need to say a word about home. I've shared my feelings about my struggle with the setting of my growing-up years, what I felt was economic, cultural, and educational deprivation. I continue to be amazed at the way mind and memory work; it's such a mystery!

I went shopping alone during a Christmas season. In the midst of the hustle and bustle of a toy department, I was momentarily smitten by painful memories of Christmas during my growing-up years in rural poverty. We had no Christmas tree or Christmas stockings. All the lights and glitter and variety of gifts I could now purchase collided in my mind

with what, in my early years of distorted assessment of my situation and
struggle, I had imagined as drab and dark. None of this could have been
mine as a child. I reflected upon what had happened in my mind and,
upon arriving home, I wrote a poem, first rehearsing in self-pity what I had
missed, but then in God-given perspective, I concluded "it was another
world and I was a child again."

> None of these fantastic toys
> had ever been mine
> But I remembered a little track
>> about two feet in diameter
>> and a little wind-up train
>> creeping around
> (It must have been zooming then)
> It provided thrills aplenty
>> until the spring
>> too tired
>> and too tightly wound
>> gave up and died
> I found it in a dresser drawer
>> (We didn't have a Christmas tree that year)
>> on Christmas morning
>> and I knew that Santa came to
>> poor boys' homes, too.
> I was a child again
>> but not really a child
> I was a man-child
>> reduced to fantasy and awe
>> by what I saw
> *I thanked God for memory*
>> *and parents who tried hard*
>> *and gave all!*

As I write this, feelings about home and what home has meant to me through the years fill me with joy.

When the opportunity came to make the around-the-world mission investigation journey, I did not want to make the journey alone. This was the kind of experience Jerry and I needed to share. But what about the children? Kevin was two, Kerry was five, and Kim was seven. How could we leave them for a month? Dare we run the risk of the possible negative emotional impact this might have on them? Reluctantly and emotionally conflicted, we decided to leave them with my parents back in rural Mississippi.

Through the years, we both have confessed a bit of residual guilt about this, even though there has never been any evidence of it being a negative experience in any way. When we talk with Kim, Kerry, and Kevin about that experience, they remember that every man in the family, and at least one aunt, smoked cigarettes, with their grandfather (whom we affectionately called "Mutt") smoking a pipe. So tobacco smoke and scent was omnipresent.

They met a lot of cousins and they laugh about one of them having twin toes. We have pictures of them with chicks being hatched. They were introduced to the sport of target shooting. They remain amazed at the fact of so many *real* guns, there never having been any guns in our home. Cans were set up on fence posts as targets; the one hitting the most cans was the champion. They joyfully remember and talk about much time spent on the sandbanks of the gravel pit nearby. The seemingly endless card games going on during the weekends introduced them to what remains a favorite family pasttime.

Kim spent the last month of her second grade there, and remembers the long school bus ride, in the company of her older cousin, Laney, who lived across the road. The distance to school was only a couple of miles, but the bus had to meander in and out of country roads to pick up all the students; so it was not a long-distance journey, but it took a long time to make it. Kerry, along with Kim, also remembers the picture of the Beatles on Laney's school notebook, and spending a lot of time with Laney, listening to her music and simply hanging out.

Interestingly, the only thing any of them remember about church was Kim's memory of the "skinny" preacher, who showed up at the house now and then, unannounced, always invited in for coffee and pie or cake. That skinny preacher was Brother Grissom, under whose preaching I had been converted and baptized.

Our family is a card-playing family. Rook, Canasta, and Spades were our favorite card games, but for most of the years it was Canasta. When Kim mentions Brother Grissom, I remember a time, long after I was ordained and serving a church, visiting my parents in Richton. We were doing what we often did, playing Canasta, when a car drove up. Momma looked out and exclaimed, "O Lord God, I do pray," (one of her favorite expressions with which she introduced many of her observations) "put up the cards, here comes the preacher." What kind of preacher did she think she was playing cards with?

Through the years since, even though there is no sign of it, and the children laugh at us for thinking it, Jerry and I often mention what a risk we were taking to leave our children for a month. Though they were with their grandparents, they hardly knew them; in fact, Kevin was so young, he would not have known them at all. My mom and dad's willingness to share their love with these children they did not know, only that they were their grandchildren, children of me, their "baby," is a telling judgment against my distorted thinking about my childhood, and one of the telling blows against the hound of hell that chased me for so many years.

My writing about home and all these joyful feelings clash with the fact of so many homeless people in my city, and the more than forty-three million people worldwide forcibly displaced as a result of conflict and persecution, the highest number since the mid-1990s. The United Nations has found it difficult to even keep an accurate count of the numbers of refugees. When in Bethlehem recently, I met adult Palestinians in the refugee camp there who were born in that camp. Refugees, aliens, illegal residents—it's one of the world's gravest political, economic, and social problems. And we Christians must stay sensitive and seek to keep the world's conscience sensitive to these, whom I'm sure Jesus would add to his list of *the least of these.*

That grave social problem serves to underscore an ongoing dilemma for us Christians, especially persons in professional Christian ministry. Jerry and I have had to deal with this throughout our lives. Our ministry has moved us often, from place to place, even across the continent. We have had to think, reflect, and pray about *moving* and the meaning of *home.* As Christians, we have a dual citizenship: residents of earth and citizens of heaven. We live in the tension of this dual citizenship. Paul made the stark claim, "But our citizenship is in heaven. And we eagerly await a Savior from there" (Phil. 3:20). In the United States we refer to some people living within our bounds as *resident aliens,* persons who belong by birth to another country, but are currently choosing to live here. That's an apt description of a Christian. We are citizens of heaven, resident aliens of earth.

Homesick

Jerry and I had no question about being in the kingdom, no question about being resident aliens, at home in Anaheim. Jerry cherishes sharing about our initial move to California, the struggle involved, but the joy of knowing God's people would greet us there and we would be at home with them. As has been the case throughout our ministry, we were at home in San Clemente and Anaheim. But still, we were homesick for the South, for our families, and our roots. But we would be guided by the call that would have to be God's call, not our selfish desires.

An invitation came to consider leading a Christian retreat ministry in Maryland. The notion that had been residing deep in our minds for years—what it would be like to live in an "intentional Christian community"—got our attention. The possibility of pursuing my interest in prayer and spiritual formation more intentionally was also compelling. We visited; the people were wonderful, the geographical setting was beautiful. We were exhilarated as we spent days in that setting and considered the possibilities of the ministry. In our minds, of course, was the thought that this was our chance—not really putting us back home, but closer.

God is so gracious. It doesn't always happen this way; in fact, it seldom happens this way. But this was such a critical emotional issue; we did not want our feelings and homesickness to determine our response to this ministry invitation. Neither of us can remember who voiced it first, or how it was voiced, but we were not in the plane long, returning to California, before we were sharing our conviction that "this is not it."

We knew we were at home where we were in Anaheim, because this offer was not God's call. We were learning, and are still learning, how to live in the kingdom *now*. Even though the fullness of the kingdom of Christ has not yet come, it is coming. We can be at home where we are, and live in great expectation and confidence because, with Paul, we *eagerly await the Savior*.

This truth of the Christian faith and way has enabled us to live with meaning and, *most of the time*, in joy, in many different places, sharing different expressions of ministry.

We didn't miss a beat as we continued our ministry in Anaheim. The possibility of getting closer to home wasn't forgotten, but Maryland was. Our prayers were not desperate, but consistent. A few months later, the letter came. Wilson Weldon, the editor of the *Upper Room*, was writing about a new ministry position. They wanted to give more focus to the possibility of the readership of the *Upper Room* praying corporately. There were more than four million readers of this daily devotional guide. Could they become a *fellowship* of prayer? Could they be more intentionally resourced in prayer and their spiritual growth with more than the magazine? They were asking me if I would consider being interviewed for the job!

I thought to myself, and later, when interviewed, I told them: the fact that I was being interviewed indicated the desolate, desperate spiritual condition of the church. I was barely an apprentice in the school of prayer. I prayed. I knew the necessity of prayer. Prayer had long been a part of my life, intensified by my experience in the civil rights struggles in Mississippi. I had been inspired and mentored in prayer by praying people like Nettie Beeson and Tom Carruth, but I was a novice.

Even with my reservations, something was burning in my soul; maybe God was calling. On the plane, returning to California from the interview, thirty-three thousand feet above God's beautiful earth, I entered into one of the most profound periods of prayer I have known. In the back of a book I had been reading, I wrote some of what I was feeling—words that I intended to share if the position actually became mine to accept.

> I want to deliberately enter the "school of prayer." I've been an auditor before, not fully matriculated, but I want to be a full-time student. I'll be willing to share my pilgrimage. I must honestly confess that what I have to share right now is not expertise, but conviction. If you want one who is committed to Christ, who believes the secret of life is what Paul said, "Yes, Christ in you, bringing with him the hope of all the glorious things to come"—if you want someone who has the deep conviction that the most pressing need of our day is God-power which is available and is tapped primarily through prayer, if you will accept me and my commitment and conviction with the full knowledge that I make no pretensions about "having already attained" in this exciting adventure, then I'll come; I'll accept the responsibility. We'll journey together and call God's people back to their heritage and hope. Along the way, we'll strive to put into their hands and heads and hearts the very best resources to assist them in learning to pray.

As I reflected upon the possibility of such a ministry, I was higher in my spirit than any plane. I never had the chance to express those reflections. Perhaps, despite my honest confession of inadequacy, they sensed my passion, and the fact that I was growing and they believed that would fit me for the task, so they invited me to take the job, and I accepted.

God Uses Others to Share in Our Calling

I knew neither Ira Galloway, then general secretary of the Board of Evangelism, nor Wilson Weldon, editor of the *Upper Room*, which was connected with the Board of Evangelism. They were the two persons primarily responsible for the job description and selecting the person for the responsibility. I was mystified by the process, especially how I came to be considered for the job in the first place. I learned later.

In 1968, I had been a part of an evangelistic crusade in Mexico, organized by the Board of Evangelism. With four other young Methodist ministers, I was assigned to Monterey. We preached every night for a week, taught in mid-morning, and in the afternoons we visited in homes, witnessing and inviting persons into a relationship with Christ and the fellowship of the church. In the early mornings, the five of us, with our host pastors, gathered for prayer. It was a rich time of fellowship and growth. I'm sure my visiting colleagues knew, as I did, that this prayer time, not our teaching and preaching, was the secret of the revival that took place that week. This was my first concentrated and extensive time of preaching through an interpreter, and it was a bumbling, humbling experience.

Ken Carter was a member of that team. He was from Texas, and had been converted, called, and mentored in ministry by Ira Gallaway. Ira called him "one of my Timothys."

Now, years later, characteristic of his style, Ira contacted a number of people, asking them for the names of people they thought could fulfill the new staff responsibility in prayer at the *Upper Room*. One of the persons he contacted was Ken Carter. According to Ira, Ken responded to his request: "I only know one person who may be able to do the job: Maxie Dunnam. I spent a week with him, preaching in Mexico, a couple of years ago."

God moves in mysterious ways, and we never know the impact we are having, or the impression we may be leaving with people. It's an indictment against me, but I confess, I had forgotten the names of the persons who participated in that week of evangelism in Mexico. Yet, one of them, Ken, whom I had forgotten, opened the door for me to be considered by Ira for this new and perhaps most transformative chapter of my life.

My Most Significant Contribution to the Church

Though I had grave reservations, because of deep feelings of glaring inadequacy, I accepted the invitation. There is a sense in which this dynamic has been characteristic of my life: God calling me, and my responding to ministries for which I was totally inadequate; and God outwitting us, proving that his will does not take us where his grace will not sustain us.

My most significant contribution to the cause of Christianity and the Christian church came out of this experience of total inadequacy: my book, *The Workbook of Living Prayer.*

When a twentieth-anniversary edition of the *Workbook* was published in 1994, I wrote in the introduction: "Through the years I've received literally thousands of letters from people who have used it and have expressed their appreciation; many of them have testified that their lives were transformed, and many others mark their commitment to full-time Christian ministry to the use of the workbook." Nothing I have done has touched more people and fostered more spiritual growth in persons than the *Workbook.*

Its origin was my inadequacy. Here I was, leading a fellowship of prayer, feeling so weak in my own practice of prayer. The Christian world has a great literature in prayer. It may be that more books have been written about prayer than any other theme of the Christian faith and way. I began to more intentionally immerse myself in this great literature. I read voraciously. I discovered that you can read any number of great books about prayer and still not pray.

So I began to pray that the Lord would give me something that would enable persons, no matter where they were on their Christian journey, to *actually pray* as they read about prayer.

The *Workbook* was the Holy Spirit's answer. It's a primer, a manual, a six-week daily guide to praying as you learn to pray. The *process*, not the content, is the genius; and that was the Spirit's gift. There is nothing new about the content. More profound content can be found in thousands of different books.

Each day of the six-week "walk" has a small segment of content; always with Scripture, because I believe you can't be a person of prayer without being a person of the Word. The lesson is brief because I believe we can best appropriate great truth in small doses.

The second aspect of the process is called "Reflecting and Recording." The purpose of this dynamic is to *force* us to center and clarify our thinking, to be specific and explicit. We are called to write something down; I call it "praying at the point of a pencil." This is important not just for appropriating the content of the day, but to demonstrate truth. On a particular day, you may be asked to go back to some previous day and consider what you recorded there. Two things are important in this approach. One, rehearsal and reconsideration are effective dynamics in the learning process. Two, in our praying, we usually are not as attentive as we should be to what is happening as a result of our praying. Going back to see where we were and what we might have prayed two or three weeks previously may show us that our prayers are being answered, or it may show us that we take our praying too lightly, because we are not attentive to the difference it may be making.

The third aspect in the process is labeled "During the Day." Actual content from the book will be the best explanation of this and the dynamic of reflecting and recording. On the very first day of the *Workbook*, the content focuses on the fact that it is natural to pray because prayer is an expression of our hunger for God. In the "Reflecting and Recording" section, this is one of the instructions: "How do you see the hunger affecting others? Think of specific persons. Name them, and in a phrase or sentence indicate how that hunger is manifesting itself."

The "During the Day" guidance for the day says: "If your mind comes back to this experience anytime during this day or night, try to remember the persons you named in whom you have seen the hunger for God working. Simply ask God to bless them and satisfy their longing. Be open to God's using you in meeting their need."

It becomes obvious, almost immediately, as you use the *Workbook*, that you can't use it honestly without praying.

I don't know anything comparable to the *Workbook* in its practicality. Though published in 1974, it is still in print and people are still using it. The publisher estimates that more than a million copies have been printed and it is printed in at least six different languages.

The truth is we don't know how many have been printed and in how many different languages. Not only with the *Workbook*, but with other books as well, I keep discovering some book I have written that has been translated for use in some other country. Though I appreciate the fact, this is certainly not the way the publishers would have it. I'm always gratified that the word is getting out and my labor matters in ways of which I am often unaware. As late as 2010, the leadership of the *Upper Room* said the *Workbook* "was one of the best-selling group resources ever published by the *Upper Room*."

For a long time, I kept the Chinese translation of *The Workbook of Living Prayer* in an obvious place in my study. It was the first book I had written to be translated into another language. I wanted to be reminded of the story behind it, to keep me aware of the possible significance of what I might be writing. A Presbyterian pastor had used the *Workbook* when it was first published in 1974. Soon thereafter, he went to Taiwan as a missionary. I visited him there in 1976, and he shared with me the fact that he had translated the *Workbook* into Mandarin, and they were getting it to leaders of the underground church in China.

Becoming a World Christian

If I am in any sense a world Christian, I became so during my ministry at the *Upper Room*. The story of the *Upper Room* is phenomenal. It began in the heart of a Sunday school teacher, Frances Craig, at Travis Park Methodist Episcopal Church in San Antonio, Texas. She encouraged her pastor, Dr. Paul Kern, to write short devotionals and publish them in their church's weekly newsletter. Kern placed daily Scripture readings alongside short encouraging notes.

Simultaneously, clergyman Grover Emmons discovered the commonality of believers around the world to serve Christ. His dream was for a devotional book that would, "cultivate an acquaintance with God"[1] for all people. Those inspirational thoughts and prayers gave life to the *Upper Room*, which by the time I became the world editor, had become the world's most widely used devotional guide.

In early 1935, the first issue was sent to the printer. In an amazing show of faith, one hundred thousand copies of that first issue (April–May–June 1935) were ordered. Shocking the many naysayers who couldn't believe such would work, it sold out quickly.

> By the seventh issue, the print run was half a million copies. Almost immediately after the magazine's publication, readers began writing and sending in devotionals that spoke of their personal faith stories. By 1938, the magazine was publishing meditations written by ordinary readers, not just invited writers.[2]

It had become a "people to people" magazine, ordinary people reaching out to one another, linked by their common faith in Jesus Christ. Less than four years later, in 1939, the print run was an astonishing one million copies. Through the years, sometimes the monthly circulation reached 3.5 and occasionally 4 million. Since this was often used by families, some ten million people were receiving the message each day. Today, the magazine is published in thirty-five languages in one hundred countries worldwide.

The ongoing story is told in *Where the World Meets to Pray* by Mary Lou Redding, published in 2009. By the time I joined the staff, printing involved more than the magazine. There were books and pamphlets; even a series entitled the Upper Room Pulpit, a collection of sermons by the nation's outstanding preachers. There had been a season when radio was used to share the daily *Upper Room* meditation. The culture of the ministry was open for creativity and different media expressions of teaching and spiritual growth.

I was called to the staff to cultivate a fellowship of prayer. As people around the world were linked by this daily, shared devotional reading, they were linked in prayer. Early on, we sought to make that explicit by adding to each day's devotional reading a prayer focus, most often suggested by the content of the devotional writing. On any given day, our millions of readers might be praying together for unity in the Christian community, or reconciliation of races, or peace, or for refugees in some ravaged land, or for the cause of education, or prison reform, or for single mothers or orphanages.

In 1977, we made the praying even more personal for our readers in the United States by establishing the Upper Room Living Prayer Center. We trained volunteers to receive prayer requests mailed or called in on a toll-free telephone line, and pray for each person by name. Phone-forwarding technology made it possible to divert calls to the trained volunteers in their homes. It was almost unbelievable. Over the years, hundreds of compassionate people volunteered to pray for persons in need, many of these volunteers signed up for two-hour blocks and faithfully served for years.

One imaginative expression of this prayer ministry was that existing prayer groups in churches across the nation and in Mexico became Upper Room Living Prayer groups by studying prescribed materials. These groups would also receive prayer requests relayed to them from our prayer center in Nashville. It was inspiring to walk into the Living Prayer Center and see a large map of the United States dotted with colored pushpins designating locations of these living prayer groups.

My ministry assignment grew out of an effort that had begun in 1949, when a small part of the staff corresponded with readers who asked for prayer, and with people who needed the magazine but could not pay for it. This group also responded to requests from military chaplains for copies of the magazine to give to service personnel, continuing a practice that began in World War II. People were not only asking to be prayed for, they were requesting resources to strengthen their own prayer life. My *Workbook of Living Prayer* was a response to my own personal need, but more crucial, to the needs of people everywhere.

Our first corporate teaching effort was the Adventure in Living Prayer retreat. Trained leaders presented this two-day model to churches throughout the United States and a network of praying churches began to form naturally. These were the churches that became extensions of the Living Prayer Center, but they were also the congregations that called for more and more spiritual growth resources.

A more expansive and concentrated model was the two-year Academy for Spiritual Formation. It was five years in the making and launched in 1983. Danny Morris was a staff member of the Board of Discipleship (former Board of Evangelism). His assignment within discipleship was very much akin to my assignment with the *Upper Room*, so we worked intimately together. He was a partner in developing the Adventure in Living Prayer and the Living Prayer Center. When the world editor and CEO of the *Upper Room* resigned in 1978, I was selected to succeed him. I recruited Danny to join our staff and assume responsibility for the work I had been doing. It was a seamless transition and gave us the opportunity to focus the *Upper Room* more concretely to the broad field of spiritual formation.

Becoming a "Catholic" Christian

Not only did I become, to whatever degree I am, a "world Christian" during my years at the *Upper Room*, I became an "ecumenical Christian," or maybe better expressed, a "catholic Christian." Again, this was basically the result of trying to make up for my own inadequacy. I mentioned earlier that my call to the *Upper Room* forced me to be more deliberate and disciplined in my own personal life of prayer, but it also introduced me to a wider dimension of spirituality than I had known.

One of perhaps the most significant persons to enter my life during this period came via the mail. The Upper Room sought to contribute meaning to our nation's celebration of America's bicentennial by publishing a volume of sermons on the theme "Under God a New Birth of Freedom?" We invited preachers to submit sermons on the theme. A collection of the best of these would be chosen, and we would write a study guide to them for corporate use in local churches.

We received a homily from a monk in a Trappist monastery in Oregon. It was too brief for our purpose, but was sensitively done, so expressive of distilled wisdom that I wrote him a letter of appreciation. That began a correspondence which made a profound impression on me. Brother Simon Reynolds was his name and he became, for a season, a kind of spiritual guide.

He was then eighty-two years old. His letters sparkled with life and were punctuated with humor. Though living in a monastery, Brother Simon seemed in touch with the world, with truth, and with the needs and feelings of persons in an uncanny, somewhat unbelievable way.

Almost immediately, I felt he was a person I wanted and needed to know. We exchanged letters every couple of months, and then, by special permission of the abbot, I spent one day with him in his monastery in Oregon. Our relationship, via letters, became intimate and personal. I prayed for him regularly; in his disciplined monastic life, he prayed for me daily.

In one of his early letters, he said, "I am a fisherman for contemplatives. In you I think I have caught one who is at least a potential." A few months later, I was in a rather serious auto accident which left me with a punctured lung and a broken leg. During my recovery time, one of his letters said,

On Monday after Mass, I got the answer to your broken leg. The Lord wants you to take more time out and choose a place for private passive contemplation. You're too active. Jesus Himself had to go up into the mountains to pray (G. K. Chesterton says, to laugh at his Apostles human mistakes: such as Peter's curiosity and the ambition of James and John to sit at his right and left in the Kingdom). All you must do is sit and listen.

Unfortunately, I am not as good a contemplative as he mentored me to be, but that was because I never disciplined my overactive nature as much as he called me to. But his mentoring was a significant influence in shaping my life.

Much of the time on the one day we were personally together was spent talking about the indwelling Christ. As indicated earlier, this notion had become a bedrock stone in my theology and in my spiritual formation. He couldn't resist talking about the *real* presence of Christ in Holy Communion.

A few months after that day together, I shared in a meaningful worship experience with Roman Catholics, but was denied the bread and wine in the celebration of Holy Communion. In a letter to Brother Simon, I expressed my pain at not being given the opportunity of sharing fully in this sacrament of life and joy. By return mail, I received this reply:

My dear Brother Maxie: I made contact this week with the very soul of you, early in the week, by mental telepathy and by letter. Wednesday and Thursday, my supraconscious started registering, "Maxie, Maxie, Maxie" by its spiritual morse dot-and-dash code. That set me Hail-Marying for the Dunnams and made me tack Jerry's "Fresh Every Morning" poster [Jerry had sent him a poster she had designed] below my daily calendar, to the left of my room door. So, it is Dunnams my coming in and Dunnams my going out.

I asked Lady Guadalupe [the patron saint of their monastery] how to tell Maxie about Jesus in the Blessed Sacrament. She said use Jerry and the word "ontological." So, He's there ontologically. Body and Blood, Soul and Divinity, whether I think of him now and then or don't. Why Jerry? Kim [our oldest daughter] was with her one month,

ontologically before either she, Jerry, or you knew it—a living existence, independent of your thought of it—there and how God willed
her to be there. As a boy in church, I remember saying, "I wish I lived
when Jesus did." The answer came immediately, "You are living with
me now, I am living here with you!" He's been living with ever since.
Sort of first-month Kim-like. I confess, I occasionally have tried to
dodge His presence. But then my whole world crashed, and I hurried
back to his energizing, chastened and secure. Therefore, I can feel your
pain in not communing completely.

He wrote a couple of more paragraphs, making the point that we must
use our imagination in appropriating faith and in cultivating our relationship with Christ. He concluded by returning to his conviction about
how imagination is operative in claiming the *real* presence, writing,
"Your Maxie image in a mirror has no Maxie substance, but it is Maxie
nonetheless."

His point about the real presence of Christ in Holy Communion is
relevant not just to the Lord's Supper, but to the whole of life. His testimony makes that point. He heard Christ say, "You are living with me
spiritually by your faith in my presence. I am living in you by the grace of
my love." And his witness was, "He's been living with ever since. Sort of
first-month Kim-like."

This metaphor of a person coming to life in a mother's womb, the egg
being fertilized before we are aware of it as a concept of the "indwelling
Christ" struck a vibrant cord. It inspired more rich reflection on Paul's
concept, which had been shaping my life since I was powerfully introduced to it by Stanley Jones. As I began the day, for more than a decade
I had been speaking a word of Paul to myself . . . sometimes aloud, sometimes simply registering it in my awareness. "Maxie, the secret is simply
this: 'Christ in you! Yes, Christ in you bringing with him the hope of all
the glorious things to come'" (Col. 1:27 Phillips). As I have continued
that practice through these forty years since, I often think of Brother

Simon and anticipate a reunion with him where the walls of the monastery and my too-active nature will not prevent deeper soul touching soul.

During my early time at the Upper Room, I knew no one within the Protestant tradition who was talking about *spiritual formation*. Brother Simon was a vivid witness that the Roman Catholics have known the importance of this aspect of the Christian faith and way, and have used formation language through the centuries. It wasn't long before we at the *Upper Room* were talking about spiritual formation and seeking to provide resources for a much broader expression of spirituality than we had known before.

I became intensely interested in the great devotional classics. The Upper Room had published a collection of little booklets—selections from some of the great spiritual writings of the ages, writers whose names I barely knew, and to whose writings I was a stranger: Julian of Norwich, William Law, Francois Fenelon, Francis of Assisi, Evelyn Underhill, and an array of others. I lived with those twenty-nine booklets and began to read these writers in fuller measure than the tiny introduction to them in those booklets. My once multivolume library has diminished significantly during the past fifteen years as I have given books away when moving, and latest, when retiring. Yet, those small pocket-sized booklets, in a little box in which they were originally packaged, are in an obvious place on a shelf in my study.

I don't remember when I last read one of those booklets, but they are there, in that recognizable package, reminding me of a significant movement and time period in my spiritual and professional journey. It was then, years ago, that I began a practice I call "keeping company with the saints."

It has been that practice, especially, that has made me a catholic Christian. And that practice has made me more authentically a Methodist/Wesleyan Christian. One of the celebrated sermons of John Wesley was his sermon on the "Catholic Spirit." Great confusion exists in our United Methodist Church today because the "catholic spirit" has been interpreted to mean "theological pluralism," and such pluralism is projected as both acceptable and desirable of what it means to be a Christian in the Methodist tradition. Taken to an extreme, there is a fallacy in this concept that would shock Mr. Wesley. The way it is too often projected suggests that a United Methodist Christian can believe almost anything about God, Jesus Christ, and the essential doctrines that relate to salvation, but this is a perversion of Wesley's idea of the catholic spirit.

He positioned a catholic spirit over against what he labeled "speculative latitudinarianism," which he called the "spawn of hell, not the offspring of heaven." This is a part of what he said:

> A man of a truly catholic spirit has not now his religion to seek. He is fixed as the sun in his judgment concerning the main branches of Christian doctrine. . . . Observe this, you who know not what spirit ye are of: who call yourselves men of the catholic spirit, only because you are of a muddy understanding, because your mind is all in a mist; because you have no settled, consistent principles, but are for jumbling all opinions together. Be convinced, that you have quite missed your way; you know not where you are. You think you are got into the very spirit of Christ when in truth; you are nearer the spirit of Antichrist. Go first, and learn the first elements of the gospel of Christ, and then shall you learn to be of a truly catholic spirit.[3]

Wesley was a "man of one book," and Scripture was the primary source of everything we are to believe or not believe. He valued tradition and reason; he was intent on an experienced, heart-felt religion; but tradition, reason, and experience were to always be in harmony with Scripture.

It is in the sense of what I believe Wesley understood and experienced that I see myself as a catholic Christian. Two involvements have cultivated and given that meaning. One was the Ecumenical Institute of Spirituality, and the other, the Methodist/Roman Catholic dialogue.

Douglas Steere was one of the cofounders of the Ecumenical Institute of Spirituality and an American Quaker ecumenist. His book, *Dimensions of Prayer*, was an important resource for me when it was first published in 1962. The civil rights struggle was intensifying in Mississippi, and I was searching for deeper grounding in a life of prayer. I was amazed that such an intellectual giant as Steere would be so boldly open to the supernatural, so deeply committed to a personal relationship with Christ, while extravagantly expressing his faith in peace movements, justice issues, social service, and spiritual enrichment conferences and retreats. Back then, I wistfully thought, I want to know persons like Douglas Steere. He seemed to understand the gospel in its wholeness. What I was experiencing and observing in Mississippi Christianity would say the gospel is almost altogether personal, with little regard for the social implications of Jesus' message.

Steere was invited to participate as an ecumenical observer in Pope John XXIII's Second Vatican Council. In 1965, he and another observer, Godfrey Diekmann, bored with the tedious proceedings of the council, took a break in a coffee shop, and there the Ecumenical Institute of Spirituality was conceived. Its mission was to bring together an equal number of Roman Catholic and Protestant scholars to talk about the horizons of spirituality as it impinges on all aspects of life.

At the *Upper Room*, I had begun to know persons like Douglas Steere because I was seeking to engage them in writing for us, inviting them to speak at conferences we were sponsoring, or gaining their wisdom for how we might serve our constituency with the very best spiritual formation resources: persons like Morton Kelsey, Doris Donnelly, Edward J. Farrell, Glenn Hinson, and Basil Pennington. Later, when I received an invitation from Douglas to become a part of the institute, I learned that some of these same people were a part of it. Because I knew I was not a scholar, I knew that my commitment and passion for formation and my relationship to some of these folks was the only reason I would have been invited.

Though passive for a season, the demon that had been most effective in draining my energy and blocking me from wholeness and meaning attacked again. He knew where I was weakest: my poor self-image and lack of self-appreciation, my feelings of having been cheated culturally and educationally. His whisper in my consciousness roared and ravaged my mind: "Who do you think you are to share fellowship with, much less be involved in serious conversation, with persons like these?"

How deceptive are our minds and emotions! The demon was effective. I found all sorts of excuses not to accept the invitation; even deliberately making plans for the time frame in which I knew the group would be meeting. But Douglas was as spiritually sensitive as he was mentally brilliant. He was humble and patient, never pushy! Somehow, on an occasion, he heard that I was speaking at Bay View Assembly, not a long way from his home on Lake Michigan; he wrote me a note (that seemed to be the Quaker way, writing notes rather than using the phone) inviting me to spend an afternoon and night with him, after I finished my speaking engagement at Bay View. He was so gracious I couldn't say no.

The peace and quiet of that home, made so by the spirit of both Douglas and his wife, Dorothy, was palatable. Everything about the setting and the experience was simple, nothing overstated. Dorothy was as charming in her simplicity and conversation as Douglas. The evening meal was delicious, but again, simple, because our sharing was the most important thing. About 8:30, without it being an issue or a question, I knew it was bedtime. As he bade me good night, Douglas said he would be happy for me to join him at 6:30 in the morning in his study; he would be there in silence and prayer.

I was tentative in mind and spirit as I entered his study that morning, frightened at how I would function in prayer with this spiritual giant. There was no functioning; only silence as, in the Quaker style, we listened and waited on the Lord. The only words we spoke were as he rose, indicating Dorothy would be ready for us at breakfast. "I do hope you will join us for the meeting of the institute this year."

Well I did, that year and the next three years. I was becoming a catholic Christian.

While at the *Upper Room* I became involved with the World Methodist Council. Joe Hale, the general secretary, had become a friend when he was a staff member of the Board of Evangelism; his invitation and urging got me involved. In 1992, I was appointed by the Executive Committee of the Council to be a member of the Joint Commission for Dialogue between the Roman Catholic Church and the World Methodist Council.

The Methodist/Roman Catholic dialogue was established after the Second Vatican Council. In 1966, the Vatican asked the World Methodist Council to begin a series of dialogues. The International Dialogue Commission works in five-year series of meetings, in harmony with the meetings of the World Methodist Council. These statements are then presented to the Council and to the Vatican.

My participation as a member of this commission was 1992–1996. I entered that dialogue with little confidence, but I was not resistant as I had been with the Ecumenical Institute of Spirituality. I had discovered a oneness in Christ with people whose religious tradition and practices were foreign to me. This became more pronounced in the Roman Catholic dialogue because it was not Roman Catholics and Protestants in general; it was Roman Catholics and Methodists, and this dialogue was made up of people not just from the United States, but from around the world.

My two favorite persons in the dialogue were Dr. Francis Frost and Dr. José Míguez Bonino. Father Francis was a Roman Catholic priest, a professor of theology in Switzerland. Dr. Bonino was a Methodist minister, a professor and leading theological voice in Argentina, world-renowned as a pioneer of Latin American liberation theology.

I had my arguments with liberation theology, but was intrigued and committed to the primary plank in that system: *God's preferential option on behalf of the poor.* Many of the political expressions of it in Latin America were seen as Marxist, and it often involved support of violence. Yet, I was intrigued with and committed to the foundation plank. Who can argue? Scripture is clear; God has taken a preferential option on behalf of the poor and powerless.

This preferential option for the poor and vulnerable includes all who are marginalized in society, including unborn children, persons with disabilities, the elderly and terminally ill, and victims of injustice and oppression. The prophets of the Old Testament made that clear. Jesus taught that on the day of judgment the primary question to each of us will be, "Well, what about the poor? How did you treat them?"

I was enriched by Bonino's sharing of his own involvement and interpretation of this theology—the theology that was a fiery center of debate and controversy for at least three decades of the twentieth century and has influenced our understanding of Christian discipleship. He so winsomely, and I believe rightly, insisted, "The poor have the most urgent moral claim on the conscience of the nation." Our moral test as a society is "how we treat our most vulnerable members."

Though he was a fellow Methodist and his was one of the first Protestant voices in the liberation theology movement, and being with him was a positive corrective to my caricature of the whole movement, I felt as close, sometimes closer, to Father Francis than to him. There was something more personal about Father Francis for me. Though separated from him by layer after layer of his Roman Catholic tradition, heart touched heart when we talked of the redeeming love of Christ, the call of Scripture to holiness, and the ongoing mission of the church to be Christ's presence in the world.

A theological statement is produced out of each of the five-year dialogues. The goal was to find doctrinal agreements between Methodists and Catholics. I have never been committed to one church institutionally, but am deeply committed to "one Lord, one faith, one baptism." Our group focused on what are usually called, in theological terms, "revelation" and "faith." Out of this dialogue came, "The Word of Life: A Statement on Revelation and Faith," a witness to the "oneness" of Christians in the core of the "faith once and for all delivered to the saints."

I became the senior minister of Christ United Methodist Church in Memphis, Tennessee, in 1982. On November 17, 1982, James Francis Stafford, now James Francis Cardinal Stafford, was appointed the second bishop of Memphis by Pope John Paul II. He was installed on January 17,

1983. Ira Gallaway, who was primarily responsible for recruiting me from the pastorate in California to the staff at the *Upper Room*, had been a participant in the Methodist/Roman Catholic dialogue, the five years preceding me on the dialogue team. When he heard that Bishop Stafford was being installed as bishop of Memphis, he wanted to come to the service because Bishop Stafford had been a part of his dialogue team.

Ira and I attended the installation service. We had no intention of sharing in the Eucharist, but we found ourselves in the line with the faithful, approaching the altar. I'm not sure what happened. The bishop did not know me, but he recognized Ira, and delivered the consecrated bread to us. I have been served the sacrament a few times by a priest in the Roman Catholic Church, but only this once by a bishop.

Bishop Stafford was committed to evangelization of the African American community, and we became friends because of mutual commitment to the underserved of our city. Like me, Bishop Stafford was also inspired by Mother Teresa. He had been with her in retreats, and he invited her to come to Memphis for a special witness for the life of the unborn. He invited some Protestants to the service.

The service was held in the Mid-South Coliseum. More than eight thousand people were there. A striking thing happened as Mother Teresa and her nuns entered. It was amazing, because I have seen what happens regularly in that coliseum. I'm a University of Memphis Tiger basketball fan, and I go to all the basketball games I can. I've also attended concerts at the coliseum and it's bedlam—applause, screaming, yelling, the ultimate in noisy, enthusiastic response to what's going on. But when Mother Teresa and her nuns came out on the floor of that coliseum, a wondrous holy hush descended upon that crowd. You could hear the nuns walking on the floor; had they not been walking, you may have heard a pin drop. It was a kind of eerie quietness that spoke of reverence and awe. This tiny, stoop-backed, wrinkled, dried-up little woman, evoked that holy hush from that mass of people.

I know that response is to what people know about her and her ministry, but I can't help but believe it's also to her very person. She is humility incarnate. Throughout that two-hour mass, for the most part, she was in prayer. For a good part of the time, completely removed from what was going on around her, she buried her face in her hands and became even more stooped, as she rested her elbows on her knees and cradled her head in deep prayer.

After the mass, she spoke. She spoke simply, but her words penetrated the conscience of the audience because her words flowed out of a life of prayer and service. She called us to prayer, and to a life of tender mercy—which she would say are inseparable. She punctuated her brief talk with some personal experiences. She told of walking on the streets of Calcutta, and seeing something moving in a ditch. She had to look carefully to see that it was an emaciated man, still alive, but his whole body was covered with worms. She took him back to their center that cares for the dying. She said it took them three hours to pick the worms off the man, clean him up, give him a bath, some simple food, and introduce him to love—love and prayer with no strings attached.

The man did die. But he died with dignity, knowing that he was loved, which is the ministry of Mother Teresa and her sisters. As he lay dying, he looked up at Mother Teresa and said, "I came here as an animal, I leave in death as an angel." And he smiled as he died.

Though she had already impacted my life, I had never met her. But this day I did, though briefly. Jerry and I had the opportunity of shaking hands with her, looking into those deep, compassionate eyes, and having her speak a simple word of blessing, as we received a prayer medal from her. I carried that medal in my pocket for two years before I lost it; and I have often prayed that the person who found it would discover the story of Mother Teresa.

By this time in my discipleship walk, my quest was clearer than ever. I passionately wanted to know who Jesus is and who I was in relation to him. Bishop Stafford preached the homily for the mass that day. He told of having been with Mother Teresa a few weeks earlier. They were walking along an enclosed cloister, in a convent where they were together for a retreat. They were in silence. Mother Teresa stopped for a long time before a statue of the crucified Christ, and he could hear her whispering in earnest prayer: "I thirst . . . I thirst . . . I thirst."

In that snapshot of this saint of God, Bishop Stafford said he discovered her secret. It was in her desire—her burning thirst for more of Christ. Again, that has been my passion, not always acted on and in the kind of discipline required, but at my core: the desire to know who Jesus is and who I am in relation to him.

As with all my total ministry, Jerry was a working partner (not passive) in our involvement in the World Methodist Council. Joe Hale, the general secretary of the World Methodist Council, gives a description of Jerry's involvement:

Shortly after we moved to North Carolina and our work with the World Methodist Council began, Maxie and Jerry Dunnam were in our home for dinner. Our son was in grade school at the time. Jerry was sitting at the dining room table, scribbling something. He intently watched her, first draw a few simple lines, then add color with some pens she had, and a picture emerged. It was of the children of the world, holding hands across the page dressed as they would appear in their respective countries. Jerry drew the picture for our son, but it ended up on the wall of my office. I looked at it every day I was there for twenty-five years.

The children of the world on the wall, for me, represented our future in the World Methodist Council. Jerry's simple drawing has helped shape my thinking about what was important and most important to do in life.

A few years later, on a far larger scale, Jerry did something for world Methodism. World Methodist Conferences have met regularly at either five- or ten-year intervals since 1881. Every world meeting has featured some kind of opening processional. In recent years, representatives carried the flags of their nation into meeting halls or stadiums in grand opening ceremonies.

The 1991 World Methodist Conference was the first of these meetings ever to be held in Africa. Jerry was centrally involved in advance preparations for the meeting. She conceived something for Nairobi that was new and dramatic. She envisioned each national church being asked to create in advance some artistic representation of their church in the year before coming to the conference, something that would uniquely represent their church and world region. For this to work, Jerry knew a framework of different shapes and carefully assigned colors would need to be sent to artists and committees in national churches. Overall coordination, she felt, was the key to freedom and creativity in national content, and design would be the task of each of the eighty national member churches.

The overall result was a spectacular array of color, coordinated style, and central to everything, an international artistry that was stunning. On one day of the Nairobi Conference, these banners were carried through the streets of the city in a great procession, led by Archbishop Desmond Tutu, dancing in the African style, with Jerry along with him, followed by leaders of the international churches, greeted by thousands of Kenyans.

The artistry of Jerry Dunnam, seen so dramatically in Kenya, has been a part of every world conference since. She brought the elements of World Methodist diversity front and center in World Methodist meetings.

The Upper Room Cursillo (Walk to Emmaus)

God has used the Walk to Emmaus in amazing ways, and it has spread around the world. More than 1.5 million people have experienced the

Walk. It is now in forty countries outside the United States, with eighty-seven local communities of the Walk that minister in an ongoing way. There are more than five hundred communities in the United States. Chrysalis, a youth expression of the Walk, now has more than thirty communities in eleven countries.

I'm sure my becoming more a world and catholic Christian opened me to different expressions of spirituality and resources for growth in our spirituality. The Walk to Emmaus grew out of the Roman Catholic Cursillo. As I traveled about the nation, I was often asked, "Do you know about *cursillo*?" I not only didn't know about it, it was a strange word, pronounced "cur-see-yo." I later learned it's a Spanish word for "short course."

People would talk glowingly about what the experience had meant to them personally, and how it was transforming their congregation. The word was coming so often and from so many different directions, I decided I had better find out more. I learned that a Roman Catholic bishop, Juan Hervás, had developed the three-day event, consisting of fifteen talks given by clergy and lay leaders in response to what he felt was a "crisis of faith" in the Catholic Church in Spain. It was an effort to teach the core of the faith and challenge persons to embody God's grace in their congregations and in the world. The first Cursillo was held in Spain in 1948.

American airmen brought the Cursillo from Spain to the Americas. The first Cursillo weekend was held in Texas in 1961. As a result of Vatican II, Christians from other denominations were invited to Catholic Cursillos. The first Episcopal Cursillo was held in 1969, and soon other mainline denominations began having Cursillo weekends.

God moves in mysterious ways, and his hand creatively intervenes through people. Ira Galloway, who had brought me to the staff of the *Upper Room*, had left the Board of Discipleship to become senior minister of First United Methodist Church in Peoria, Illinois. He invited me to lead an Adventure in Living Prayer in his congregation and to test my initial work on *The Workbook of Living Prayer*. I learned that weekend that there was a dynamic Roman Catholic Cursillo in Peoria, and that it was very ecumenical. Ira had participated, and his associate minister, Bob Wood, was very active in the community.

It was difficult to resist thinking that God may be saying something to me about Cursillo. Again, Jerry was a working partner in ministry. I went back to Nashville, and immediately engaged her and Danny Morris and his wife, Rosalie, in conversation. Our conclusion: we needed to check Cursillo out personally. The model is that men and women go on separate weekends; if married, both husband and wife must make the commitment to go. Danny and Rosalie went to Miami; Jerry and I to Peoria. Danny always seemed to get the more exotic place, but I wanted to test if it could play in Peoria.

It did; it played in Peoria *and* Miami. The four of us were convinced that the Cursillo was a spiritual formation model we wanted to make available to our *Upper Room* constituency. My Cursillo experience was comparable in impact to my experience with Stanley Jones in the Christian ashram years before.

God's grace (*grace* being the operative word) was working overtime. Father Tom Hensler was the spiritual leader of the Peoria Cursillo. He was Catholic (spelled with a capital "C"), he was also "catholic" (spelled with a lowercase "c"), and he added more meaning to my being a catholic Christian. Father Tom joyfully agreed to engage the Catholic Peoria Cursillo community to help us model two ecumenical Cursillo weekends.

This was the beginning of the Upper Room Cursillo. The Peoria community numbered them as a part of their ongoing Cursillo ministry. These weekends were Cursillo #108 held on April 21–24 and #110 held on May 19–22 at the St. Augustine Cursillo Center in 1977.

In 1978, the first Upper Room Cursillo was held in Nashville. We were so convinced of the potential of this movement for spiritual renewal that we invited Bob Wood, the associate minister of the United Methodist Church in Peoria, to join our Upper Room staff and direct this program as it spread across the nation, and literally across the world. Within a few years, the Upper Room Cursillo became the Walk to Emmaus. The prayer to the Holy Spirit has become as much a part of pilgrims on the Walk to Emmaus as the Serenity Prayer is to the recovering community.

> Come, Holy Spirit, fill the hearts of your faithful and kindle in us the fire of your love. Send forth your Spirit and we shall be created. And you shall renew the face of the earth. O God, who by the light of the Holy Spirit did instruct the hearts of the faithful, grant that by the same Holy Spirit we may be truly wise and ever enjoy your consolations. Through Christ our Lord. Amen.

Launching Multiple Ministry Expressions

We had a saying in Mississippi that things were moving "at breakneck speed." As the 1980s began, I was trying to keep up with the speed at which the Upper Room was moving. We had a creative staff and our work in spiritual formation was being affirmed around the world. We had proven our capacity to adapt and to take advantage of the fresh expressions of communication that were breaking out.

Exploring new approaches to the devotional life, the staff called for something less structured than the *Upper Room* daily guide, something younger, maybe "edgy" and "under thirty." The Upper Room's first new periodical in thirty-five years was born: *Alive Now*. Art, poetry, fiction, and personal witness vignettes were all used for multiple appeal. It was launched in 1971.

A decade later, in 1981, another bold dream was made a reality. A new magazine, this time for children, was launched, responding to the desire to lead children into a deeper life with God. The magazine was named *Pockets*.

Jerry played a significant role in the early stages. For the first two years, her The Meeting Tree was a regular feature of the magazine. Nothing Jerry has done combined her two greatest gifts so completely: art and storytelling. You can't be with Jerry too long before you realize she loves a good story, not only hearing one, but sharing one. Her sharing is always lively, and if there is not a fun aspect to the true story, she will usually add one. A friend said of her, "She can make a funeral sound fun." Keeping the story true to the bare facts is not a guiding principle for her. While enjoying embellishing a good story to make it a great story, she doesn't stray from the basic facts. She believes the goal of a great story is to lift up, not put down. More often than not, her humor points back to herself.

The Meeting Tree was "the most wonderful climbing tree you have ever seen." It was in Sally's backyard. Sally is the host in the story, and Jerry's imaginative tale begins with Sally having to move from the farm and the animals she loved to the city, because her father had been killed in an accident, and her mother had to now work and support Sally and Joshua and Dianne, her little brother and sister. Sally discovered the tree in her backyard the morning after her first night in the city, having "cried all night until there were no tears left inside."

In the initial installment of the story, Jerry set the stage for monthly sharing about The Meeting Tree and what it was all about with these words of Sally:

> Have you ever been sad like that? It hurts, doesn't it? Well, the next morning I went to explore the backyard and there it was! The biggest, most wonderful tree I'd ever seen. I knew there was something very special about it the moment I saw it. It was as if this tree could understand how sad I felt. I climbed up there where I am now, and this is still my favorite spot! Anyway, I felt that I could tell this tree anything, and it would cry with me or laugh with me. But always it would understand and listen.[4]

That's the way it began, and each month Jerry would tell the story of children gathering around, up, in, or under the Meeting Tree, to share their happiness or sadness, their troubles with parents or friends. It was Jerry's way of teaching children about relationships, God's love and forgiveness, the need to share and to be honest in sharing. Her art (she painted each person that was featured) captured the character and personality of the child. Dianne, Sally's sister, was shy, so when she first appeared in the story, she was peeping from behind a tree. Marty was often at the Meeting Tree, but he couldn't climb it because he was in a wheelchair, yet always smiling. (The children had cleared the alley so Marty, in his wheelchair, could get to the Meeting Tree.)

Though often subtle, the lessons were always clear. The magazine's primary purpose was to lead children into a deeper life with God. The Meeting Tree sought to do just that. Very early in the series, Sally shared about Toby, and makes it clear what the Meeting Tree is all about.

> Toby said before I moved in he used to come sit in this tree and talk to God. He told me it was not the tree that understood me but that it was God listening to all my feelings. He said this tree was a meeting place to talk with God, and that's how my own adventure of talking with God and listening to God got started.[5]

Jerry is an affirming person. She pays attention. Whereas I am often in a hurry, even when relating to others, Jerry never is. She gives her time and attention freely. She regularly engages people she doesn't know in conversations . . . in a checkout line at the grocery story, or in the parking lot—especially if she thinks that person might need encouragement. Hardly a day passes that she doesn't tell me at the close of the day about some conversation she has had with some stranger.

This gift of affirmation is present in The Meeting Tree. Not only does she affirm different ethnicities and persons with physical limitations, two of the main characters are Roger and Rick, the sons of Freddy, the teenager who became a part of our family when he was sixteen. Each of them has a piece of original art from The Meeting Tree that is clearly a portrait of them.

I left the Upper Room in 1982, just before the Academy for Spiritual Formation was launched. Danny Morris and I had worked on this for five years, believing that a more disciplined, more concentrated, more demanding model of formation training was needed. The model was rooted in community and involved worship, silence, lectures, and small groups over a weekend. Two expressions of the academy emerged, one over a two-year, the other over a five-year period. Participants meet quarterly to learn and share in depth when they are together, returning to their homes to live out what they have learned.

I don't have many ministry regrets, but one of them is that I did not have the opportunity of sharing in the full expression of the Academy for Spiritual Formation.

CHAPTER NINE

In the Shadow of Giants

In March 1982, we were spending a weekend with Jerry's parents in Atlanta. An astonishing story headlined the news on Sunday morning before we joined her parents listening to their favorite television preacher. A fifteen-year-old, Leslie Gattas, had been rescued from the man who had abducted her from her home in Memphis. From November 1981 to March 1982, her kidnapping was a nationwide mystery. It was the Memphis version of the Lindbergh baby kidnapping—a prominent family, a child taken from its bed, the agonizing period of not knowing.

It was one of Memphis's most notorious crimes, made so in part because the kidnapper had kept the young lady captive in a crawl space of the balcony of Christ United Methodist Church for 119 days. You can imagine my shock. I was going to preach my first sermon as pastor of that congregation the next Sunday.

I then remembered. When I had preached at the church some time before, I found a note on the desk in the pastor's office: "Please help me, I'm here. Leslie." When I inquired about the note I was told that such notes had been found in different places on the campus. They told me sketchily that a kidnapping had taken place in the city. They had concluded the notes were from an ongoing jokester, because they had reported these notes to the police; they had searched the entire property, even using dogs, but had found nothing.

The news was now reporting that Earnest Stubblefield kidnapped Leslie Gattas from her home, intending to seek a $25,000 ransom. For four months in the crawl space with a kidnapper, the high school sophomore relied on her instincts to stay alive.

After the rescue, Leslie shared that at about 10:30 p.m. each night, when all activities at the church were over and most of the lights out, she and her kidnapper would creep downstairs. Sometimes they would go into the sanctuary. He would allow her to sit on the front pew and pray, but he would sneer, "Your God ain't so good. He can't help you now. The only one who can help you is me." She later testified that listening to the music, the singing, and the preaching in Sunday worship was a sustaining dynamic.

She wrote the notes when she could, most of the time in the ladies' room while he waited outside. As they moved about, when he wasn't looking, before the beam of his flashlight swept past, she stuffed them in Bibles, under pews, in desks, under books, desperately hoping they would be found. She kept a pencil in her jeans pocket and scribbled plea after plea for help; but the folks at the church, after the search by police, became used to finding the notes and began to disregard them.

The kidnapper and his victim would also go to the church gym/fellowship hall where they usually found food in the refrigerator. It was the food issue that led two maintenance employees of the church to do a stakeout near the hall in the middle of the night. They thought young people were coming into the gym to play and were helping themselves to the food.

Their stakeout was successful, not in confronting young people they thought were having a good time, but shocked by a huge three-hundred-pound man with a teenage girl firmly in tow. They attacked him with baseball bats and sought to subdue him, but he got away. They had the prize, though; Leslie's prayers had finally been answered.

My time of discernment in accepting the bishop's appointment to the church had already been filled with intense emotional issues. As I have already discussed, my time at the Upper Room was rich and rewarding. Apart from the challenge of personal growth and opportunities for groundbreaking creativity, there was a kind of romantic, adventurous dimension to it. For a country boy from Mississippi, it was heady, traveling the world and meeting some of the world's leading Christian writers, teachers, and preachers.

But I was first of all a pastor. That was the primary plank in the foundation of my calling. My bishop, Ed Tullis, knew that. He had been the chair of committee that guided the work of the Upper Room for the General Board of Discipleship of our United Methodist Church, when I was elected world editor of the *Upper Room*. He knew my story and he knew preaching the gospel was my primary passion.

I was speaking at an evangelism conference in Nashville, and Jerry was leading a workshop on mime and clowning as a ministry, when I got the call from Bishop Tullis. Could Jerry and I come to his home for coffee with him and his wife, Mary Jane?

It's not easy for an outsider to United Methodism to understand the role of a bishop; in fact, even insiders don't always understand it, especially the relationship between a bishop and his clergy/pastors. Bishops in our church are not *ordained* as bishops are in the Roman Catholic, Orthodox, and Anglican churches. Our bishops' ordination is the same as all clergy. As ordained elders, they are elected by peers and representative laypersons to be bishops, and are *consecrated* (set apart) to perform the ministry of a bishop.

They are at once equal to, yet with authority over, the clergy who serve in the conference (geographical area) over which they preside. This system sets the stage for mixed emotions, confused understandings, and sometimes conflicted relationships. Early in my ministry, there was more than a hint of awe in my relationship to bishops. For a season, I'm sure that had to do with the authority issue. But that changed; I continued to respect authority, but it was more than respect. My bishop, the one under whose authority and oversight I served, had been given a special responsibility by the church for deploying me in ministry for the sake of the best expression of the kingdom.

This feeling came into play significantly when Bishop Tullis called, requesting a meeting with Jerry and me. We had become friends through the years, as our paths crossed before he became my bishop. Jerry and I had led a retreat for ministers and their spouses when he was the bishop of the South Carolina Conference. His wife, Mary Jane, had been responsible for that event and Jerry and I were impressed with her warmth, simplicity, and her deep concern for clergy families.

The bishop had since been reassigned, and had moved to the Nashville area from South Carolina. I had transferred my membership from Southern California to this area when I joined the staff of the Upper Room. He wanted us to come to his home for coffee as soon as we finished our session. I looked at Jerry as we rang the doorbell, and noticed that she still had some of the white clown paint on her neck. We had the sense that this was to be more than a friendly visit when he greeted us at the door with a huge file beneath his arm. And it was. He wanted to talk with us about the possibility of my becoming the senior minister of Christ United Methodist Church in Memphis.

A couple of months before, Bishop Mel Wheatley had talked with me about assuming the leadership of one of the best-known United Methodist churches in the nation. It didn't take me long to say no to that possibility. But he was not *my* bishop, and I did not feel he had the kind of authority Bishop Tullis had for me.

I had been affirmed by the possibility of serving the nationally known church another bishop had offered, and rejoiced that the person I recommended for that position was chosen. Interestingly, because he was *my bishop*, I felt compelled to continue the conversation with Bishop Tullis and the congregation in Memphis. And there we were in Atlanta that Sunday morning, on the verge of beginning our ministry in Memphis, when we heard the bizarre news of a young woman being rescued from her abductor who had taken up residency in the attic of the sanctuary of the church of which I was now the pastor.

In terms of emotional heaviness, and the ongoing life of the congregation, the revelation of this notorious crime was the least of my concerns. The position I was filling at the church had opened by the death of their beloved senior minister, Dr. Harold Beaty.

Christ Church was one of those successful church plants that took place in the fifties and sixties. Memphis was a well-churched city. Bellevue Baptist Church and pastor R. G. Lee were known in Baptist circles across the nation. People talked about his identifying sermon, "Payday Someday." Calvary Episcopal Church, downtown, only a few blocks from the Mississippi River, was a leading parish in the Episcopal world. But the population was growing and there was only one direction for it to go, away from the river, to the east. So new congregations were planted; they were churches that grew and became influential in the city: Second Presbyterian, Holy Communion Episcopal, and Christ United Methodist.

Christ Methodist worship began in a theater. That became a kind of metaphor for creativity and a desire to take the gospel to the people. The theater marquis announced that *To Hell and Back* was the film being shown on the first Sunday that church was held there. The sermon that day seemed planned to offer an alternative: "The Birth of a Church." Dr. Charles Grant, from Kentucky, became the founding pastor, and preached that sermon on June 19, 1955. It was a phenomenal beginning. Six hundred people became charter members. Dr. Grant was an outstanding evangelistic preacher, and during his fourteen years as senior minister, the church grew rapidly.

Dr. Harold Beaty, from South Georgia, followed him as senior minister in June 1969. The church had grown to more than 2,500. Dr. Beaty served

until his tragic death on November 6, 1981. The sermon he had prepared
to preach the coming Sunday was entitled "Up to Jerusalem," and his
manuscript began:

> Mark records in the tenth chapter of his gospel, "They were in the way
> going up to Jerusalem, and Jesus went before them; and they were
> amazed; and as they followed, they were afraid" (Mark 10:32). Here is
> a distinct turning point in the gospel story. The Galilean days came to
> an end. No more crowds will gather on the sandy beach to hear Jesus
> speak, no more jaunts for Jesus and his friends across the lake. No more
> quiet evenings in Capernaum, no more nights under the Galilean sky.
> He leaves behind the hills, the villages, and the people he has served
> for months. He moves toward Jerusalem, where hostility, danger, and
> death await. Knowing what lies ahead, Jesus met it head-on. In the
> process Jesus taught a great lesson about life.
>
> However hard we work to avoid suffering, heartache, and pain, it
> inevitably comes. Like Jesus, the wise accept this fact and deal with it
> realistically. The foolish hide their heads in the sand and hope it will go
> away. In her novel *So Big*, Edna Ferber has an elderly housewife say to a
> young woman who is trying to avoid trouble: "You can't run away from
> life, Deane; you can't run far enough." No one can escape life; we must
> all deal with it one way or another.

Many people in the congregation knew Dr. Beaty was speaking with
authority, from experience. His wife had been mentally and emotionally
troubled for some time. Rather than being healed, her condition wors-
ened. One wonders what kind of thoughts and premonitions Dr. Beaty
might have had, even as he prepared his sermon. On the Friday evening
before he was to preach that sermon on Sunday, his wife took his life, and
then her own.

Both ministers were deeply loved. Dr. Grant had a more evangelistic style. People who knew and loved them both talked about Grant's
powerful evangelistic preaching and formal style that came across as

sternness, and Beaty's personal warmth and pastoral concern. Dr. Beaty had a PhD in communication. Both were popular and effective public speakers.

So here I was, following in the steps of two very effective, deeply loved pastors; one who played the unique role of founding the church, the other who had died tragically and was living as a kind of ghostly presence everywhere in the church.

I had not served as a pastor for ten years. My last church was a large neighborhood multi-staff, multi-worship services congregation, but Christ Church was becoming more a regional church, serving the city. My primary credibility in the mind of most was that I had headed the ministries of the Upper Room. Few Methodists would not know about the *Upper Room*, the world's most widely read devotional magazine, though they might be unaware of the expansive spiritual formation ministries of the organization. They knew I had written a number of books, and were proud to call me "Doctor," though that was an honorary degree. But I was not Dr. Grant, and I certainly was not their beloved Dr. Beaty, whose death they were still grieving.

My first big mistake came rather soon. Our most popular ministry was with youth. The first building project of the church included a gymnasium, not only for the young people, but also as an instrument of reaching the unchurched community. We had a full-time recreation and youth ministry staff. The heads of each of those ministries were husband and wife, Dale and Sandra Brady. Sandra was smitten with cancer.

The people knew my commitment to prayer. I had written *The Workbook of Living Prayer*; they knew I believed in prayer as a healing power. But that was not enough to save them from many questions and concerns when they learned that we had held a healing service for Sandra. She was hospitalized and some of us, who had from time to time gathered in small groups to pray for her healing, felt a need to come together for a special healing service. It was not a big, publicized service; just a word-of-mouth announcement that we would gather in Reeves Chapel to pray for Sandra. About one hundred people gathered. I gave a brief teaching on healing, and then invited our lay leader, Tom Dyer, to come forward to represent Sandra. We gathered round, in our minds and hearts laying hands on Sandra as we laid hands on him, and prayed. It was a very simple, brief, straightforward service of prayer for the healing of this one we loved.

I couldn't believe the stir this caused. People were talking about the unusual *secret* prayer service that had been held. Within a week, the chair of the Staff-Parish Relations Committee called for an appointment. "We didn't know Oral Roberts had come to town," he greeted me. He was teasing, but the issue was obviously serious enough that a layperson had organized a group to oppose "that sort of thing," and had contacted the Staff-Parish Relations Committee to register their feelings. The oppositional layperson closed his formal report against me to the Staff-Parish Relations Committee with these words:

> There are a large number of unhappy members and the only difference has been the appearance of a new senior minister. In the twenty-eight-year history of this church, there has been only one year of dissent to this degree. The church has embraced extremists over the years. Some of these individuals could not embrace the church and left.

I shared with D. A. Noel, the chair, all that had happened at the prayer service, and readily agreed that I should have talked more about it, that the church needed more teaching on the subject of healing, and that there was not anything *un*-Methodist that I was doing or was committed to. That seemed to be enough for him to answer my critics. I became more deliberate in my teaching and before I left the congregation, twelve years later, there was a regular, weekly healing service.

I had failed in leadership. Two things were obvious: one, it was not fair to the congregation for me to have a service of healing without preparation through teaching and witnessing; and, two, the mainline church had surrendered a significant aspect of her call: to preach, teach, and *heal*. The ministry of healing belongs to the whole body of Christ. To be sure, there are individuals who have been given a special gift of healing. Even so, healing is a ministry of the entire congregation. We must not allow the ministry of healing to be exercised solely by television evangelists who too often come off as superficial and self-promotional.

This is a part of our understanding of the priesthood of all believers. As baptized Christians, we are *priests*. This is a cardinal principle of Scripture and was one of the big sparks that started the fire of the Protestant Reformation. We are constantly in need of claiming that principle. A priest has a two fold function. He/she speaks *to God for the people* (that's our ministry of prayer) and *to the people for God* (that's our ministry of witness . . . in word, deed, and sign). We Christians are all priests.

More than forty times in John's gospel, Jesus mentions the importance of his having been sent by the Father. He saw himself as "the sent one." God had to have someone to represent God, so he sent Jesus. Likewise, Jesus needs us to represent him, just as he represented the Father. The language could not be clearer: "As the Father has sent me, I am sending you" (John 20:21); "he always lives to intercede for them" (Heb. 7:25), then certainly the same call is upon us. When we pray, we are joining Jesus in his ministry. Our intercession becomes the *intercession* of Jesus. Isn't that exciting? God calls us to prayer, which means that prayer is not our idea; it is God's idea. In prayer we become partners in God's kingdom enterprise. God has designed his economy in a way that makes our praying a primary channel through which he accomplishes what he wishes in the world. Healing and health is certainly a part of his will for his children.

As had been the case for many years, prayer was a primary focus of my teaching and ministry. I often begin my teaching on prayer with the question: "What if there are some things God either cannot or will not do unless and until people pray?" On the surface, some may respond that I am questioning the sovereignty of God. Not so; I am affirming God's sovereignty. Scripture and Christian history confirm the fact that God's promises to act in history and in our personal lives are often connected with conditions we are to meet. Many times that condition is prayer. The classic example of it in the Old Testament is 2 Chronicles 7:14: "If my people, who are called by my name, will humble themselves and pray and seek my face and turn from their wicked ways [those are the conditions, then the promise], then I will hear from heaven, and I will forgive their sin and will heal their land." The classic example in the New Testament is Jesus' own promise: "If you abide in me, and my words abide in you [those are the conditions], ask for whatever you wish, and it will be done for you" (John 15:7 NRSV). In God's sovereignty, he gives us freedom; he calls us to partner with him in his kingdom enterprise. One of the ways we do that is through our praying.

It became clear to me rather quickly in my life in Christ Church that we need to find a way to focus the need for spiritual formation and the priesthood of all believers in a corporate fashion. We had started the Emmaus Walk at the Upper Room, and I had witnessed its power across the nation. I felt this would be a powerful renewal and spiritual formation instrument for our church. But I didn't want it to be a Christ Church movement, or restricted to Methodists, or any single denomination. I wanted it to be ecumenical, open to all and impacting the entire Christian community. I didn't know how that could happen, but I knew it had to involve other churches and other pastors.

At that point, I didn't know the Christian leadership of the city, so I prayed and waited . . . impatiently, of course, because patience is not one of my virtues. I'm glad I waited and prayed because one day Dot and Harold Goodwin showed up at our door. Harold was the pastor of Decatur Trinity Christian Church. They told Jerry and me that they were burned out in ministry. They had attended a renewal conference in Kansas City, and heard about the Emmaus Walk. When they inquired more about it, someone told them that I had been involved in the founding of the movement, and that I was in their backyard in Memphis. So here they were, offering, no, begging for a chance to be involved. They were honest and open, which was so characteristic; they wanted it for themselves and their own spiritual renewal, as well as for their congregation.

That was the beginning of years of rewarding, enriching partnership in ministry. The Emmaus Walk greatly impacted our city. Even now, as I look around Christ Church, the people I see formed by the Emmaus Walk are everywhere. Christian leaders in Memphis witness to the difference this movement made in their churches. People often credit Jerry and me for bringing Emmaus to Memphis, but really it could not have happened without Harold and Dot. For more than thirty years they were the spiritual shepherds of this dynamic movement in Memphis.

The Congregation as Evangelist

In 1992, I was invited to give the Denman Lectures, a lectureship honoring Harry Denman, established by the Foundation for Evangelism. Harry is a legendary figure, described by Billy Graham as the most committed and effective personal evangelist he had known. Harry was a layperson who became the general secretary of the Board of Evangelism of the Methodist Church.

He personified evangelism. Long before anyone was calling into question a narrow definition of evangelism as personal witnessing and/ or preaching alone, Harry was practicing holistic evangelism—giving his money away, living a simple life characterized by his one suit and his tiny satchel with an extra shirt and a change of underwear, sharing food with prisoners at Thanksgiving and Christmas—that is, actually going to the jails to spend the holidays there as an act of love and oneness. His vocation as a Christian was *evangelist*. Bishop Earl Hunt, in his foreword to my published lectures, *Congregational Evangelism*, described him as "one of the most influential and picturesque evangelists in the history of the church."[1]

The only reason I can think might have led to my being invited to give those lectures was the growth of our church in the ten years I had been there. The congregation numbered a bit more than three thousand members when I became senior minister in 1982. When I left in 1994, the membership had doubled. Membership numbers are important because numbers represent people. Whatever creativity and impact possibly present in my lectures was my claim that the congregation should be the evangelist. Indeed, I made it clear that Christ Church had demonstrated my claim.

As always, I was nervous in preparing and delivering the lectures, but I was excited because it gave me the opportunity to share the story of a congregation that had claimed her identity as evangelist. The congregation believed with me that evangelism is the demonstration and proclamation of the gospel. We remembered that the evangelistic activity of the early church was not limited to preaching. Everything the church was called to be and do in its worship, witness, fellowship, and service was infused and informed by evangelism. Everything the church does should contribute to its evangelistic task. It's a matter of the Christian community sharing the good news of a Savior with those who do not know him.

In the beginning of the lectures, I affirmed three difference-making assertions: (1) *What you think about Christ determines what you do about evangelism.* If we don't have confidence in the gospel, and if we are not solidly convicted about the uniqueness of Christ as Savior and Lord, it is not likely that evangelism will have much priority in our personal ministry and/or in our congregation; (2) *What we do about evangelism is shaped by what we think about grace.* If we think grace is limited, or that all people are automatically saved, we will not likely proclaim the message of grace, with urgency, to all people. If, on the other hand, we realize that grace is unlimited, and that salvation can be accepted or rejected, we will share urgently and with all; and (3) *What we think Jesus can do for a person will determine what we do about evangelism.* If we have confidence in the gospel, we will not diminish the possibility of the forgiving, transforming, empowering work of Christ in the life of any person. These affirmations shaped my leadership.

Mission and Visioning

Early after my arrival at Christ Church, we established a Joel Committee, named after the prophet Joel. We wanted to "see visions and dream dreams." It was my thought that I would be spending the balance of my ministry in this church. We needed to be clear about mission and vision. At the core of our thinking was a commitment to the Great Commandment of love and service of neighbor, and the Great Commission of taking the gospel throughout the world.

Our mission clearly indicated our commitment to Christ and his centrality in our life together. This was our mission statement:

C: Celebrate Christ in worship
H: Honor Christ in all we do
R: Reveal Christ in our witness and fellowship
I: Instruct persons for discipleship and ministry
S: Serve persons in Christ's name
T: Transform the world by spreading scriptural holiness

Our values were: Christ is central; people are primary; discipleship is demanded; and mission is intentional.

While we had gotten off to a bumpy start with a portion of the congregation being upset with my leading a healing service, and some misunderstanding my strong emphasis on the Emmaus Walk, we were beginning to hit a stride of walking together as kingdom people. But that didn't mean the leader didn't stumble. My next stumble was due to a lack of boldness.

A Roman Catholic college for women was located across the street from the church . . . wonderful buildings on a huge piece of property. Pauline Hord, a prayer warrior in the congregation, came to see me one day to express her belief that Christ Church should purchase that property. I knew little about the school and the property and nothing about the possibility that it might be for sale. Sadly, in retrospect, I knew too little about Pauline.

In the months ahead, I was inspired by what I learned about Pauline. She was one of a few people I have known who clearly and beautifully wed a vital personal prayer life with passionate concern for neighbor and social issues. The witness of Frank Laubach and his commitment to literacy had influenced her. As a public school teacher, she learned his literacy method, "Each One Teach One," and began going to prisons to teach prisoners to read and witness to them about Jesus' love.

I soon learned that she was currently working with our public schools, training teachers in a new literacy method. She was giving three days a week, four or five hours a day, to teaching this new method of literacy in model programs. Also, though in her early seventies, she was driving ninety miles one way to Parchman Prison, in Mississippi, to teach prisoners to read and write. Along with this, she ministered to them in a more encompassing way as she shared her love and faith, and witnessed to the power of the gospel.

I was just getting to know Pauline when she came to tell me about the property across the street, and invited me to prayer walk with her around the property. As time went on I discovered that she was the most unique blending of prayer and personal piety, with servant ministry and social concern, I have known. She was always engaged with groups in prayer and hardly a week would pass that I did not receive a call from her, telling me of some particular need in our congregation or in our city . . . a need that might call for emergency housing because of fire, or medical attention, or intervention at court for a young man accused of selling drugs. She seemed to know everything going on, and never hesitated to engage the congregation and me in response. As she aged, she could no longer drive, but she didn't want to give up her ministry in Parchman so we recruited a driver to take her to the prison every Wednesday.

President George H. W. Bush had begun a program called Points of Light, calling citizens to exercise positive and creative influence and service in the areas where they lived. In different cities and communities in America, people were recognized for being *points of light*. I nominated Pauline for that honor, and her story was told in our daily newspaper. President Bush came to Memphis, and as a part of his visit, wanted to honor the seven most outstanding *points of light* in our city—the people who had done the most for the sake of humankind. Pauline was one of those selected.

The president wanted to have lunch with the seven, but he made a mistake. He set the luncheon for Wednesday. You should have heard Pauline tell the story. When she got the call from the White House, she was overwhelmed, not believing what was happening . . . a call from the White House! Momentarily she was speechless. But when she got the message clearly, without hesitation, she responded: "Wednesday, you say? Please tell the president I'm sorry. I can't be with him on Wednesday. That's the day I go to Parchman to teach prisoners to read and write."

In the beginning, I did not know the character of this woman, thus my stumbling in leadership. When Pauline visited to tell me about the college across the street, she suggested that we might prayer walk the campus, and seek God's guidance about the possibility of the church somehow obtaining it. I responded and a number of times we walked the campus and prayed. She was rather clear about it, but I wasn't. The hindrance was my lack of openness to the Spirit's leading. I had not been in the congregation long; early on we had gone through the confusion and questioning about my leadership, I was not yet confident enough about potential growth and the financial stewardship commitment of the congregation. Also, I still lacked clarity about my own vision for the church's future.

We missed the opportunity, and have since been plagued with parking and building space problems. The college has long since closed. In its place are upscale retail and commercial buildings that have adequate space for their enterprises. Wouldn't the Lord be more pleased if ministries in his name had replaced the college?

Because of folks like Pauline, I soon had a clear picture of the nature of evangelism, which is the task of the individual and the congregation. I called it "discipleship evangelism." We cannot claim Jesus as Savior without a willingness to surrender to him as Lord. To think of faith which does not include fidelity to Christ's call to walk in newness of life, and to share that life with others, is a distortion of the gospel. Faith that does not give attention to holy living and ethical issues—to telling the truth, seeking to live morally clean lives, shunning evil, fighting personal immorality and social injustice, feeding the hungry, caring for the needy, seeking the lost, suffering for those to whom the world has said no—that kind of faith is faith without works and is dead (see James 2:26).

The goal of every church should be to have a congregation of disciples who are on a mission of discipleship, disciples making disciples. Pauline was an incandescent model. Though I stumbled in my leadership by not being as sensitive and visionary as she was about the property, it didn't take long for me to realize that if I was facing a grave issue and needed prayer, Pauline was the first person I called. And I always paid attention to the needs to which she was calling to my attention.

Witness through Worship

For Christ Church, worship was a huge dimension of our witness. Many congregations experience tension over worship, and we had some tension, but nothing that came close to what has been called "worship war." We had two Sunday morning services, 8:30 and 11:00. Our growth in attendance, especially at the 11:00 a.m. service, had grown to the point we were talking about expanding the sanctuary, redesigning, or building a new one. That didn't materialize, but we did build a fellowship hall, a youth gym with fellowship and study space, a chapel to seat two hundred, a parlor, and office facilities.

Everybody has a different worship style they prefer. There is no shortage of opinions on how worship should be done. Since both our Sunday worship services were traditional, we added a 9:45 contemporary worship service. Because of attendance we were able to meet in the new Wilson Chapel for only two weeks before moving into the Fellowship Hall, where the service soon grew to 500–600 persons weekly.

If you use the war metaphor in talking about worship, there are many battles to be fought: hymns, choirs, bands, volume, style, and presentation. Do we incorporate artistic elements like spoken word or dramatic readings of Scripture? Or just sing the songs? How do you guard against the leaders primarily becoming performers?

Then you have the lyrics of the songs/hymns themselves. Are they theologically accurate? Some older songs have a great message, but champions of contemporary worship deem them painfully boring and out of date in their musical setting. Some newer songs sound cool, but often lack the depth of the hymns so many grew up hearing. Preacher friends tell me of people who left their church because the worship style changed. When the musical style wasn't what they wanted, they left to find a church with a style they appreciated. I'm sure some of this happened at Christ Church, but it must have been minor; it was unnoted. I consider two things we did about our worship life as two of the most significant contributors to our growth.

First, we added the contemporary service on Sunday morning. The second was the addition of a Saturday night worship service. This move was an effort not to satisfy particular worship style tastes, but to reach people. We realized that a large segment of the population in Memphis could not worship with us on Sunday if they wanted to. Nurses and other medical workers, service providers such as hotel staff, firemen, policemen, and others had to work on Sunday. Who was responding to them?

Rick Kirchoff was serving as our executive minister, beginning in 1991, and played a major role in assisting in establishing this Saturday night service. We called it "Saturday Night Alive." To engage and involve the congregation in this new outreach, I called for at least 150 persons to "seed" this new worship service. We wanted people present in this service to welcome the new people who would be coming. More than two hundred people responded in commitment to attending the service weekly for at least eight weeks.

We decided the service should be contemporary, with music with a Memphis sound, informal come-as-you-are dress, and with no assumption that the audience would be familiar with church. We recruited persons who were involved in the Memphis music scene. Two of them were Bill McMath and Bobby Manuel, both known across the city, playing in clubs and recording studios. Both testified to the transforming nature of their involvement and became members of the congregation. The service was at 5:00 p.m., allowing Saturday evening freedom. This was especially meaningful for our musicians because some of them had other Saturday evening music commitments.

The music ingredient of this service grew under the leadership of Sharon Beth Hutchinson, and a band evolved which named itself the Lord's Most Dangerous Band. A descriptive phrase was often used to describe the service: "A Holy Happening Hospitality Place, Where Faith Finds Rhythm and the Message Is Grace." Within three weeks, the service was having between four and five hundred in weekly attendance.

This service, along with our outreach to the recovering community, made us one of the most welcoming congregations in the city. When we built new facilities, we set aside space for Christians in recovery. At that time, no mainline congregation in the city was having contemporary worship, and nothing like Saturday Night Alive.

CHAPTER TEN

A Church Shaped by the Great Commission

At the end of the first chapter of the Acts of the Apostles, there is a curious, little-noticed story of how the eleven remaining apostles filled the vacancy in the band of the Twelve left by Judas's suicide. The choice came down to two: a man named "Joseph, called Barsabbas (also known as Justus) and Matthias. . . . Then they cast lots, and the lot fell to Matthias: so he was added to the eleven apostles" (Acts 1:23, 26). But Matthias was never heard from again! What happened? Had some sort of mistake been made? Were the apostles not as careful as they ought to have been? Had they been sitting in a meeting all day, trying to make the decision, and they were tired and weary? One could think that they would have settled for almost anybody. Matthias's election was done so quickly that one gets the impression he became an apostle almost by accident.

Unfortunately, that condition has not changed in the Christian church. We pay too little attention to the matter of discipleship. I made that case in the Denman Lectures: *the intimate connection between evangelism and discipleship.* From the beginning at Christ Church, I desired deeply to lead a congregation whose life was shaped by the Great Commission. That commission is clear: "Therefore go and make disciples

of all nations, baptizing them in the name of the Father and of the Son
and of the Holy Spirit, and teaching them to obey everything I have
commanded you. And surely I am with you always, to the very end of the
age" (Matt. 28:19–20). Thus we have Jesus' charge and marching orders.

A disciple is one who subscribes to the teachings of a master and
assists in spreading them. Discipline for the Christian is the way we train
ourselves or allow the Spirit to train us to be like Jesus, to appropriate his
Spirit, and to cultivate the power to live his life in the world.

I mentioned earlier that the congregation doubled during my time
as pastor at Christ Church, but membership does not always mean discipleship. Yet, the commission of Jesus is clear, "Go therefore and make
disciples."

Stephen Covey, the leadership guru of *Seven Habits* fame, has popular-
ized the phrase, "Beginning with the end in mind." The bottom line of the
Great Commission is discipleship. That's the end we must keep in mind.

The telling manifestation of not "beginning with the end in mind"
as we think of the Great Commission is, first of all, a dichotomy between
evangelism and social transformation; and second, an evangelism void of
discipleship. Os Guinness prophetically observed that the result of these
two failures is a church that has lost its impact by becoming "privately
engaging, socially irrelevant."[1]

Despite the clarity, the church has missed the point that the command
of Jesus is to make disciples. The evangelical church has been guilty of
making converts, but not making disciples. The mainline church seeks
to make disciples without first making converts. Both groups perpetuate
within the church a great omission of the Great Commission. Salvation is
far more than forgiveness of our sins; it is also a matter of thorough moral
and spiritual transformation. But also, to seek to make disciples apart
from a personal relationship with Christ that begins with repentance and
justification blocks the process of discipleship before it begins. Salvation
and discipleship is an act of the whole person, involving the mind, the will,
and the affections, issuing in a changed life, committed to live according

to the law of love in obedience to Jesus Christ the Lord. Scripture calls this the life of holiness or sanctification.

I sought to stay aware of this failure of the church in relation to discipleship. We sought never to separate conversion from discipleship; always seeking to connect personal and social dimensions of the faith, intimacy with Christ, and engagement with culture in transformative ways.

As an expression of this understanding and commitment, in 1986, our youth minister, James Loftin, launched SOS (Service Over Self). As an expression of Christ's love, SOS sought to empower people and transform neighborhoods by utilizing volunteers to renovate the homes of the economically disadvantaged and some of the most vulnerable homeowners in Memphis. Since then, SOS has repaired more than nine hundred homes in the inner city of Memphis, and has engaged more than twenty-four thousand volunteers.

The ministry began with home repair camps for junior and senior high school youth and college students of our local congregation. It has developed into a program that brings youth from all over the nation in week-long spiritual renewal/serving events throughout the summer, as well as during spring breaks. Through partnerships with other organizations and residents within the communities served, SOS helps play a vital role in the holistic Christian community development of the neighborhoods. All of the work is done with the gospel at the heart of motivation, believing that Jesus preached the gospel in both word and deed. He commands us to "repent and believe the good news" (Mark 1:15); he also reaches out and heals lepers (see Matthew 8:3). One is not a means to the other, but both have equal weight. Actions validate our words and our message must be filled with selfless compassion. The mission is to introduce homeowners, campers, volunteers, and neighborhoods to the One who can change our home and our heart—Jesus Christ.

From a small beginning dream of discipleship, now each year SOS hosts more than fifteen hundred high school and junior high campers from all over the nation, believing that this is one sure way to develop a new generation of urban ministry leaders to serve our most vulnerable communities.

I mention it now, because it can't be said too often, Jerry and I have always seen our life together as a ministry partnership. Some of her involvements are clear expressions of what we sought to do in the congregation in expressing evangelism and discipleship. She became a volunteer chaplain, serving the women of the Shelby County Jail. It entailed being an advocate for the disenfranchised, solving problems like emergency childcare, and sometimes simply making a phone call to a friend or family member for the person detained. Inmate phone lines were often too long and the need too urgent.

The officers would connect her with those who had special needs and she was a go-between for the women and the officers. However, her most meaningful experiences were in prayer with the women. A vivid memory is of a first-time inmate who had killed her abusive husband. Jerry recounts, embracing her, rocking her back and forth, weeping and praying together as the woman cried out loud in anguish for God to forgive her. It was an intercessory work: connecting, meeting, and being present as the Lord's emissary.

Not seeing herself as a Bible teacher, Jerry recruited her friend, Linda Richmond, a Christ Church member, to teach a Bible class. Jerry engaged women in our suburban congregation to pray for the women in jail. She invited the inmates to share their concerns in writing and she delivered those to an intercessor who would pray for that particular person.

Corporate prayer was going on by the women for those in jail and their families, as well as the guards. When this had gone on for about two months, some of the inmates asked, "Why not make intercession a two-way process? Why not invite the women in your congregation to share their needs and allow us to pray for them?" Lights on! It was a powerful dynamic: upper-middle class (primarily white) women praying for and being prayed for by poor (primarily African American), incarcerated women. Light was taken into a dark place, but now light was shining from that dark place into the dark places in the lives of persons who presumably were living in the light.

One day Jerry said to me, "You travel to Chicago, Los Angeles, Atlanta, and over the nation to preach, why don't you come and preach to the women in jail?" Why hadn't I thought of that? There was a weekly worship service every Thursday evening in the jail. I had preached all over the world, but that was my first experience of jail preaching. Different ministers on our staff and our Lord's Most Dangerous Band took our monthly turn providing for that service. What meaning . . . taking light into a dark place! And amazingly, receiving light out of that dark place.

Millard Fuller, the founder of Habitat for Humanity, inspired one of those expressions. He preached one Sunday in the worship services of our church. At lunch following, he sensed a particular interest on Jerry's part. He shared with her the fact that within a few weeks a group was going to walk from Americus, Georgia, the headquarters of Habitat, to Kansas City, where the International Board Meeting was to take place. They would walk to raise money as well as to raise national awareness of the need for housing for the working poor. He invited Jerry to join them on the walk. "No way!" she exclaimed. She was not in shape for that. He assured her that if she could get into shape to walk twelve miles in a day, she could join them wherever they were on the walk.

That day arrived and, with backpack and bed role, she took a bus, joining them on the road for the last week of their walk into Kansas City.

President Jimmy Carter was the most famous person at that meeting, but my perception is that he was not nearly as excited as Jerry. But she could not stay for the enrichment of the meeting. Our first grandchild, Nathan, was being born in Connecticut, and that excitement trumped Habitat; she didn't walk, but flew there for that miraculous event.

Her Habitat excitement, however, was translated into action. She raised money for the first Habitat house our church built in Memphis, served on the local board, and inspired our congregation to respond to this critical need of the working poor. By the time we left Christ

Church in 1994, our congregation was building two houses a year for the working poor.

Because of this kind of life and ministry, the United Negro College Fund and LeMoyne-Owen College, in Memphis, presented her the 2012 Althea B. Price Women of Distinction Award. I keep this award close to the picture of Jerry and me with E. Stanley Jones, reminding me that the partnership that began years ago and was tested in Mississippi, has not only survived, it has thrived prayerfully, joyfully, and hopefully with much kingdom meaning.

Her life as a minister's wife has been unique because of the nature of her giftedness and the nature of my ministry. Though always supportive of my ministry, and often sharing that ministry in a unique partnership, she has been true to her self, and to God's special gifting.

The Body of Christ in the World

As the body of Christ, the church is Christ's incarnation in the world, a servant reaching out to be the eyes, the voice, and the hands of Jesus. When those images fulfill themselves in the life of the church, the church itself becomes the evangelist. In reflection, this is a Trinitarian understanding of evangelism—centered in Jesus Christ, empowered by the Holy Spirit, and ultimately grounded in the God of all creation. The power and purpose of this God—alive and active throughout history, named in Scripture and worshiped today as Father, Son, and Holy Spirit—is what finally accounts theologically for the kind of evangelism that we were seeking to express.

The more intentional we became, the more two audiences clamored for attention: the poor and the recovering community. Our response to these specific audiences demonstrated the witness of the church as fellowship and as servant, the people of God as the body of Christ.

When we built new buildings, we set aside three large rooms that would be used primarily for Alcoholics Anonymous, Narcotics

Anonymous, and other groups that were reaching out to addicted folks. It did not take much sensitivity to realize that the number of people needing this help was mind-boggling. We knew the statistics; fifteen million alcoholics in the United States, with maybe as many millions addicted to other drugs. Sometimes when I speak at conferences, and plan to touch on this issue, I will ask how many people in the audience have a family member or a close family friend who has a problem with alcohol or some other drug. Always, more than 50 percent will raise their hands and often as many as 90 percent. When I ask the additional question, "How many of you know someone who is either in Alcoholics Anonymous or some other twelve-step recovery program?" more than half the audience will raise hands. I saw more transformation taking place through our Christians in Recovery and other twelve-step programs than I saw anywhere else.

We took our ministry role in the city seriously, always wanting to share resources and make a prophetic witness. One of the ways we did this was through what we called "celebrations." Two or three times a year, we would bring nationally known persons as speakers at these celebrations. Often we were deliberate in connecting these celebrations with the ministry focus of our congregation. We had Chuck Colson for a weekend conference, focusing on evangelism and prison ministry. Some of the most memorable events and conferences related to our commitment to the recovering community. One of these was U.S. Senator Harold Hughes from Iowa. Another was Kitty Dukakis. But the most exciting of our celebrations was when Father Joseph Martin spoke. He was probably the best-known person in the United States speaking on the AA circuit.

Our church was packed to overflowing the night he came, and I had never felt our church was more like what the church ought to be, in terms of who was present that night. There were black folks and white folks, rich folks and poor folks, young and old, well-dressed and rather shabbily dressed, liberal and conservative. It was a conglomeration of humanity, and I thought, *Jesus would be pleased with this.*

One of my treasured Christmas cards had this sentence penned below the formal printed greeting: "I came to this church a drunk, and you accepted me. I'm still a drunk and you accept me. But, praise God, I'm recovering—and it is the fellowship and acceptance of the church that is empowering my change."

I was so convinced of the monumental problem of addiction, and believed so deeply that if the church was rooted and grounded in the love of God it would purposefully reach out to this audience. I wrote *The Workbook on Christians Under Construction and in Recovery* in 1993. I made the case that alcoholism is a disease, and though maybe not afflicted by the disease, none of us are free from the afflictions that go with addictions. We need to recognize that we are all either under construction or in recovery if we are on the Christian pilgrimage. Probably more than anything else, our reaching out to the recovering community identified us as a place of hospitality and grace.

The second audience that clamored for our attention was the poor. We sought to resist the normal tendency to institutionalize our concern for the poor; too much of that had been done already. We build hospitals to express our concerns for the sick, orphanages to express our concerns for the orphans, homes for widows to express our concerns for the widows, and hand over our responsibilities to these institutions, absolving ourselves of costly personal involvement. In the process these institutions grow independently from the church and many lose their original sense of mission. We sought to express our concern in personal involvement, in the style of servanthood, not removed philanthropy.

One story gives a hint of our effort. When we became convicted about the need to do evangelism among the poor black people of our city, we learned rather quickly that we could not do this ourselves in terms of the kind of identification needed for evangelism. We looked around, located Billie Joe Jackson, a preacher who happened to be a Baptist, in Pine Bluff, Arkansas. He had worked with Prison Fellowship, was streetwise, and had a heart for the poor. We invited him to be a part of our staff, convinced that when we give attention to this audience, the style must be incarnational.

Billie Joe began talking about economic evangelism. He started a program, which he called "Willing Workers." It was a program, which picked up poor people off the street—primarily black men—who had no jobs. He would link them with people in our church who had short-term jobs to be done. But he did more than that. Those who became his willing workers were a part of a prayer study group that would meet weekly; those who were willing were also linked in a prayer partnership with some person in our church.

That partnership was more than prayer; it was a ministry of encouragement and support. It required the partner from our congregation to be available to help in every way possible the person who was looking for a way to make a living and to get his or her life in order.

One of the first persons that became a part of the Willing Workers program was a man named Charles Hall. Charles was not long out of jail and had no family. He was living from hand to mouth and sleeping wherever he could. I don't even know how Billie Joe located him, but he became a willing worker. He was assigned Fred Mills as a prayer partner. Fred met with Charles once a week, tutored him in a lot of different skills, discovered him to be a very responsible person, and suggested to us that he was the kind of person who would be a good maintenance staff person for our church, and we hired him.

Other significant things began to happen in Charles's life. He was converted and accepted Christ as his personal Savior. One of the great joys of my life was to share in his baptism. Along the way, he married a woman who had three children. During that time, our church had started working with Habitat for Humanity. We had participated with other churches and groups in building houses for the working poor. Then we took it on ourselves to raise the money and build a house by ourselves and Charles Hall bought it. It's one of the most complete stories I've ever been a part of.

I resigned as president of Asbury Seminary after ten years. The trustees convinced me to continue my relationship with Asbury by serving as chancellor. We didn't need to live in Wilmore to do that work, so we moved to Memphis in 2004. I worked as chancellor for six years. I resigned when the bishop invited me to become interim minister of Christ Church in 2010.

Soon after assuming that responsibility, we honored persons who had longtime service on the staff of the church. One of those persons was Charles Hall. The service was especially meaningful to me because I knew his story. After more than twenty years, he was still working in our church. As I shared in honoring him that day, I remembered my participation in his baptism, and I thanked God for Billie Joe Jackson, Fred Mills, and a congregation that was the evangelist for Charles.

The stories don't always turn out that way, and nobody knows that better than I. We fail far more than we succeed. But, we're not promised success in our ministry; we are called to be faithful and that calling is pretty clear according to Jesus: "Inasmuch as you did it unto the least of these—the poor, the homeless, the prisoner—you've done it unto me" (Matt. 25:40, author's paraphrase).

Contemporary church growth research shows that between 75 and 80 percent of those who become Christian disciples do so because of the testimony, deeds, and encouragement of someone they trust. George Morris and Eddie Fox, in their book *Faith-Sharing*, remind us that there are three crucial issues revealed in this statistic. Effective faith-sharing involves a proper balance of word, deed, and encouragement. Word is proclamation and/or testimony. Deed is faithful Christian lifestyle and service. Encouragement is active initiative on the part of the faith-sharer. The Christian must take the initiative and do as Jesus commanded, "Go." Christians must go to the people, love the people, share Word and life with the people, listen to the people, and offer Christ to the people.

We sought to take this seriously at Christ Church. If 75 to 80 percent of those who become Christian disciples do so because of the testimony, deeds, and encouragement of someone they trust, then person-to-person faith-sharing must be the highest priority, and we must train our people in this ministry. Christians must be equipped not only with personal knowledge of Jesus Christ and a knowledge of the gospel, they must also know how to relate to another person in such a way that trust develops.

As a reminder of this, I kept an old worship bulletin from our church on December 30, 1984. The first act of praise in our worship service that day was a solo entitled "Sing Your Praises to the Lord." Don Halpern composed this selection, and he sang it that day. The chorus goes:

> When you're lost and alone and have no place you can go,
> Nothing has worked out as planned.
> There's one who is greater, there's one who is waiting,
> Just let Jesus take your hand.
> Sing Alleluia, Alleluia
> Sing your praises to the Lord.

Now that may not sound like great poetry, and the music to which it had been set was nothing more than ordinary, but had you been in the service, and had you known the story, you would be thrilled as I continue to be.

Don was a bearded young man, who played a classical guitar beautifully. I met him about a year preceding his singing in our worship team. He was Jewish. He made an appointment to see me one day, and I was amazed that he wanted to talk about Christianity and the church.

He came back two or three times. Then one Sunday morning, we were celebrating Holy Communion and I saw Don Halpern approaching the altar to receive the elements of bread and wine. The next Sunday he walked down the aisle and made a public profession of faith in Jesus Christ. I didn't baptize him that Sunday because I wanted to talk more. I knew what a big step it was for a Jew to make a profession of faith in Christ. We talked more during the week and the following Sunday not only did we baptize him, we baptized his two children.

During the Christmas season, after his profession of faith, Don sang and played "Gentle Mary Laid Her Child." What a witness! On the following Sunday, he was singing, "There's one who is greater, there's one who is waiting, just let Jesus take your hand"—singing about the Messiah.

When he sang for us in that worship service, I thought about how he came to be in our church. It wasn't this preacher who won him to Christ. It was Martha and Don Helm, a young lay couple that had had a transforming conversion experience in our church. They were Don Halpern's neighbors. Their lives were so transformed by Christ that they captured Don's attention; their performance and their profession spoke to this young Jewish person, and their witness is really what won him.

Martha and Don embodied the personal kind of evangelism as a crucial part of what we have talked about: the congregation as evangelist, with persons witnessing in word and deed, centered in Christ, waiting on the power and timing of the Holy Spirit, growing in the grace of full discipleship, sharing in the congregation as evangelist.

A City Divided

On October 3, 1991, Dr. Willie Herenton defeated incumbent Dick Hackett by just 142 votes to be elected the city's first black mayor. "This victory tonight represents a new beginning for Memphis," Dr. Willie Herenton told his supporters at an election-night party at the famous Peabody Hotel. He had already made history as the city's first black public school superintendent. This victory would make him the first elected African American mayor in the city's 172-year history.

The jubilation could have been short-lived. White incumbent Hackett had a huge lead as early returns poured in, but things changed rapidly as the results of inner-city precincts began coming in. The dynamic of race and the pervasive black/white tension was dramatically expressed as the vote lead flip-flopped through the night. As the evening and the reporting went on, the confidence of the Hackett team changed into a somber panic.

That panic spread throughout the community during the next few days. The narrow 142-vote victory was being challenged in the public arena and the talk of a recount was setting the city on edge.

Hackett had done a good job and was deeply appreciated by the white community. Though we shared that appreciation, some of us thought that a recount would throw the city into further panic, and possibly trigger destructive racial unrest and explosive civil upheaval. The racial divide was already deadly deep, and to question Herenton's election would have turned the divide into a glaring bottomless chasm. Long polarized in racial division, the city's majority-black population was hungry for change, and were celebrating what appeared to be a stunning reversal of power in their city where Dr. Martin Luther King Jr. was assassinated. If the Christian community ever needed to speak, it was now.

There were different pastor organizations in the city, but no single organization that would speak with a common voice that might be respected and received. It was clear that the voting had taken place along racial lines. The more I thought about it, the more I felt the ministers of the city, primarily representing the white establishment, needed to speak to the issue. The white community needed to hear a call to accept the verdict of the election, and to move to reconciliation and commitment for the sake of our community.

I wrote an eight-paragraph letter expressing the desperate need for the "city's constituents to get together and turn this city into a community." I wanted the message to be an open letter to the citizens, but primarily addressing the white community. I knew it would not be impactful unless it had representative leaders of the clergy community. The two I thought absolutely essential were my two closest clergy friends in the city, Adrian Rogers, pastor of the 22,500 member Bellevue Baptist Church, the most influential conservative voice in the city, and Doug Bailey, rector of Calvary Episcopal Church, in the heart of downtown Memphis, recognized as one of the most influential liberal Christian leaders. If I got these two friends, others would readily join us and perhaps we could calm the troubled waters.

It was an arduous task. I spent almost two days, by phone and fax, sharing the letter with Adrian and Doug. Language meant different things to them, and both were persons of integrity and did not want that integrity compromised. When we had perfected the letter, I limited the cosigners to a dozen of the county's most influential clergy leaders in order that we could get it in the Sunday paper as a quarter-page advertisement. The election had taken place the previous Tuesday. The cost of the ad was $2,428.99, paid for by the churches.

A reporter got hold of the ad and wrote an article, which called attention to the ad, making it more powerful. We expressed our thanks to God for "the leadership of Mayor Hackett, and . . . his unselfish devotion to our city." The big message was a call for reconciliation and unity, saying, God "has been powerfully at work in recent historical events such as the crumbling of the Berlin Wall and the independence movement in the Soviet Union. That same God will enable us to achieve unity in our city."

Dr. Herenton credited that statement with calming the raging waters, saving the city from destructive turmoil, and making his beginning work as mayor successful.

CHAPTER ELEVEN

Grandfather of Resistance

In 1992, a few ministers and I had an opportunity to visit Russia at a time when significant governmental and political change was taking place. We had the opportunity to visit with President Mikhail Gorbachev. He led a movement, shocking the country, announcing the ability for citizens to freely voice their opinions and the need to democratize his country's political system and decentralize its economy.

For decades, the United States and the Soviet Union had been competing with each other over who could amass the largest, most lethal stockpile of nuclear weapons. Gorbachev realized that the Soviet Union's economy was seriously suffering from the excessive spending on nuclear weapons, so he began meeting with President Ronald Reagan in an effort to end the arms race. Some thought it miraculous; not only did they eventually work out a deal where each county would stop making new nuclear weapons, they would actually eliminate many weapons they had accumulated.

Gorbachev had been the general secretary of the Communist Party of the Soviet Union from 1985 to 1991, and was president of the Soviet Union from 1990 to 1991. Because of his leadership direction and the ending of the Soviet Union's postwar domination of eastern Europe, and his efforts to end the arms race, Gorbachev was awarded the Nobel Peace Prize in 1990.

Because of the creative leadership of Leonard Sweet, then president of United Theological Seminary, we ministers were there to give spiritual support to the Christians who had been oppressed for decades throughout Eastern Europe, but also to gain information about the exciting happenings that were changing Russia. We were wondering how these monumental changes could open the way for the church to minister more extensively in that section of the world.

Gorbachev's presidency was coming to an end; he resigned his post on December 25, 1991, but we felt he was an important voice, and represented a new kind of leadership. We wanted an audience with him. Amazingly, we got it, but only for thirty minutes.

We had been told by his managers that they only had time for five questions. There were twenty-one of us, so everything had to be orchestrated around that limitation. Our group decided that we would devise questions that we would like to ask President Gorbachev as the interview progressed, then we assigned those questions to different members of our group. Because we were Christian and wanted him to know that was an explicit part of who we were, we sought a way that we might communicate that to him. After much discussion we concluded that the question should be non-threatening or defensive and would be put to him any time in the conversation that seemed appropriate. The question would go something like, "Mr. President, we're Christian ministers, therefore we are persons of prayer. Are there personal needs and concerns for which you would like for us to pray?"

We assigned that question to be asked by Dr. Sundo Kim, the only non-American minister in our group. He was the pastor of the largest Methodist Church in the world. Dr. Kim had become a friend during my years at the Upper Room; I had preached in his church in Seoul, and he had preached in our church in Memphis. He was seated to the immediate right of Gorbachev, who was at the head of the table, and I was on Dr. Kim's right. It was providential that we assigned that question to Dr. Kim because none of us Americans would have been as bold as he was.

The president was gracious and warmly engaged our questions and conversation, even extending our time from thirty minutes to an hour. When the conversation was wearing down, and we knew it was time for the interview to come to a close, everybody turned to Dr. Kim. Instead of asking the question he had been assigned, he said something like this, "Mr. President, we understand that you were baptized when you were a baby, and that your mother has been praying for you every day since." I'm not sure how he asked the question then, but it was something to this effect: "Do you think that because of her prayers, God is working in your life?"

Gorbachev is a very charming man, and has a wonderful sense of humor, but you could tell he was surprised and that the question was burrowing deep into his soul. It was a tense moment. It seemed longer than I am sure it actually was before he responded, "Yes, I was baptized when I was a baby. When I was born, my parents named me Victor." After a pause and again, what appeared to be serious reflection, he added, "Isn't that a great name, Victor?" Again, there was a pause before he continued, less frustrated and with humor, "But when I was baptized my grandfather changed my name. Maybe that's the reason what has happened lately would not have happened [opposition was growing against him throughout the country and he had resigned the presidency]. I'm no longer Victor." He chuckled lightly and continued, "My grandfather named me Mikhail, in English that is Michael."

He surprised us by going on to say, "I've looked in the Old Testament, your Bible, and I understand the name Michael in Hebrew means 'God's person.'" And with a sort of impish smile he said, "But that's not really a bad name, is it?"

Dr. Kim was not going to let it end there. He spoke again, thanking the president for his sharing, but added, "We are sure your mother's prayers have been a great source of strength and meaning in your life, and we want you to know we will be praying for you as you assume a new path of leadership." Turning to me he said, "In fact, I'm going to ask Dr. Dunnam to pray for you right now."

Until then, I had never felt the impact of John Wesley's word, "A Methodist preacher must always be prepared to pray, preach, and die."

I prayed!

I came away from that meeting more convinced that naming and the need to be named is one of the most crucial of human needs. I was also excited about the boldness of Dr. Kim and his call to prayer, and confirmed in my conviction about what I had been teaching about prayer: that a primary dynamic of prayer is naming and being named. I believe that's what prayer is all about.

The activity of God in history is naming. Creation itself is a naming event; the height of creation, the creation and naming of Adam and Eve. That naming continues throughout the Old Testament, then reaches its Mount Everest height in the incarnation. God took upon himself flesh, blood, and bone to become one of us, and he was named, Jesus. But even beyond the incarnation, the naming goes on, reaching a beautiful climax in the tender word spoken by Jesus in the fifteenth chapter of John. After he had given the marvelous analogy of the vine and the branches, Jesus said, "Greater love has no one than this: to lay down one's life for one's friends," and then he gave us that amazing word, taking the business of naming to its ultimate, when he said to his followers, "I no longer call you servants, because a servant does not know his master's business. Instead, I have called you friends, for everything that I learned from my Father I have made known to you" (vv. 13, 15). So this is the work of God in history—naming.

Yet, not only so, this is what Christian prayer is all about. Naming and being named. Prayer is relationship. It is meeting. It is being with God. It is a personal relationship where you and God move from a greeting of politeness to an embrace of love. Prayer becomes most real when we name God in the first person singular, when God becomes more than the remote "He," or "the Almighty," and becomes the intimate and unique "Thou" or "You."

The second dynamic of prayer is that we name ourselves as we are before God. This is the confessional dimension of prayer. By "confession" I don't mean the deliberate verbalizing of our sins and failures, though this is an essential part of it. I mean locating ourselves as we are before God.

There is more. Not only do we name God as he is in our experience and, not only do we name ourselves before God, we allow God to name us as we are and as he is calling us to be. In prayer, we wait in the presence of the Lord to be named by him, not to get a change of names, but to be spoken to by God; to be impacted by God's Spirit, to receive his blessing or his judgment, his comfort or his challenge. We listen to receive his word. We wait for his power and his guidance—the heightened perception and insight that is ours when we live with him. Prayer is always incomplete without this dynamic of listening to God, allowing God to name us.

Other Names

My name has been a source of interest through the years. People often assume Maxie is a nickname, or short for my formal name. I have some fun thinking what it would be like to be called Maxwell or Maximillian. Many folks who hear my name or see it in print think I am female and Maxie is short for Maxine. That thought comes more naturally when they hear my wife's name, Jerry; they think she is the male and I the female. I get mail regularly to "Ms. Maxine Dunnam."

But, as I will share shortly, I have been given other names as well.

The General Conference is the only body that can officially speak for the United Methodist Church. It is a representative governing body, fashioned somewhat like the United States Congress. There is an equal number of clergy and lay people, elected by their peers in the conferences from which they come. (An Annual Conference in United Methodism is a geographical area of the church, and is presided over by a bishop.)

The doctrine and discipline of the Methodist Church are determined by General Conference, which consists of representative persons from these Annual Conferences.

Issues of human sexuality have been front and center of General Conference concern for more than forty years, centering on homosexual *practice*. The Methodist Church is very clear that every person is of sacred worth, and that the church must minister to all persons, while affirming that "the *practice* of homosexuality is incompatible with Christian teaching."[1]

Therefore, practicing homosexual persons cannot be ordained to ministry within the church. The more strident the issue has become, the more specific the language has evolved. Thus marriage is clearly defined as between "one man and one woman."

Throughout this long struggle within the church, I have been strongly supportive of the official position, which I believe is firmly based on Scripture and the tradition of the universal church for all her history. In the early years of the struggle, my position on this issue was disarming and confusing to the so-called liberal wing of the church. My stand on civil rights in Mississippi and my move to California because of that struggle was known, and I was affirmed and praised by the liberals.

In Mississippi, I was considered liberal, but in California, because of my strong commitment to scriptural authority and an evangelical expression of the faith, I was generally considered conservative. Yet, because Orange County is one of the most conservative counties in California, and the two congregations I served in California were both located in that county, there were times when I was considered liberal because of my stand on issues like fair housing and immigration.

Labels are never adequate, and I don't know anyone who really likes them. They can be harmful. Too often we use them to "put people in their place" in a hurtful way. They are not only inadequate for descriptive purposes, they are too often destructive.

Believing all this, and not knowing whether I'm a liberal conservative or a conservative liberal, I wore proudly the social media label that was given me at the 2008 General Conference. Social media has changed the dynamic of this body that assembles every four years. Everybody has cell phones, and texting is going on as discussion and debate is taking place. Official conference members are seated in a restricted, designated area, but with cell phones, delegates may be paying as much attention to non-delegates outside the bar of the conference, as to the formal discussion. There are always persons who are not elected delegates who have influence throughout the church, and with social media, their voices are heard, and shared even as General Conference is in session.

I have never discovered who started it, but someone, via texting, labeled me the "Grandfather of Resistance" and that label became rather pervasive among the social media crowd at that General Conference. I'm not sure why, but I have almost relished that label. Maybe it's pride. To be given a title certainly says that someone is recognizing what you are doing, whether they understand it rightly or not.

To resist means to "withstand, to actively oppose, to fight against." Whether perceived as negative or positive is dependent upon the beholder. The bare truth is: I have expressed a good deal of resistance throughout my life.

An Enclave of Resistance

In September 2002, Our Lady of the Angels, the Los Angeles Catholic Cathedral, was dedicated. Unlike the European cathedrals of old which took generations to complete, construction crews took only three years from the time of excavation in 1999 to build the cathedral.

Located in the heart of downtown Los Angeles, the eleven-story structure stands along the famous Hollywood freeway, the most heavily traveled highway in the nation. So like ancient cathedrals, this one also sits in the midst of the hustle and bustle of the city.

The architect was world-famous José Rafael Moneo from Spain. To design this place of prayer and worship, Moneo said he had to create "buffering, intermediating spaces," such as "plazas, staircases, [and] colonnades."[2] His post-modern design used almost no right angles and the resulting complex geometry created unexpected, mysterious spaces for worshipers.

There were models of the cathedral at the groundbreaking service and on the basis of the models a *Los Angeles Times* reporter wrote a review of the cathedral. This is a part of what the reporter said: "Moneo is creating an alternate world to the everyday world that surrounds the cathedral, a testimony to the grandeur of the human spirit, an antidote to a world that is increasingly spiritually empty." Then he wrote this sentence: "The cathedral, set in the midst of the secular city, will be an enclave of resistance."[3]

What an image . . . the church, *an enclave of resistance.*

The church has never been able consistently to understand what it means to be "in the world but not of the world." We've known, at every period of our history, that the very nature of the church provoked some form of resistance. There is always the sense in which God's kingdom ideals are in conflict with the world in which the kingdom is set.

I learned early on that I had to be careful about the nature and focus of my resistance. We must not deceive ourselves into thinking that if we can get the right king on the throne—if we can elect the right president, the right congress, the right governor—if we can put "our people" in places of political power, then we can win the battle. There can be no kingdom without a king, and the kingdom to which we're committed has only one King—Jesus.

So I have believed the church needs to think more of transformation than of confrontation. Even so, there are occasions when we have to confront, and I have never been comfortable with that.

Our task as an enclave of resistance is to subvert the calloused, materialistic, secular culture of which we are a part—to subvert that culture at its root by living as though we believed that we do not live by bread alone. We believe that there is a kingdom reality of love in which all those things that are expressed in Romans 12 are operative. Our love is without hypocrisy. We abhor what is evil and we cling to what is good. In honor we give preference to one another. We are able to rejoice in hope, but also able to be patient in tribulation. We attend to the needs of others and we give ourselves to hospitality. We bless those who persecute us; we rejoice with those who rejoice and we weep with those who weep. We associate with the humble and we do not see ourselves as wise in our own opinions. We don't confront evil with evil but we seek to overcome evil with good (see Romans 12).

My personal expression of resistance has been two-sided. On one side, I have prayed, preached, and acted for the church to be more resistant, to be "an enclave of resistance," not being shaped by, but shaping culture. I have resisted cultural forces that I believed were opposing the gospel and the kingdom message of the church. This *resistance* began in the first years of my ministry in Mississippi, in my involvement in the civil rights crisis. That resistance continues today in my conviction that public education is the civil rights issue of the twenty-first century. The church has a role to play, not in establishing more and more private schools that the underserved cannot access, but in advocating for and participating in guaranteeing that a child's zip code should not determine the child's opportunity for quality education.

On another side, I have resisted forces within the church that I believed were wrongly expressing the faith, questioning the authority of Scripture, and denigrating the person and work of Christ, making inclusiveness and pluralism redemptive within themselves. This has been an ongoing struggle in mainline Protestant denominations for almost a century now. Dr. Thomas Oden, a widely respected theologian, has chronicled the struggle in his book *Turning Around the Mainline*. In his introduction, Oden recalled an issue of *Christianity Today* that had a cover illustration portraying a huge ocean liner being slowly pushed into a new direction by a tiny tugboat. He said this was a "glimpse into the irony of believers within the mainline. What was previously regarded as a highly unlikely reversal is in fact occurring: the turnaround of the mainline."[4]

I shared his optimism when the book was written. There were signs that renewal groups within different denominations who were resisting the break of their church with classic Christian tradition and the orthodox expressions of faith in the historic creeds (i.e., Apostles' and Nicene Creeds) were turning the ship around. But no sign of the turn is obvious in reality. For me, and a huge portion of the membership of United Methodism, the ship of the church is still off-course in many ways.

That doesn't mean we haven't been ardent in our efforts. In April of 1994, I joined Bishop William R. Cannon and Dr. Oden in convening a meeting of ninety-two church leaders in Atlanta, to discuss what we believed was a crisis within our United Methodist Church. We called for a "Consultation on the Future of the Church." A movement grew out of that gathering committed to advancing doctrinal renewal and enabling the United Methodist Church to retrieve its classical doctrinal identity, and live it out as disciples of Jesus Christ. The sign of grave concern about the church's swing away from "the faith that was once for all entrusted to God's holy people" (Jude 1:3), and the Methodist/ Wesleyan expression of that faith, was confirmed by the fact that very soon what began in a very small way became the Confessing Movement within the United Methodist Church with a known constituency of more than five hundred thousand and with more than three thousand Confessing churches at its peak.

The invitation we extended to the whole church expressed our concern and hope:

> The United Methodist Church is at a crossroads. We face either the
> peril of abandoning the Christian faith, thereby becoming unfaithful
> disciples of Jesus Christ, or embracing the promise of becoming God's
> instrument of a new awakening of vital Christianity. The causes of the

crisis are complex and multiple. However we believe that the central reason is our abandonment of the truth of the gospel of Jesus Christ as revealed in Scripture and asserted in the classic Christian tradition and historic ecumenical creeds. Specifically we have equivocated regarding the person of Jesus Christ and his atoning work as the unique Savior of the world. We have been distracted by false gospels. We have compromised in our mission to declare the true gospel to all people and spread scriptural holiness. For the sake of the kingdom of God, it is now time for action.

One would have been hard put to find anyone who would deny that the mainline church was living from crisis to crisis to crisis; what was disputed was our belief that the crisis had to do with the loss of theological bearings, biblical grounding, and historical continuity with the apostolic teaching. Rather than exercising cultural wisdom, we were being seduced by current cultural swings.

We stated our goals and strategies:

The Confessing Movement is a witness of United Methodist lay men and women, clergy and congregations who pledge unequivocal and confident allegiance to Jesus Christ according to the "faith once and for all delivered to the saints" (Jude 3) . . . . The faith centers on Jesus Christ, fully God and full man; and on his life, death, resurrection, ascension, and promised return as attested in Holy Scripture.

We made very clear our perspective on Christian social responsibility.

We reject widespread and often unchallenged practices in and by the church that rebel against the lordship of Jesus Christ. For example: experimenting with pagan ritual and practice; consuming the world's goods without regard for the poor; accommodating the periling patterns of sexual promiscuity, serial marriage, resigning ourselves to the practices of racial and gender prejudice; condoning homosexual

practice; ignoring the church's long-standing protection of the unborn
and the mother.

The Confessing Movement, as an organization, was a latecomer to the
battle within United Methodism. *Good News*, which began as a magazine
with its first issue in the spring of 1967, was a forerunner. Very quickly
the magazine developed into a populace movement of what Charles
Keysor, the editor, called a silent majority within the church—those who
believed that the church had veered far off-course in its doctrine and
mission. Through the years since, Good News, as a movement, has been a
voice, sometimes too shrill, but always with courage and integrity, for the
renewal of the Methodist movement.

What was at the core of the mission of the Confessing Movement
defined the nature of my resistance. Signal events in the life of the church
and responses to those events have been expressions of my part in resistance. In 1987, I joined some friends who were described as pastors of
seven of the most significant churches in the denomination to issue an
invitation to persons concerned about the church to gather in Houston to
discuss strategy for the upcoming 1988 General Conference.

Eighty-seven key pastors and laypersons joined us in Houston. We
issued a statement, which came to be known as the Houston Declaration,
addressing the issues confronting the church, which we thought would be
critical as the General Conference met in 1988. We affirmed the primacy of
Scripture, the importance of the doctrine of the Trinity, and the language
used in the liturgy of the church in affirming that doctrine. Because
human sexuality and the practice of homosexuality was becoming the
presenting issue (on the surface, the critical issue), we underscored the
necessity for sexual purity in the clergy.

We mailed this declaration to fifty-five thousand United Methodist
clergy and lay leaders. More than sixteen thousand responded, 94 percent
of them expressing support. We placed a paid ad in the *United Methodist*

Reporter, and fifty-eight thousand persons responded, all except eighty-seven expressing support.

Until that time, this was the clearest sign that doctrinal integrity, which we were calling for, and which had been ignored for years, was on the hearts and minds of the people of our United Methodist churches. Richard John Neuhaus, a Roman Catholic priest and respected and trusted observer of the landscape of religion in America, commented on the response generated in large part by the Houston Declaration that a new reality was being surfaced. In "A New Methodism Afoot," an article in the April 1988 *Religion & Society Report*, he referred to Methodism as the "most American of America's churches," which in recent years he said, "had been noted for changing its 'solid' Wesleyan heritage for both silly and serious elements of American culture."[5] He predicted, I believe wistfully, that "our wandering in the theological wilderness might be coming to an end."

In 1972, the General Conference of the United Methodist Church that had come into being by the union of the Methodist Church and the Evangelical United Brethren Church in 1968 had affirmed a new theological statement. This statement established four main sources and guidelines for Christian theology: Scripture, tradition, experience, and reason. This came to be known and the Wesleyan "quadrilateral," and continues to be debated.

The liberal forces of the church defined those guidelines to give them equal standing in interpreting not only doctrinal/theological issues, but also ethical and moral conduct. It was the prevailing teaching of these revisionist interpreters, basically giving *experience* as much authority in determining the mind, discipline, and doctrine of the church as Scripture, that generated the debate that culminated in a new doctrinal statement coming from the 1988 General Conference. This statement, still the official statement of the church, affirms the primacy of Scripture and makes clear that Scripture is the ultimate authority of the church.

While Neuhaus's statement about "A New Methodism Afoot" was true, the fulfillment of the prediction was a long way off, and in fact, is still to be realized.

With the primacy of Scripture in the book, it was clear immediately, and continues to be obvious, that the matter of authority is still the issue. Before the next General Conference in 1992, it became clear that the "enclave of resistance" needed to express itself as it had done preceding the 1988 General Conference. Having the primacy of Scripture *in the book*, though an ally in our struggle for theological integrity, did not end the struggle. The commitment to theological pluralism was especially embedded in the DNA of the program boards of the church, and in most of the seminaries of the church.

Gratified by the success of the Houston Declaration, we decided to speak to the church in that fashion again. As my friend, Bill Hinson, senior minister of First UMC in Houston, had hosted a gathering there, I hosted a similar gathering at Christ United Methodist Church in Memphis. Many of the participants had been a part of the Houston gathering. A Memphis Declaration came out of our gathering. Our primary concern was doctrine. We affirmed that Jesus is God's only one complete and suffi-cient sacrifice for our salvation, and while baptism is a means of grace, it does not replace the personal necessity of having to accept Jesus Christ as Savior and Lord. We again called for holiness of life and the strengthening of legislation related to homosexual practice.

We may have been too confident in the wake of the Houston Declaration, and we were certainly not politically savvy. We addressed too many issues, including structural ones such as moving the Board of Global Missions out of New York, doing away with the General Council of Ministries, and establishing a new General Board of Evangelism. Though we had more than 199,000 signatures by the time of General Conference, this did not have the impact of the Houston Declaration.

Following the 1992 General Conference, the church continued to struggle publicly with social issues, particularly the practice of homosexuality and abortion, but doctrinal/theological issues were becoming publicly conflictual. The February issue of *Circuit Rider*, a monthly magazine for United Methodist clergy, focused on this stirring. The editor, Keith I. Pohl, wrote that "the issue of an inclusive versus and exclusive view of salvation is at the apex of that which divides many groups in the UMC and an issue that will determine the direction of the denomination as a global church in the twenty-first century."

Though I believe and have always preached that this gospel is *inclusive* of all; grace is not limited and the invitation is to "whosoever will," I was invited to make the case for an *exclusive* view of salvation. This was the heart of the Protestant Reformation: salvation comes by grace through faith in Jesus Christ. I made my case forthrightly: Jesus Christ is God's unique and complete revelation of God's being and provides God's salvation for all humankind. This conviction shapes us as the body of Christ, and it becomes both the motive and power for evangelism, for mission, and ministry, and must be the "bottom line" conviction that we carry into all ecumenical dialogue.

Even now, more than thirty years later, I wonder why I ever agreed to write, knowing that John B. Cobb Jr., professor emeritus at the Claremont School of Theology and one of the United Methodist Church's foremost theologians, was selected by *Circuit Rider* to make the so-called inclusive case. His central point was, "We view each community of faith individually with joy and gratitude as having its own irreplaceable role to play in the economy of God's salvation of the world."

But trembling and nervously, I would do it again. To be sure, God may use anything, any person, and any movement he chooses to accomplish his purposes, but that does not diminish, and it certainly doesn't nullify what he has chosen to do in "the fullness of time" (Gal. 4:4 NRSV) in sending his Son as his unique and complete revelation and providing God's salvation for all humankind. No other religion, nor anything else, does that. Jesus' claim is *exclusive*, "I am the way, the truth and the life, no one comes to the Father, but by me" (John 14:6, author's paraphrase).

But his invitation is *inclusive*: "Come unto me, *all* . . ." (Matt. 11:28 KJV; emphasis added).

This kind of ongoing dialogue, and the impact of the different organized efforts that led to the Houston and the Memphis Declarations, led leaders of the Good News Movement to realize that while there were more and more persons sharing the core concerns of Good News, they would not be publicly identified with Good News, because it was considered an outsider group. It had been unfairly and harshly criticized. No bishops, pastors of large congregations, seminary leaders, or program board leaders had formally and openly identified with them. Wisely, they concluded there must be a way to work with these persons for the cause of renewal.

A small group of Good News leaders invited Bishop William R. Cannon, Dr. Thomas Oden, and me to discuss the theological crisis of the church, and to explore a different approach to renewal. So, my *resistance* witness continued in the establishment of the Confessing Movement, which I previously discussed.

The General Conference at which I got that social media title, Grandfather of Resistance, was tense and stressful. The division of the church over human sexuality, and particularly the practice of homosexuality, was severe. The gay caucus was constantly disrupting the conference with demonstrations. It was a painful time. One of our most outstanding clergy leaders, a friend, had invited me to cosponsor a resolution which would insert into the *Discipline* a long statement acknowledging that the church was divided on the issue of homosexuality, though the General Conference held the position that "the practice of homosexuality was incompatible with Christian teaching."

I refused to do so. The church was divided on many issues, and the body charged with the governance of the church had to make decisions. And when we do, we don't present them with an acknowledgment that we are divided. It is because we are divided that we make decisions after we have prayed and conferenced together, and those decisions, given our governance, have to be accepted as the mind of the church. When my friend presented his resolution, I opposed it and it failed. That gave support for the label I was given, Grandfather of Resistance.

There is something shameful, maybe even sinful, about the fact that I have given so much time to resistance to what I have believed has been an unfaithful church, when I could have been spending more energy resisting the forces of darkness outside the church, and the forces that are numb to the condition of poverty in which millions are living and dying; numb to the racism that treats some as less than human because of their skin color; numb to the fact that in some places in the world persons are persecuted and are dying defending the faith that we discount and compromise; numb to the fact that too often the location of a child's home determines the quality of his or her educational opportunity.

In my heart, and when I have been at my best in my thinking, I have wanted my resistance to be against that which contradicted the Spirit and way of Jesus, as I have wanted my advocacy to reflect my commitment to loving Jesus and loving like Jesus.

CHAPTER TWELVE

From Addition to Multiplication

The providence of God is an ongoing theme of Scripture. The story of Joseph is a classic example. His jealous brothers were going to kill him, but had a more attractive opportunity; they sold him into slavery. He ended up in Egypt, found favor with Pharaoh, and became one of the trusted officials in Pharaoh's court.

A strange irony of fate (the providence of God, of course) brought Joseph and his brothers, who had betrayed him, together again. A famine had ravaged the land of Canaan and the people were without food. Jacob, Joseph's father, sent his sons to Egypt seeking to buy food from Pharaoh. It was soon revealed that the person with whom they had to deal was the brother they had sold into slavery. The tables were turned: here they were asking food from the brother they had sold into slavery.

When it came to Pharaoh's attention that Joseph's brothers had come, it pleased him. He instructed Joseph to bring the whole family away from Canaan, promising to give them the goods of all the land of Egypt.

This ongoing theme of Scripture, God's providence, is expressed in powerful ways, especially in the Psalms. Psalm 37 is one of the most beautiful expressions of it. Note a portion of that psalm: "Trust in the Lord, and do good; dwell in the land and enjoy safe pasture . . . Commit your way to the Lord; trust in him and he will do this: He will make your righteous reward shine like the dawn, your vindication like the noonday sun" (vv. 3, 5–6).

The word *providence* comes from the same root as our word "provide." Our God is a power greater than all powers and that power is baptized in love. God's providence is flavored by God's grace. So the psalmist could be confident. "Delight yourself in the LORD, and he will give you the desires of your heart" (Ps. 37:4 NRSV). The apostle Paul expressed the same confidence, testifying to his commitment no matter what his circumstances were. In the midst of plenty or want, whether hungry or well-fed, he affirmed, "I can do all things through him who strengthens me" (Phil. 4:13 NRSV). He could assure the Philippians, "My God will fully satisfy every need of yours according to his riches . . . in Christ Jesus" (4:19 NRSV).

It is the consistent witness of Scripture: we are children of God our Father, who will provide and care for us. Here is an extra dimension of that truth: God often provides in surprising ways, which makes us echo Brother Lawrence, "God, you have outwitted me!"

I experienced this most dramatically in my vocational journey related to the presidency of Asbury Seminary. Such an expression of ministry was never a part of my thinking. I am certainly not an academic, either in training or temperament. I have had to work diligently to cultivate the reflective aspect of my spirituality. I have always considered my education limited and inadequate. My elementary and high school experience was in rural Mississippi, and Mississippi has not been known for commitment to education. My college (then, Mississippi Southern College; now, University of Southern Mississippi) at that time, was not on par with the other two major state universities. I received my graduate theological education at Candler School of Theology, Emory University, an outstanding training center for Methodist clergy. Yet, I did not take full educational advantage of that season at Emory. More than anything else, I wanted to be a preacher, and felt I needed to preach, not in the future, but *now*. I had served as pastor of three small Methodist congregations during most of my college years, and then in seminary, I became the organizing pastor of a congregation in suburban Atlanta. I gave more attention to sermon preparation and pastoral duties than to classes and lectures at Emory.

Some readers may possibly imagine how unbelievable it was for me when I was nominated to receive an honorary doctor of divinity degree from Asbury Seminary. My work in spiritual formation at the Upper Room was becoming known across the church; my books and publications were being used not only by the Methodist/Wesleyan family of churches, but by many denominations. I'm sure this is how I came to the attention of the faculty and administration of Asbury.

Not only did Asbury confer upon me the honorary DD degree, in 1982 I was invited to serve as a trustee. Dr. David McKenna was serving as the fourth president of the school. An outstanding educator and administrator, he shepherded the school through one of its most creative periods. I became chair of the trustees in 1992, and had the privilege of working intimately with Dr. McKenna.

This was a time of leadership growth for me. I had managed a huge budget and staff at the Upper Room and was now leading a large congregation, so to work collegially with such an outstanding leader as David in the enterprise of theological education was rich. I'm certain it enhanced my ministry at Christ Church.

In May 1993, I was shocked by Dr. McKenna's announcement that he would be retiring in June 1994. It had become the tradition of the seminary that the chair of the trustees lead the search team for a new president. I felt the awesome responsibility, but I was excited. Though not a denominationally owned and operated school, Asbury was educating more persons for United Methodist ministry than any of the thirteen official United Methodist seminaries. Primarily serving the Wesleyan/ Methodist family of Christians (Free Methodist, Nazarene, Salvation

Army, Wesleyan, and others), our community was made up of multiple evangelical denominations and students from around the world. What a challenging opportunity for someone to lead this school into such a promising future!

We engaged consultants to assist with the search process, which went on for almost the entire year. Two candidates were eventually selected from a large field of applicants—both outstanding leaders, nationally known in their academic discipline, both popular published authors, both widely sought for teaching, preaching, and conference leading. I was thrilled, knowing that one of these would be a very able successor to Dr. McKenna, and Asbury would not miss a step in providing the church with the very best in ministry training.

I would have been happy with either of the candidates, and I believe either candidate would have done an excellent job, but the selection committee was equally divided, and could not agree corporately on either. Unable to agree, they decided to return to the search. In the midst of that perplexing situation, I was surprised as the question began to arise, "What about Maxie?"

"Well, what about him?" was my response. I had no interest and no inclination to even consider the possibility. But the conversation grew, and when it was clear that the committee had to continue the search, I resigned the committee.

This period was an emotional roller coaster for Jerry and me, and for the leadership of Christ Church. Almost a year before, we had gone through the decision-making anguish of whether to "stand" for election as a bishop. In the United Methodist Church, bishops are elected by the Jurisdictional Conference, which consists of lay and clergy members of the churches within the jurisdiction. A kind of de facto practice has become common in Annual Conferences of the jurisdictions. The first clergy person elected to the General Conference is thought to be the person that should be considered the conference's candidate for the episcopacy. Of course, that person has to declare willingness and intention.

I had been elected to lead the conference delegation for the 1992 General and Jurisdictional Conferences. The immediate assumption was that I would be our conference's candidate to stand for election as bishop. Naturally, those who encouraged me to go in this direction were certain I would be elected.

So strong were the thoughts and encouragement that this was to be the climatic expression of my vocation that Jerry and I had to give it serious consideration, deep prayer, and engagement with trusted friends in discernment. I vividly remember a prayer time that centered on this issue. We were in London with the Executive Committee of the World Methodist Council. A part of the decision for the meeting in London was the opportunity to dedicate the new sculpted memorial to John Wesley's heart-warming experience on Aldersgate Street. This experience changed the course of his life, and was the pivotal event that contributed to the birth of the Methodist movement.

The dedication service not only celebrated Wesley's experience, it called the participants to prayer and personal commitment. The possible call to the episcopacy tumbled in mine and Jerry's minds. Some of the persons who were urging me to consider this possibility were in the group. More earnestly than ever before, Jerry and I prayed Wesley's Covenant Prayer, a prayer used for the renewal of the believer's covenant with God. Jerry and I knelt at the base of that monument and prayed,

> I am no longer my own, but thine.
> Put me to what thou wilt, rank me with whom thou wilt.
> Put me to doing, put me to suffering.
> Let me be employed for thee or laid aside for thee,
> exalted for thee or brought low for thee.
> Let me be full, let me be empty.
> Let me have all things, let me have nothing.
> I freely and heartily yield all things to thy pleasure and disposal.
> And now, O glorious and blessed God, Father, Son and Holy Spirit,

thou art mine, and I am thine.

So be it.

And the covenant which I have made on earth,

let it be ratified in heaven.

Amen.[1]

We returned to Memphis, divided in our minds. I continued to struggle, but Jerry's struggle was different. She was so certain that I was going to be elected bishop that, when she got home, she spent a day crying and praying, making more explicit her surrender to whatever future God had in store for us. A big part of that surrender was our home. It was the most charming place we have ever lived, an old English-style Cotswolds cottage. We stumbled upon the house when we were feeling desperate and discouraged about a place to live when we had accepted the call to the ministry of Christ Church. In our understanding, "miracle" is a better word than stumble. So much life, so much ministry, so many family events had taken place there.

Jerry was certain that she was going to have to give it up, so she went from room to room, recalling life in each room, and surrendering the room, praying that it would mean as much to the next residents as to us.

But it was not to be. I became certain that I was not being called to be a bishop, and shared that conviction with our delegation so they could nominate someone else. Jerry breathed a sigh of deep relief. She would not be leaving her treasured home.

I, too, felt relieved and energized to continue my ministry at Christ Church. Very few, fellow clergy especially, could understand my decision. I was so appreciative of the few that did. Claude Young, book editor of the United Methodist Church, understood and wrote,

Dear Maxie, I would be happy for you to be my bishop at any time. However, I am happier still to read that you wish to be responsive to "a higher call," one that you do not feel at this particular time. Your priorities are right. You model what all United Methodist clergy should practice. If you should sense a call from God, you will have my support and vote.

My friend, Bishop Reuben Job, who had followed me as editor of the *Upper Room* and had been elected bishop from that position, wrote me a note, so pointed, which meant most to me,

> *Dear Maxie,*
> *You have listened.*
> *You have obeyed.*
> *God honors faithfulness.*
> *My prayers continue.*

I could live confidently with that, and I did; but now, here we were, almost a year later, in a similar vocational struggle. After an initial period of conversation with the Asbury trustees, I said no. The leadership of Christ Church knew what was happening, so as soon as I told the trustees, I shared this with the leadership, and we settled into our ongoing ministry that was so meaningful and rewarding.

Four of my most-trusted friends, persons who shared my life most intimately, and from whom I had sought counsel often in the past, were not convinced I had made the right decision. The Asbury trustees had not settled on any candidates, and some of them were still urging me to reconsider. One of them kept insisting, "Heretofore your ministry has been a ministry of addition; at Asbury it will be a ministry of multiplication." That grabbed my imagination ... influencing young men and women who would be ministering years after I was gone. My friends insisted that I should at least have an interview with the search committee. I agreed and told Jerry we had to at least submit to an interview. She was confident that I should. When we made the decision to accept the trustees' call to the presidency, she said she knew what her praying and surrendering the house a year before was all about, and she could leave it freely.

Even so, I accepted the presidency of Asbury kicking and screaming. It was not what I wanted to do. Jerry and I were blissfully happy and our lives were filled with meaning. I didn't want to give up preaching to the same people Sunday after Sunday, being present as pastor in the deepest, most significant times of peoples' lives: baptisms, marriages, deaths. Jerry had her own ministry—counseling and encouraging women in jail; inspiring, organizing, and working with Habitat for Humanity, which grew into our own congregation's ministry of providing housing for the working poor; a clown and mime troop that ministered in worship, but particularly in hospitals and nursing homes.

The congregation was growing, having reached well more than five thousand in membership. Our outreach ministry in Memphis and around the world was expanding and increasing in effectiveness. I had a unique and popular television/radio ministry called *Perceptions*, seen and heard by thousands every day. Hardly a day would pass without a specific affirming response to this special ministry. More than 60 percent of the people who joined our church visited for the first time because they heard *Perceptions*. Not only did we not want to leave our congregation, we did not want to leave our city where twelve years as a pastor and preacher had been so rich and rewarding. And, as if that were not enough, two of our three adult children, Kerry and Kevin, were living in Memphis. We didn't want to leave them.

I struggled with the trustees' invitation to become their president. They were clear that they were being led by God. But I was far from clear. Jerry discerned the call before I did. Why could I not receive this as God's call? They were all so sure.

I struggled. If this was God's call, I thought, God was asking too much. But finally it came clear. It is enough to say that I felt the move to be God's will, and I was not pleased at all. I responded reluctantly, even grudgingly. I yielded, but without excitement, anticipation, or joy. My attitude was, "This is what I *have to do*." So, I gritted my teeth and accepted the call.

God outwitted me! The richness of our life in that community of learning, worship, and prayer was indescribable. Almost every week, I had the privilege of hearing the witness of some student who was passionately in love with Jesus and desirous of pleasing him. I discovered soon that I was participating in a kingdom enterprise that was sending persons to the ends of the earth to live and proclaim the gospel, and spread scriptural holiness across the land. I could not have imagined such joy and meaning as I had during those years at Asbury. And I had thought I was giving up something . . . sacrificing. God outwitted me!

That has been the dynamic of our faith journey—God has outwitted us. The whole of my ministry life has involved my being called to places and positions of ministry for which I was woefully inadequate. Who I am today, and whatever I have accomplished for the kingdom, flow from those occasions when I have responded to God's call with fear and trembling, knowing that unless I lived in his presence and received his power I would fail. Connected with my personal commitment has been Jerry's journey, and her willingness to follow God's call for us as partners in ministry.

When I arrived at the seminary, the question began pressing me: What is your vision for the seminary? Believing that the absolute essential of leadership is honesty and humility, I had to respond, "I have no unique vision. I have been in governance leadership here, and I see no need at this time in our history to change. So we are going to stand firm and move forward." That was the theme of my inaugural address and my presidency: "Standing Firm, Moving Forward."

While I believe, as I have stated, that my greatest contribution to the church is *The Workbook of Living Prayer*, it can well be argued that my greatest contribution to Asbury was my pastoral presence. Who I was, a pastor/preacher, was my greatest gift. I believed that one of the problems of modern theological education was that it had distanced itself from the church, becoming too much a university academic model (graduate theological education), and not a servant of the church.

I was elected to the presidency February 1994, to take office July 1, 1994. I spent two months, after finishing my work at Christ Church just after Easter, reading everything I could find about educational leadership, especially theological education leadership. I visited seminary presidents. My most fruitful visit was with David Hubbard, perhaps the most outstanding seminary leader of the day. He was on the verge of retirement, having served Fuller Theological Seminary for thirty years. He confirmed my conviction about honesty and humility being essential for leaders, by saying more than once during our two days together, "Maxie, don't promise too much." His most signal overall advice was, "stay close to your trustees; you will achieve little or nothing without their guidance and support."

My primary equipping for general leadership came from my experience leading the ministries of the Upper Room and as senior minister of Christ Church. Equipping for leadership in the specific area of theological education came from my work as a trustee of Asbury (1982–1994) under the presidency of David McKenna.

At the beginning of my first school year, I invited our Asbury extensive constituency to participate in a four-day prayer vigil. I knew the school and I needed prayer. Thousands of persons across the nation responded to my invitation. One day, in my office, I was reading some of those responses, and came upon one that had a personal note written on the commitment card, "Always prepare your lessons, always show up on time, always be a good boy." I searched for the name of the writer, and there it was, Murdoc Dunnam, my father. I didn't know he had gotten the invitation to join the vigil. He had no understanding of what my job as president was, but he knew I had to prepare, show up, and be "a good boy." I kept that note in my office middle desk drawer during my ten years at Asbury.

Because of her health, my mother was never able to visit us at Asbury, but after she died, my father came. I was preaching in chapel the week he was there. I introduced him during the service, and afterward students gathered round him and were gushing about his son, their president. One of them asked, "And how would you rate that sermon today?"

Without hesitation, he responded, "Oh . . . maybe a B." I don't think he was judging my sermon, or comparing it to the sermons he had heard his Free Will Baptist father preach, or those of Brother Grissom, under whose preaching we were both converted and baptized. Unknowingly, maybe, yet clearly, he was telling those students to keep things in perspective. Character and calling, not position and performance, are what matter most.

Exercising Pastoral Ministry in an Academic Community

Shortly before my second year as president, I took a twenty-four-hour retreat at the Abbey of Gethsemani, the Trappist monastery near Bardstown, Kentucky, not far from Asbury. This time was for my own spiritual preparation for our new academic year. God convicted me about my prayer pattern. I would pray for the students and faculty, generally, and when I heard of special needs, but I needed to be more intentional and more systematic. The Holy Spirit gave me the pattern. I would divide the school year calendar into forty weeks (early September through early June), and each week I would pray for a number of the students and faculty, the number each week enabling me to pray for every person in the community over the course of the year.

The week before I was to pray for persons, they would receive a letter from me, telling them I was going to be praying for them, and inviting them to share their concerns or joys so that I could name them specifically before the Lord during the week I was praying for them. I knew it was through these students that God was going to do his mighty work in the future, and they needed prayer. I also soon learned that their present needs were great, and many of them were carrying heavy burdens.

In my years at the *Upper Room*, my colleague, John Birkbeck, the editor of our British edition, introduced me to some of the great Scot preachers. One of those was Robert Murray M'Cheyne, who had a very short, but extraordinary life. He spent two hours daily in meditation and prayer. On Sundays, though preaching, he would spend six hours in prayer and devotional reading. He died at age thirty, having suffered ill health much of his life, yet his devout life and passionate ministry continued to inspire believers. His passion and commitment, as well as the secret of his influence in the lives of so many, is revealed in his conviction: "The greatest need of my congregation is my own personal holiness."

I believe that is true for all of us who would be pastoral leaders. So I insisted that Asbury could fulfill its mission only as it placed a high priority on the students' spiritual formation. More than anything, the church needs leaders who are formed by Christ into his own likeness. Character is as crucial as calling. How we function in ministry must flow out of who we are, thus the expression of our own personal holiness. If our students left the seminary without being rooted and grounded in prayer, and the disciplines of spiritual formation, we would have failed them.

God outwits us in all sorts of ways. Earlier I shared the struggles of my mild involvement in the civil rights movement in Mississippi. Relationships were strained, some shattered. There was anger, frustration, confusion, and pain. Trust was diminished and, for some, obliterated.

Yet, for the most part, reconciliation was the most powerful dynamic. There were instances where the people with whom I had the closest relationship could not accept my position on the issues and felt betrayed by the actions I was taking. One relationship became a kind of parable of friendship and Christian community. Roy Anderson was a building contractor. He was small in stature, but oh so big in spirit. He, his wife, "Weezie," and three children were charter members of the church.

The congregation built four buildings in the five years I was there: in the beginning a multipurpose worship/fellowship space, then a prayer chapel, a sanctuary, and education space. Roy was the contractor for all these buildings, so we spent a lot of time together. He never called me anything but "Preacher." Apart from my children and grandchildren addressing me as "Pop," Roy calling me "Preacher" has been most meaningful.

Roy did not agree with me on the civil rights issues, but he never lost trust in me, and there was never a wedge in our friendship. Through the years after leaving the Gulfport Church, and going to California, then all the years following, now and then I would get a telephone call with the greeting, "Preacher," and Roy would be on the line, catching up, sharing a family or personal concern.

When I was seeking to firmly establish prayer and spiritual formation as an essential dimension of the academic and practical life of the seminary, I felt we needed to give concrete expression to it. The best way to do that was to establish an endowed chair (a teaching role and position). I turned to Roy for funding, and he responded. Both he had Weezie have died, but at Asbury Seminary there is "The Roy and Weezie Anderson Chair of Prayer and Spiritual Formation" that memorializes them.

God outwits us. Out of a congregation that struggled with a tough, anguishing, divisive issue, a relationship survived out of which the resources came to bless generations of young persons preparing for Christian ministry, which, when true to Christ, is a ministry of reconciliation.

On the Cutting Edge

God outwits us. A man without a cell phone or a laptop computer became the president of a seminary that became the model for the use of technology in theological education. That's right. When I answered the call to Asbury I had not begun to use a cell phone. Only for a brief season, before cell phones, I had a big CB (citizens band radio) that I sometimes used in my car. I was not just passive about technology, I was actively resistant, in terms of my personal involvement.

During the months between finishing my work at Christ Church and assuming the responsibility at Asbury, I spent some time with Robert Buckman, a member of our congregation in Memphis. Bob was the CEO of Buckman Labs, a global specialty chemical company, who had innovatively used technology not only for communication, but for the education of his employees around the globe. He became an authority, and wrote a book on *Building a Knowledge-Driven Organization*. Though I was technologically limited, I was reading enough to know that major educational breakthroughs were coming through technology. Bob became a mentor/consultant. As I left Memphis for Asbury, Bob gave me my first laptop computer, urging me to at least get involved at that level.

I knew that meant more than what was on the surface. My predecessor at Asbury had launched serious conversations about technology. Out of these conversations already begun, in my second year, during the spring term of the 1995–96 school year, the seminary entered into a semester-long visioning process. Out of this process, a task force, sparked and headed by Dr. Leslie Andrew, forged an initial statement of vision for a global virtual campus.

God outwits us. Because he was so committed to the seminary, and to organizations moving from hoarding knowledge to sharing it, Bob and his wife, Joyce, made a gift to fund the establishment of a virtual campus, which was launched in 1997. While the church debated how much technology-based education could count in academic degree requirements for ordination, Asbury pursued and actualized her vision. After a few years, those who had questioned were applauding, and the Association of Theological Schools was referring member schools to Asbury as a model for effective use of technology in theological education.

Dreams and visions open an institution to further dreams and visions. And often, when a dream is realized, the new situation demands adjustment and change, and stimulates a new vision.

By the mid-1990s, the student body had grown to the point that the administration had to seriously consider how to faithfully move into the future. The technology issue was stirring, and by the time our virtual campus was established, other options were on the table. We could limit enrollment, or expand the Kentucky campus, or we could establish another campus.

Wilmore, the small town (3,600 in the 2010 census) where Asbury Theological Seminary is located, was settled in 1779 by Revolutionary War soldiers from Virginia, Pennsylvania, and Maryland. It is situated near the Big Bend of the Kentucky River and the breathtaking limestone formations of the Kentucky Palisades. The magnificent High Bridge railroad structure that spans the river was considered an engineering marvel of its time and featured by the Smithsonian Institution. It is an honored landmark, and when built in 1877, was the highest railroad trestle in the world. The quaint turn-of-the-century downtown, which features architecture from the 1890s, surprises potential students who visit and charms the parents who accompany them. My predecessor president, David McKenna, was fond of saying, "Wilmore is not the end of the world, but you can see it from here."

When we began to deal with the growth questions confronting us, we had to deal with location. Though through the years we had no lack of international students from Africa, India, and countries around the world, we found it difficult to attract and keep U.S. urban ethnic students. Robert Bridges, vice president of development, and I became convinced that we did need another campus. My position was grounded in the conviction that, as a seminary, given our strong Wesleyan identity, we should be evangelistic in sharing our perspective and mission. I was also convinced we needed to be in an urban setting in order to expand our mission geographically, ethnically, and demographically. I remembered my stumbling in leadership back at Christ Church when we failed to purchase the Catholic college across the street, and Pauline Horde's dependence on the Lord. This inspired my boldness.

We chose Orlando, Florida, which a national magazine had recently designated the new American metropolis. What mattered most was that Orlando had led the nation in population growth of Hispanics and African Americans. Our goal was to deliver theological education in a multiracial, multicultural, multidenominational urban center. With a campus in urban Orlando, and with classes in English and Spanish, the seminary would also be in a better position to prepare Christian leaders for Central and South America.

I recruited Steve Harper to be the founding dean. Steve had been professor of spiritual formation and Wesley studies at the seminary in Wilmore for nine years, but was serving as the dean of the Upper Room Chapel and directing Pathways, a spiritual formation initiative of the Upper Room. Sixty-five students made up our first class on the Florida campus when we opened in the fall of 1999. When I retired from the presidency in 2004, the trustees named the campus in my honor. In 2015, the Florida-Dunnam campus was home for 189 students, with an average of 250 students taking classes at any given time. The significance of this is realized when you know that the average seminary in the United States is 150 students. The two campuses combined numbered fifteen hundred, among the five largest seminaries in the nation.

I learned long before I went to Asbury as president that one of our greatest problems in the mainline church is the theological training of our ministers. America's seminaries were producing ministers who did not believe the historical doctrines of Christianity. At the root of these changes was a denial of the divine inspiration of the Bible, which was one of the chief characteristics of theological liberalism that was shaped by the universities in Europe, especially in Germany, where philosophical rationalism and biblical criticism were ascendant.

In 1920, in an article in the *Pentecostal Herald*, Dr. H. C. Morrison hinted of his intention of beginning a seminary in response to this rampant denial of classic, orthodox Christian faith.

> We have many pastors today who have practically given up the orthodox faith; they do not hesitate to deny the inspiration of a large portion of the Holy Scripture. They deny . . . the fall of man, the existence of original sin, the depravity of the race, the need of regeneration, the future punishment of the wicked. . . . They are the most dangerous class of skeptics that have assailed the Church.[2]

In the fall of 1923, Dr. Morrison followed through with his concern and founded Asbury Seminary. In the first *Bulletin*, the school's core theological beliefs were stated, at the center of which was this statement: "All our teaching will range around the Bible as an inspired book; around the Cross as the center of Redemption's plan; around Jesus Christ as the Incarnate Son of God who died that he might bring us to God." The statement concluded, "In these days of tragic unbelief we must build a School of Theology at Asbury where Divinity students will grow in faith and grace as well as in intellectual attainments, and where they can acquire a sound Theological training consistent with a sound Gospel faith."[3]

In assuming the presidency, I knew the faithful history of the seminary, which in large part had been swimming against the tide of classic American Protestant liberal theology, and I was committed to standing firm and moving forward: communicating the uncompromising truth of historic, biblical Christian faith through the most progressive, relevant means available.

I learned rather quickly that the secret of being faithful in my commitment, and in leading the seminary in its faithfulness, was faculty selection. I came to the seminary at a time when the student population was growing and we also had faculty retirements. I had the responsibility and the good pleasure of adding twenty-four new faculty. The process involved faculty search committees who made recommendations to the president, with final confirmation made by the trustees.

As I related to students who were called to teaching vocations, the negative reality of the broad theological milieu in which the seminary had been living became stark. Most of the universities to which these students would have to go to pursue PhDs in biblical studies and theology were the schools characterized by the negative factors that had led to the founding of Asbury in the first place. One way to guarantee professors that would carry on the spiritual and theological tradition of Asbury would be to train some of them ourselves.

I began to pray and float with the faculty and trustees the idea of our offering PhD degrees in biblical studies and theology. We had at least two of the nation's outstanding Old and New Testament scholars, along with outstanding ones in other disciplines. We had a problem with which most seminary presidents are familiar. The cost of offering PhD degrees is far greater than the normal master's degree offerings. After I left the presidency, and began working in development as chancellor, the notion continued to plague me and I continued to pray and seek a way for the seminary to add this dimension to its offering to the church.

I have two ties on my closet tie rack, both the same design. One has a navy blue field, the other a rich red field. The color fields are broken up by diagonal stripes, and the spaces outlined by those stripes are filled with white ducks. I have had them since my work with the seminary. I still wear them now and then, and I call them my *gratitude* ties. They are gifts from Paul Amos, one of the founders and longtime president of Aflac Insurance. The ducks on my ties are the famous Aflac ducks. I wear them as a reminder of the ways God outwits us, because Paul and his wife, Jean, provided the resources to fund two PhD degree programs at Asbury.

And I thought God was being unfair, calling me to leave a ministry so full of meaning and joy, to a task for which I was woefully incapable. I remembered what one of my trusted friends who helped me discern the call had said, "heretofore your ministry has been a ministry of addition; at Asbury it will be a ministry of multiplication." I continue to find that abundantly true, as I regularly receive communication from all over the world from persons who graduated from Asbury, many of them during my presidency.

God outwits us, not only by accepting us where we are, but by not leaving us as we are. God's grace is sufficient, but God outwits us by giving us far more than we ask, think, or even imagine.

CHAPTER THIRTEEN

Retirement?
What Is That?

My friend Robert White relayed a story to me about his grandfather, who was a fireman in Mobile, Alabama. It was back before everything was mechanized. The fire wagons, with huge tanks of water, were pulled by horses. The fire chief's buggy was pulled by Ole Dan, a handsome horse, worthy of a place in a parade. When the fire department became mechanized, they had to find homes for the horses. Robert's grandfather asked for Ole Dan. He had a beautiful pasture in which there was a small lake with plenty of water. He was given the horse, and Ole Dan retired in style to a veritable horse paradise.

Ole Dan was well-behaved, but there was one problem: whenever he heard the fire siren there wasn't a fence or gate that could hold him. He would jump the fence and go to the fire. After they learned there was no stopping him, when the siren sounded they would go straight to the fire where they would find Ole Dan, standing quietly by the fire truck. He was doing what he was trained to do; when the siren sounded, go to the fire.

Robert reminded me, "and you and I . . . these old war horse preachers . . . regardless of how old or how comfortable we might be, when the siren sounds we have to go to the fire. Why? That is what God called us to do and what we are trained to do, to pull people from the fire" (see Jude 22–23).

After sharing the story, Robert wrote, "Old war horse, I'm glad to know you are still alive and kicking. I am too, except sometimes I do the kicking and sometimes I'm the one that gets kicked."

Robert was one of sixteen in our graduating class from Richton High School. Like me, he came from a poor family, lived out in the country, and rode the bus to school. He was pudgy, more than a little overweight. We couldn't have gotten away with it today, and shouldn't have gotten away with it then; some of us called him "Tonnage." I may have given him that name, thinking it was more respectful than "Fatso" or "Fat Man." And the truth is, he wasn't overweight enough to be "Fatso," but he was heavy.

We showed up for school one Monday morning, early in eleventh grade, and there was a note on the main bulletin board. In his own hand, on notebook paper, Robert was sharing his testimony. In revival services during the weekend, he had been converted, and he wanted us to know. I have never forgotten that. What boldness! I didn't make that kind of declaration when I was converted and baptized.

After graduation from high school, I lost contact with Robert; in fact, I lost contact with almost all the persons with whom I was in high school. But I heard that Robert, like me, had become a preacher. Through the years, when I would see someone from high school, I would ask about Robert. Some would tell me they had seen him, heard him preach, or had seen someone who had seen him. We had not been the closest friends in high school, but there was something that caused me to want to make contact . . . maybe it was that I never forgot his bold testimony!

I never actively sought to contact him until we were both in our mid-seventies. I was visiting in Richton, and inquired to someone about Robert. They had heard him preach in Petal, a town near Richton, and knew someone who would have contact information. I followed through, after all my years of wondering about him, made personal contact, and we made a plan to meet for an all-day reunion. It was glorious. Amazingly, there were parallels on our pathways. Early in his ministry, he had been a church planter as had I. He was an evangelist for his denomination; I had worked for more than twenty years as chair of evangelism for the World Methodist Council. He had been the president of the only seminary of his denomination; I had been a seminary president for ten years. He had been the general superintendent of his denomination; I had been invited to seek to be a bishop in my church, but felt no calling for it. He was now retired, but going as strongly as ever; so with me. Thus, his sharing the fire horse story, and addressing me as "old war horse."

I haven't done it yet, but maybe I will also follow through with the other fourteen in my high school class. Did any of them remember Robert's testimony? I want them to *know* that Robert lived out his conversion in a fruitful, faithful way, and his ministry was rewarded richly.

When I accepted the presidency of Asbury, I was sixty, and I made a commitment to myself to retire at seventy. I kept that commitment to retire from the presidency, but I accepted the trustees' invitation to become chancellor and work in development and some of our international involvements. Not wanting to stay in Wilmore, in the immediate community of the new president, I knew it was best to move.

The obvious place for us was back in Memphis. We had lived there longer than any other place during our ministry, and we had a strong network of Christian friends. More emotionally driving, was that our middle daughter, Kerry, and her husband and son were there. I have this notion that if at all possible, senior people, if they have children, need to live out their last years near at least one of them. In healthy families, most children want to be attentive to their aging parents. Parents need to make that as easy for them as possible. Our oldest daughter, Kim, was in West Lafayette, Indiana, where winter is worse than uninviting. Our youngest, son Kevin, was in Pensacola, Florida. He was unmarried, and his work in real-estate development offered no guarantee as to where he might be even five years ahead. The decision was easy for us. We had invested twelve years in Memphis, our ministry at Christ Church and in the city had been rich and meaningful, Kerry was there, so Memphis was our landing place.

We moved to Memphis in 2004. I worked as chancellor for Asbury for six years. I resigned when the bishop invited me to become interim senior minister at Christ Church in 2010. They were searching for a new senior minister, and didn't want to rush the process. Bill Bouknight, who served as senior minister at Christ Church for thirteen years, following me when I became president at Asbury, began a tradition of inviting me to preach on Low Sunday (the Sunday following Easter) every year. So I had maintained a casual connection with the congregation; I was not a total stranger even to the folks who were not there during my active ministry.

It was a good year for Jerry and me, and I thought, what a good way to close my active ministry. But closing my active ministry was not to be.

It's amazing what media can do in branding and imaging. Christ Church was known for her heart for the city. As indicated earlier, during my years earlier as senior minister I had a radio/television program called *Perceptions*, which was carried on two television and two radio stations. That much media exposure made me known throughout the city. Amazingly, I was still known years later when I returned.

Even before I became interim minister at Christ Church, while still engaged as Asbury's chancellor, I was involved in the city. That involvement became more intense when I became interim minister. I discovered that the city had not changed much in the years I had been gone; it continued to be a very troubled city. A national magazine recently featured an article claiming Memphis to be one of the least-favorite cites in America in which to live. Poverty and the huge racial divide play a monumental role in our many troubles. In 2015, it was named as the third most dangerous city in the United States in which to live.

Many of our problems were focused on public education. There were two public school districts in the metropolitan area: one, Memphis, primarily "the city," which was 85 percent black and poor; the other,

Shelby County, "suburbia," which was 70 percent white and economically middle and upper-middle class. In early 2011, the Memphis City School Board surrendered its charter, which action was confirmed by a public referendum and a federal court order, forcing the creation of one school district to serve the city and the county. The process represented, at the time, the largest school district consolidation in American history, and it came with major challenges of bridging chasms in race and class.

The Holy Spirit led me, with others, to believe that a huge part of the reconciliation/redemptive ministry to which Christ-followers are called is public education. Christians are called to represent Jesus' care for "the least of these."

Almost from her beginning, Christ Church has been concerned about education. We have an outstanding Christian Day School that has been operational for many years. Through the years we have tried hard to serve some of the underserved population in Memphis through that school, but we have never been successful.

During my years as senior minister, a small group established Shepherd's School, intentionally designed to serve the underserved. A group of committed persons explored the experimental work of Marva Collins, an education pioneer in Chicago. She had become frustrated with the classroom approach at the public school where she taught, and established Westside Preparatory School where she gained wide acclaim for her novel approach to teaching.

Under her guidance, Westside Preparatory School flourished and became nationally known for its success in taking children from impoverished neighborhoods who were often considered unteachable and turning them into solid students.

We modeled Shepherd's School in Memphis, as much as possible, after her efforts in Chicago. It was reasonably successful, survived for five or six years, and evolved into the Neighborhood School, which continues today.

That school was never intimately connected with Christ Church. But the conviction for educationally serving the underserved was growing in the minds and hearts of people in the congregation. In 2010, Christ Church took a bold step and established Cornerstone Prep, a private, explicitly Christian school, with focused attention on providing education for the underserved children of our city. We located in Binghampton, an underserved neighborhood in which our church had been serving for twenty years. Again, we sought guidance, spent a year in planning, and sent our leaders to places around the nation where effective urban education was taking place, and sought to model similar effectiveness. We began with thirty-three pre-kindergarten students.

From the beginning Cornerstone Prep had amazing results in providing education, proving that where a child lives does not determine learning potential. The educational measurements exceeded national norms in every area, so our little school received state and even national attention.

Great efforts at educational reform were going on in our city. Memphis was becoming a kind of epicenter for reform in public education, and it was desperately needed. In 2011, 950 of Tennessee's 1,750 public schools failed to make Adequate Yearly Progress (AYP). In the concentrated educational reform efforts of our state, eighty-five of these failing schools were targeted for intervention by the state. Our governor, through the Department of Education, established the Achievement School District, a district of these failing schools, and named a superintendent of that non-geographical district, charging him to reclaim those schools for effective education. Sixty-nine of those failing schools were in Memphis. Lester School was the worst of the sixty-nine.

Some of us had already begun to feel that Lester School, located in Binghampton, had to have our attention if we were going to be faithful in our witness in that neighborhood. Often, when I was driving near the neighborhood, I would prayer drive around the property. Some of our church members began to tutor and mentor there. When the superintendent of the failing school district began to make it known that some of these failing schools might become charter schools, the Board of

Directors of Cornerstone Prep made the bold, courageous decision to offer to take responsibility for Lester School.

In order to accomplish this, Cornerstone Prep would have to give up being an explicitly Christian private school and become a public charter school. This change in status would allow Cornerstone Prep to serve the larger public good in a manner currently not possible, to serve more than eight hundred Binghampton families. After a lengthy interview, application, and approval process, Cornerstone was given the responsibility for a failing school in the neighborhood where our church had for years focused its missional work.

Jesus said, "unless a grain of wheat falls into the earth and dies, it remains just a single grain; but if it dies, it bears much fruit" (John 12:24 NRSV). As those seeking to be missionally faithful, we believed that Cornerstone Prep had to die as an explicitly Christian school in order to serve a desperate and needy community. We were not giving up our Christian mission; we were pursuing that mission in a different way. What we were able to do in explicit Christian witness and teaching in the classroom, we would now do after school and in other creative ways. The biggest Christian witness would be putting our compassion and concern for the children into practice, and affirming all the students as valuable as any other child in the county.

We closed down Cornerstone as originally constituted, with sixty-six students, and opened with 325 in pre-kindergarten through third at Lester School. In the fall of 2015, we were given the additional responsibility for grades four through six, and what began as a "grain of wheat," willing to be buried in the ground, became an education effort serving 1,400 students.

Playing Second Fiddle

When Christ Church, in consulting with the Methodist bishop, had selected a new senior minister, I was asked to continue as an associate minister. The Staff-Parish Relations Committee, which is the official body in the congregation that works with the pastors and staff in making these decisions, made it clear to me that this was the desire of Shane Stanford, the new senior minister. I had grave reservations. One, I had a long history with many of the people in the congregation, had just finished a year as their pastor, and did not want the dynamic of that to slow or sideline the process of the congregation's acceptance of Shane's leadership. Two, I was working my way to retirement and knew that with my experience in the church and the city, and my workaholic nature, this would not be something I could give myself only partially to. I also knew that Shane would have to be very secure in his identity and confidence for such a relationship to work.

Shane is one of the most effective communicators I have known. He is a powerful preacher; his power is in his suffering. Born a hemophiliac, as a teenager he received a bad transfusion and is HIV positive. All sorts of outflowing health issues from that has made suffering his lot. He has had heart surgery and has lost almost half the sight in one eye. Balancing medications is a constant problem. Yet, he is transparent, uncomplaining, and clear in his convictions and commitments. His book, a kind of memoir, *A Positive Life*, is inspiring and challenging.

He convinced me that my staying on the staff as an associate (consulting and mentoring) and leading some of the creative ministries he had in mind, was his desire and earnest wish. My title evolved into director of Christ Church Global, our ministry of taking the gospel, through the resources of Christ Church, across the street and around the world. The primary focus was training leadership and making creative use of technology.

Early in this decision-making process, I was confronted and challenged by Scripture. In mine and Jerry's morning devotional time together, we use different translations for our reading. We have found that different renderings of texts enliven our devotional time. At that time we were using The Message (Eugene Peterson's translation of the

New Testament). In our reading, we came to chapter 12 of Romans. In the NIV, the translation I use most, verses 9 and 10 read: "Love must be sincere. Hate what is evil; cling to what is good. Be devoted to one another in love. Honor one another above yourselves." Good, clear, challenging. But that day Peterson's translation was, "Love from the center of who you are; don't fake it. Run for dear life from evil; hold on for dear life to good. Be good friends who love deeply; practice playing second fiddle."

More than challenging, it was God's word for me, and confirmed the decision to continue in ministry with Christ Church as an associate with Shane. What clinched it was the last portion: *practice playing second fiddle.* This term alludes to the part of second violin in an orchestra. Although many would argue that "second fiddle" is as important as first violin, it is the idea of subordinacy that is suggested in the figurative term, *playing second fiddle.* If you play second fiddle to someone, that person is usually in a stronger position, or is more important than you. To be sure, I have had those who were in authority over me: bishops, district superintendents, trustees; but in terms of everyday work life and responsibility, with the exception of a couple of situations early in my ministry life, I have always been *in charge.* Could I close my ministry life playing second fiddle?

I spent some days reflecting and praying. I concluded what should not have taken me so long. Playing second fiddle is one of the chief defining marks of a Christian and ultimately gives us an attractive distinctive. At the core of my understanding of the Christian life is my experience of the indwelling Christ. The Bible tells us emphatically that our walk with Jesus is one where we empty ourselves and then fill ourselves back up with Christ. The apostle Paul was always talking about how it was no longer he who lived, but Christ who lived in him, and that he actually died daily to be a follower of Jesus. Even Jesus himself states that his followers are those who deny themselves, and even lose themselves for his sake. Denying our wants is not an easy thing. It may, in fact, cause a lot of stress. I knew all that, and had preached it with conviction for more than fifty years; now was my chance to practice it: playing second fiddle in a very concrete way.

Memphis is a very troubled city. We have a huge impoverished population, and the racial divide impacts every governmental and civic decision that is made. We suffer low corporate self-esteem, not least because it was our city in which Dr. Martin Luther King Jr. was killed. Yet our city is the setting of some of the most exciting mission and ministry expressions I know.

To highlight the problem/need factor and to affirm the exciting ministries that are going on, Shane and I created a thirty-minute television program called *We Believe in Memphis*. We begin the program, spending eight to ten minutes addressing the intersection of the Christian faith and everyday life, focusing on a problem in the city (e.g., poverty, juvenile crime, homelessness, hunger, parentless children). We follow our conversation with an interview with some person or persons who are working to address the problem/issue we have discussed.

Two dynamics are obvious: one, we address problems and social issues from a Christian perspective; two, we present a positive witness to which people respond and become involved. The city knows the church cares.

"The Arc of the Moral Universe Is Long, but It Bends toward Justice"

Medgar Evers was one of the heroes of the civil rights struggle in Mississippi. In late 1954, he was named NAACP's first field secretary for the state. In that position, he helped organize boycotts and set up local chapters of the NAACP. In 1962, he was involved in one of the most dramatic events in the struggle, helping in James Meredith's efforts to enroll in the University of Mississippi.

Early in the morning of June 12, 1963, after a long evening meeting with NAACP lawyers that had gone past midnight, he pulled into his driveway in Jackson, Mississippi. He was carrying NAACP T-shirts that read, "Jim Crow Must Go." Out of the darkness came a bullet that ripped through his heart. He managed to get to the doorway before collapsing.

He was taken to the hospital, but was refused entry because of his race. He was admitted after the hospital staff learned who he was, and died an hour later. He was buried on June 19 in Arlington National Cemetery, with military honors before a crowd of more than three thousand.

Fifty years later, on June 9, 2013, the Mississippi Annual Conference was meeting in Jackson, the capital city where Evers had worked and had been assassinated. The Emma Elzy Award had been established to celebrate reconciliation and honor persons who had contributed significantly to the improvement of race relations in Mississippi. Because it was the fiftieth anniversary of Medgar Evers's death, and because he had been one of the heroes in the civil rights movement in the state, he was recognized and honored as his wife, Myrlie Evers, was invited to present the Emma Elzy Award.

The award was presented to the twenty-eight ministers who, fifty years before, had presented their "Born of Conviction" statement to the church in Mississippi. Dr. Joseph Reiff, who was writing a book on "the 28" and the impact of their statement, was present. He described the event in his book, *Born of Conviction.*

Eight of the twenty-eight signers who were still living were present. I was invited, along with Keith Tonkel, to accept the award for "the 28." I referred to the word of Brother Lawrence, about which I spoke in the introduction, "God, you have outwitted me," saying,

Fifty years ago, some young men, now old men, signed a statement, and now this Annual Conference is saying, "We appreciate that." God outwits us. That's the storyline of the Christian faith and way: God continually outwits us. There have been times since that occasion when many of us left the state, when I have been most pleased with the faithfulness of people like Keith Tonkel who stayed in the state, and there have been occasions when I have felt guilty for having left, and wondered what God was doing with that. But God outwits us. When you think about the contribution that those who left the state have made to the whole church, you know what I mean when I say, God outwits us. Two of those persons became presidents of seminaries. Two of them became deans of seminaries; three of them became pastors of some of the largest churches in the denomination.

In his book, *Born of Conviction*, Reiff wrote:

Although Dunnam did briefly praise the signers who stayed [in Mississippi] and offered the litany of accomplishment by those who had left as an example of triumph in the face of adversity through the power of God, the critics heard it as perpetuating the narrative that the *Born of Conviction* story centers on those who left the state. . . . The persons who planned the event could not know of the emotional mine-field it would expose and they were not responsible for the Conference's lack of acknowledgment of the signers over the previous fifty years. This was the first time the Mississippi Conference had formally cele-brated the 1963 Born of Conviction witness. Fifty years of pent up feelings resulting from the lack of recognition [of those who stayed in Mississippi] could not be put to rest with one thirty minute ceremony, and the expressions of anger illustrate one central aspect of the *Born of Conviction* story: the experiential divide between the signers who left and those who stayed.[1]

I was honest in expressing my sometimes feeling of guilt for having left the state, and often wondered what pattern my ministry would have taken had I remained. In my brief statement, on that day of recognition, I mentioned the significant service of some who left to underscore how God uses all circumstance to accomplish his will, and his will does not take us where his grace will not sustain us.

In an article about the Mississippi Annual Conference recognition of "the 28," Steve Beard wrote:

History sometimes takes a long time to heal itself. The course correc-tions are often patchworked together over decades. "How long will prejudice blind the visions of men, darken their understanding, and drive bright-eyed wisdom from her sacred throne?" Dr. Martin Luther King Jr. asked in a famous speech in Montgomery, Alabama, on the steps of the state capitol after completing the march from Selma to Montgomery in 1965. Later in the speech, he answered the question with his trademark eloquence. "How long? Not long, because the arc of the moral universe is long, but it bends toward justice."[2]

We had issued our "Born of Conviction" statement a few years before King's speech. The violence surrounding the admission of James Meredith, a courageous black student, to the University of Mississippi in 1962, was pervasive across the state. Though not so pervasive, racial violence persists in our country. At the time of the Annual Conference's long-delayed witness of the "arc of the moral universe bending toward justice," I was, and still am, living under the conviction that the civil rights issue of the twenty-first century is public education. I closed my acceptance speech to the gathering that day with these words:

> My prayer is that fifty years from now, maybe, an Annual Conference will look back, and some of you will have taken a stand on behalf of those for whom God has extended preferential treatment, that is, the poor; and some of you will have taken a stand on welcoming the stranger in our midst around the issue of immigration; and some of you will see to it that we don't allow the zip code of a child to determine the quality of education provided to the child.

This celebration opened a kind of public discussion about my leadership in the general church, especially in the context of the issue of human sexuality: the support of same-sex marriage and the ordination of practicing homosexual persons, which I believe is contrary to Scripture, and was tearing the church apart. People who, maybe for the first time because it happened fifty years ago, heard of my being a coauthor of the "Born of Conviction" statement, began to ask, "Who is this? What happened to him?" From their perspective, the struggle for black freedom and the

affirmation of same-sex marriage and the ordination of practicing homosexual persons are in the same category.

Bishop Carcaño was one of those persons who connected the two
causes. She invited Frank Schaefer, a minister who had been defrocked by
his Annual Conference in Pennsylvania because of performing a same-
sex wedding, to become a part of her Cal Pac Annual Conference. She
equated her actions to Bishop Gerald Kennedy welcoming eight ministers
from Mississippi, in the wake of the "Born of Conviction" statement, to
his conference fifty years before. Some of these eight persons (not all) had
signed the "Born of Conviction" statement, which was a witness against
racism as well as a plea for the preservation of public education, during the
civil rights struggle in Mississippi in the early sixties.

As one of the persons who wrote this statement and had responded to
Bishop Kennedy's invitation to transfer from Mississippi to California, I
was troubled by Bishop Carcaño connecting Bishop Kennedy's welcome
of some of us to California to her inviting Frank Schaefer to come to that
conference. Only African Americans can make a judgment about whether
what Frank Schaffer did in performing a same-sex wedding in blatant
violation of the church's position that marriage is a lifelong covenant
between one man and one woman is comparable to those who walked
across that Selma bridge, those who have struggled and suffered, physically, emotionally, and spiritually in opposition to the dreadful sin of
racial discrimination.

In my public opposition to Bishop Carcaño, I sought to make the
case that the witness against racism in our *Discipline* is as clear as the
church's present witness against same-sex marriage and the ordination of professed practicing homosexual persons. We "Mississippi 28"
were not violating the covenant of our ordination; we were upholding it.
Personally, I knew I was keeping the covenant I made in my ordination,
but I also was convicted that I was acting in keeping with the witness
of Scripture.

The same commitment to Scripture and to the covenant of my ordination that guided me fifty years ago and has formed and guided me through the years, guides me now in my support of the church's position on marriage and ordination. As indicated in chapter 11, I understand in part why I might be labeled the Grandfather of Resistance, but what I'm committed to is biblical grounding and historical continuity with the apostolic teaching of the Christian church for two thousand years. I continue seeking to resist being seduced by current cultural swings.

Why I Have Not Quit the Ministry

It was a serendipity. As I was working on this last chapter on retirement, I came across a sermon I had preached at Trinity Methodist Church in Gulfport, sometime in 1963, before we moved from Mississippi to California. It was the title of the sermon that grabbed my attention: "Why I Have Not Quit the Ministry."

The sermon was in a file folder of articles and letters related to the reaction and response to my involvement in the civil rights struggle. Naturally, I thought, the sermon would address that issue.

My assumption was wrong. Listeners in the congregation back then would know there were emotional and intellectual connections with my current struggle, but a reader of the sermon today would not make that intimate connection.

The sermon began with reference to a then-current article in the *Saturday Evening Post*, the title of which hit me in the face: "Why I Quit the Ministry." The anonymous writer closed his article with these words:

> I still believe in Jesus Christ, I still want to serve Him. For it is He who taught me to care . . . about man, God, and the deepest questions of life. This is why I quit the ministry. The majority of today's church members refuse to care. In this refusal, most remaining members and much of their chosen church hierarchy blandly acquiesce. How then

can a minister rationalize devoting his life to the organization which results is a superficial extension of society? How can he live with himself if he does?[3]

In the sermon I was responding to that last question by sharing why I have *not* quit the ministry. To get to the core of my sermon, I said,

In my anxiety, after reading the article, I turned my mind back to the early church and Jesus. Convincingly came the words of Jesus, "You have not chosen me, but I have chosen you." Then I remembered Paul's words to the elders of the church at Ephesus. It was a farewell speech charged with emotion. First of all he made certain claims. He claimed that he had spoken fearlessly, telling them of God's will. "I have declared to both Jews and Greeks that they must turn to God in repentance and have faith in our Lord Jesus" (Acts 20:21). He expressed his claims about how he lived independently, coveting nothing, nor pandering to the fear or favor of any man. "I served the Lord with great humility and with tears and in the midst of severe testing by the plots of my Jewish opponents" (Acts 20:19).

He faced the future gallantly. "And now, compelled by the Spirit, I am going to Jerusalem, not knowing what will happen to me there. I only know that in every city the Holy Spirit warns me that prison and hardships are facing me. However, I consider my life worth nothing to me; my only aim is to finish the race and complete the task the Lord Jesus has given me—the task of testifying to the good news of God's grace" (Acts 20:22–24).

What conviction of calling! Can you imagine a man like that quitting the task to which he had given himself? No—a thousand times no; so, you have Paul, the martyr, dying in Rome, but confident that he was completing the ministry of declaring the good news of the grace of God.

I shared in chapter 6 how during that same period, in the midst of my struggles in those first years in ministry in Mississippi, I was on the verge of burnout, ready to throw in the towel. God intervened through Stanley Jones and a Christian ashram experience. Jones's understanding of the "in Christ" dynamic of the gospel was already impacting me when I preached that sermon fifty years ago. After declaring that Paul could never think of quitting, I quoted a poem, which I had found in Jones's book *In Christ*. This is a part of what the poet had Paul saying:

> From the glory and the gladness,
> > From His secret place;
> From the rapture of His Presence
> > From the radiance of His Face—
>
> Christ, the Son of God hath sent me
> > Through the midnight lands;
> Mine the mighty ordination
> > Of the pierced Hands.

The poet went on to describe how Paul wanted us to hear the gospel that offers forgiveness, affirmation of God's love, rest, and gladness, and "not alone of life eternal breathed into the dead," then said:

> But I tell you I have seen Him,
> > God's beloved Son,
> From His lips have learnt the mystery:
> > He and His are one.

There is that *in Christ* dimension of the gospel that has been the cornerstone of my theology and life: "He and His are one."

The poet sounded the note yet again as he concluded Paul's description of his journey:

> On into the depths eternal
> > Of the love and song,
> Where in God the Father's glory
> > Christ has waited long;

There to find that none beside Him
God's delight can be—
Not beside Him, Nay, but in Him,
O beloved, are we.[4]

I preached that as the reason I had not quit the ministry. I had been claimed by Christ, chosen, "mine the ordination of the pierced hands." I was living, "not beside him, nay, but *in him*."

I closed that sermon I preached years ago with these words:

Why haven't I quit the ministry? I can't quit. This is my calling. And, even though I share many of the feelings of the young man who wrote the article, I would only say to him, "You quit too soon; you used the wrong judgments; you never saw yourself in proper perspective as God's man, for whom Christ died, speaking to those for whom Christ died.

Even as I close this memoir, I have not quit the ministry. I keep on retiring, and beginning again. This time, as of this writing, Christ Church has named me minister at large. Who knows where this will take me? Wherever, God will certainly outwit me!

APPENDIX: BORN OF CONVICTION

Confronted with the grave crises precipitated by racial discord within our state in recent months, and the genuine dilemma facing persons of Christian conscience, we are compelled to voice publicly our convictions. Indeed, as Christian ministers and as native Mississippians, sharing the anguish of all our people, we have a particular obligation to speak. Thus understanding our mutual involvement in these issues, we bind ourselves together in this expression of our Christian commitment. We speak only for ourselves, though mindful that many others share these affirmations.

Born of the deep conviction of our souls as to what is morally right, we have been driven to seek the foundations of such convictions in the expressed witness of our Church. We, therefore, at the outset of this new year affirm the following:

The Church is the instrument of God's purpose. This is His Church. It is ours only as stewards under His Lordship. Effective practice of this stewardship for the minister clearly requires freedom of the pulpit. It demands for every man an atmosphere for responsible belief and free expression.

We affirm our faith in the official position of The Methodist Church on race as set forth in paragraph 2026 of the 1960 Methodist Discipline: "Our Lord Jesus Christ teaches that all men are brothers. He permits no discrimination because of race, color, or creed. 'In Christ Jesus you are all sons of God, through faith . . .' (Galatians 3:26)."

The position of The Methodist Church, long held and frequently declared, is an amplification of our Lord's teaching: "We believe that God is Father of all people and races, that Jesus Christ is His Son, that all men are brothers, and that man is of infinite worth as a child of God" (The Social Creed, Paragraph 2020).

We affirm our belief that our public school system is the most effective means of providing common education for all our children. We hold that it is an institution essential to the preservation and development of our true democracy. The Methodist Church is officially committed to the system of public school education and we concur. We are unalterably opposed to the closing of public schools on any level or to the diversion of tax funds to the support of private or sectarian schools.

In these conflicting times, the issues of race and Communism are frequently confused. Let there be no mistake. We affirm an unflinching opposition to Communism. We publicly concur in the Methodist Council of Bishops' statement of November 16, 1962, which declares:

"The basic commitment of a Methodist minister is to Jesus Christ as Lord and Savior. This sets him in permanent opposition to communism. He cannot be a Christian and a communist. In obedience to his Lord and in support of the prayer, 'Thy Kingdom come, Thy will be done on earth as it is in Heaven,' he champions justice, mercy, freedom, brotherhood, and peace. He defends the underprivileged, oppressed, and forsaken. He challenges the status quo, calling for repentance and change wherever the behavior of men falls short of the standards of Jesus Christ."

We believe that this is our task and calling as Christian ministers.

FINDING AUTHORITY IN THE OFFICIAL POSITION OF OUR CHURCH, AND BELIEVING IT TO BE IN HARMONY WITH SCRIPTURE AND GOOD CHRISTIAN CONSCIENCE, WE PUBLICLY DECLARE OURSELVES IN THESE MATTERS AND AGREE TO STAND TOGETHER IN SUPPORT OF THESE PRINCIPLES.

NOTES

Foreword

1. G. K. Chesterton, *St. Francis of Assisi* (Peabody, MA: Hendrickson Publishers, 2008), n.p.
2. Ibid.

Chapter One

1. See https://en.wikipedia.org/wiki/Great_Depression.
2. Maxie Dunnam, *Barefoot Days of the Soul* (Waco, TX: Word, 1975), 11–12.
3. Jack Bertram, *The Clarion-Ledger* (June 12, 2001).
4. See https://en.wikipedia.org/wiki/McComb,_Mississippi.
5. Bertha Gober. Copyright © 1963. webspinner@crmvet.org.
6. Maxie Dunnam, *Dancing at My Funeral* (Atlanta, GA: Forum House Publishers, 1973), 8–9.
7. Ibid, 9.

Chapter Two

1. Carl Gustav Boberg, "How Great Thou Art," translated by Stuart K. Hine (Sweden: *Sanningsvittnet*, 1891).
2. The Baptismal Covenant I, *The United Methodist Hymnal* (Nashville, TN: The United Methodist Publishing House, 1989), 33.
3. Ibid, 36.

Chapter Three

1. Geoffrey Chaucer, "Prologue," *The Canterbury Tales*, l. 1–4.
2. Robert Burns, "To a Louse, On Seeing One on a Lady's Bonnet at Church," *Poems, Chiefly in the Scottish Dialect* (Kilmarnock, Scotland: 1786), l.
3. See https://en.wikipedia.org/wiki/Central_United_Methodist_Church _(Detroit).
4. Ibid.

Chapter Four

1. See http://www.christianity.com/church/church-history/timeline/1701 -1800/john-wesleys-heart-strangely-warmed-11630227.html.
2. Maxie Dunnam, *Dancing at My Funeral* (Atlanta, GA: Forum House Publishers, 1973), 67.

Chapter Six

1. Quoted in "A Riveting Look at Racial Hatred in Mississippi," by Eric Arnesen, June l, 2003.
2. See https://mcc.org/learn/about.
3. Joseph T. Reiff, "Born of Conviction: White Methodist Witness to Mississippi's Closed Society," in *Courage to Bear Witness: Essays in Honor of Gene L. Davenport*, edited by L. Edward Phillips and Billy Vaughan (Wipf & Stock Publishing, 2009), 124.
4. Joseph T. Reiff, *Born of Conviction: White Methodists and Mississippi's Closed Society* (Oxford University Press, 2015), xviii.
5. Ibid., 86.

Chapter Seven

1. Article draft, Oct. 1963.
2. "Methodists: The Challenge of Fortune," *Time* (May 8, 1964).
3. I made numerous speeches the first year I was in California to clergy, congregations, etc. This would have been common content in many of my speeches.

4. Frank Laubach, *Letters by a Modern Mystic* (Westwood, NJ: Fleming H. Revell, 1958), 27–28.

5. Brother Andrew and Al Janssen, *Light Force: A Stirring Account of the Church Caught in the Middle East Crossfire* (London: Hodder & Stoughton, 2004), 103–04.

Chapter Eight

1. See http://www.upperroom.org/en/about/history.
2. Ibid.
3. John Wesley, *Fifty-Three Sermons*, "Catholic Spirit," 502.
4. *Pockets*, vol. 1 no. 1 Nov./Dec. 1981, *The Upper Room*, Nashville, 11.
5. Ibid.

Chapter Nine

1. Maxie Dunnam, *Congregational Evangelism* (Nashville, TN: Discipleship Resources, 1992), ix.

Chapter Ten

1. Os Guinness, *The Gravedigger File* (Downers Grove, IL: InterVarsity Press, 1983), 80.

Chapter Eleven

1. *The Book of Discipline of the United Methodist Church*, 2012, paragraph 161 F, 161.
2. http://www.olacathedral.org/.
3. Roman Catholic Archbishop of Los Angeles, "Architecture: Overview," 2002–2004, http://www.olacathedral.org/ 2 December 2004.
4. Thomas Oden, *Turning Around the Mainline: How Renewal Movements Are Changing the Church* (Grand Rapids, MI: Baker Books, 2006), 11.
5. Richard John Neuhaus, "A New Methodism Afoot," *The Religion & Society Report* 5, no 4, April 1988: 2.

Chapter Twelve

1. "A Covenant Prayer in the Wesleyan Tradition," *The United Methodist Hymnal*, (Nashville, TN: The United Methodist Publishing House, 1989), 607.
2. March 10, 1920.
3. *Bulletin* of Asbury Theological Seminary, 1923–1924, 5–6.

Chapter Thirteen

1. Joseph Reiff, *Born of Conviction: White Methodists and Mississippi's Closed Society* (Oxford University Press, 2015), 239.
2. Steve Beard, "The Long Arc Toward Justice," *Good News* (July/Aug. 2013).
3. Alfred Balk, writing for an anonymous clergyman, *Saturday Evening Post*, November 17, 1962.
4. Lois Buck, "In Christ—The Gospel According to Paul," in E. Stanley Jones, *In Christ* (Nashville, TN: Abingdon Press, 1961), 5–6.

CPSIA information can be obtained
at www.ICGtesting.com
Printed in the USA
LVOW13s1043281217
560730LV00012B/11/P